SMALL
TOWN
JOY

Published by 404 Ink Limited
www.404Ink.com
hello@404ink.com

Please note: Some references include URLs which may change or be unavailable
after publication of this book. All references within endnotes were accessible and
accurate as of February 2025 but may experience link rot from there on in.

Excerpt of 'Love' by Edwin Morgan (*Centenary Selected Poems*, ed. Hamish Whyte, 2020)
is reprinted by permission of Carcanet Press and the Estate of Edwin Morgan.

Editing: Kirstyn Smith
Copy editing: Heather McDaid & Laura Jones-Rivera
Typesetting: Laura Jones-Rivera
Cover design: Kara McHale
Co-founders and publishers of 404 Ink:
Heather McDaid & Laura Jones-Rivera

Print ISBN: 978-1-916637-00-9
Ebook ISBN: 978-1-916637-01-6

EU GPSR Authorised Representative
LOGOS EUROPE, 9 rue Nicolas Poussin, 17000, LA ROCHELLE, France
E-mail: Contact@logoseurope.eu

Printed and bound in Great Britain by Clays Ltd, Elcograf S.p.A.

404 Ink acknowledges and is thankful for support from
Creative Scotland in the publication of this title.

MIX
Paper | Supporting
responsible forestry
FSC® C018072

LOTTERY FUNDED

SMALL TOWN JOY

FROM GLAM ROCK TO HYPERPOP: HOW QUEER MUSIC CHANGED THE SOUND OF SCOTLAND

CARRIE MARSHALL

SMALL TOWN JOY

FROM GLAM ROCK
TO HYPERPOP,
HOW QUEER MUSIC
CHANGED THE SOUND
OF SCOTLAND

CARRIE MARSHALL

FOR SOPHIE AND ADAM,
THE BEATS OF MY HEART;
AND IN LOVING MEMORY OF MUM,
WHO WOULD HAVE BEEN SO PROUD.

"Love rules. Love laughs. Love marches. Love
is the wolf that guards the gate.
Love is the food of music, art, poetry. It
fills us and fuels us and fires us to create."

Edwin Morgan, 'Love',
from *Love and a Life*

CONTENTS

A NOTE ON LANGUAGE AND CONTENT

I n this book you'll find me, and others, using the word "queer" a lot. It's not a word used lightly, because it's a word with a terrible history of being used against us. But it's also a word that since the early 1970s has been defiantly reclaimed by the very people it had been used against – "We're here! We're queer! Get used to it!" – and which today is used proudly, much like other marginalised communities have reclaimed the slurs once used to dehumanise them.

Reclaiming such words is intended to draw the sting, to drain those words of their poison, to take them back from people who have no right to use them. "Queer" is used in these pages in that spirit. I apologise if that makes some parts of this book difficult for some readers.

As an umbrella term to describe people who don't correspond to stereotypical ideas of gender and of sexuality, "queer" is really useful when you're writing about musicians who are no longer around to tell you who they are. Our understanding of gender and sexuality is much more nuanced today, so while many of the people you'll encounter in these pages might not have defined themselves using words such as pan, trans, non-binary, asexual or gender-fluid, or would have interpreted some of those descriptions differently than we do today, or may have used words that have since fallen out of favour, they lived lives where their sexuality, their gender presentation, or both, would clearly have fitted under the queer umbrella. Because it's such an inclusive term, it enables me to describe people without trying to force labels onto them that they might well have rejected.

For simplicity and readability's sake, I'll be using the acronym LGBTQ+ as shorthand for everybody under the queer umbrella unless I'm directly quoting someone else. I know some people prefer longer acronyms such as QUILTBAG (queer/questioning, intersex/indigender, lesbian, trans/trans-gender/two-spirit, bisexual, asexual, gay/genderqueer/gender non-conforming) or LGBTQQIP2SAA (lesbian, gay, bisexual, transgender, queer, questioning, intersex, pansexual, two-spirit, asexual, and ally), but I find that they take me out of whatever I'm reading. QUILTBAG sounds like it should be a BBC Two sitcom where the lead character keeps breaking the fourth wall and talking to the viewer, while LGBTQQIP2SAA feels to me like the name of a TikTok band whose music largely consists of glitchy videogame music and autotuned screaming.

As for the content, *Small Town Joy* is primarily about love, pride and joy, but, of course, any book about LGBTQ+ people is going to talk about some very dark events and include some terrible things said and done by terrible people. Reader discretion is advised.

INTRODUCTION

All your favourite music is queer.

I should probably explain.

The music you love might not be made by queer musicians, or be made specifically for queer listeners, or address queer themes, but queerness is in its DNA.

Queer people have been making music for as long as there has been music. Tchaikovsky,[1] Chopin,[2] Schubert,[3] Handel,[4] and Britten[5] are all believed to have been gay or bi, and while western pop and rock music quickly distanced itself from its primarily Black and queer roots, almost all of it owes its existence to the raucous "bulldaggers" of 1920s Harlem, the masculine-presenting Black lesbian blues and jazz singers who messed with gender roles and put queerness at the centre of their most celebrated, most sexual songs, and to the music made by the queer Black musicians that would follow them.

In the 1930s, Sister Rosetta Tharpe, a bisexual woman, took queer and gospel music and created rock'n'roll. She forged a template mixing the sacred and the profane that would be made even more explicit in the 1950s by two queer artists, Minnie Willie Mae "Big Mama" Thornton and former drag queen "Little" Richard Penniman, who first performed as Princess LaVonne.

Penniman's image and act were borrowed from and shaped by two queer performers who were known as The Prince of the Blues and The Queen of Rock'n'Roll respectively. The prince was Billy Wright, a gospel singer and female impersonator who would perform in drag at the tent shows of the time, refining the make-up skills and tricks he would pass on to Penniman; and the queen was a kinetic, dramatic piano player born Eskew Reeder, Jr. but much better known as the bewigged, heavily made-up Esquerita. Esquerita was the pioneer – he would later be credited by the B-52's Ricky Wilson as a key musical influence and both Mick Jones of The Clash (on *Big Audio Dynamite*'s 'Esquerita') and Adam Ant ('Miss Thing', from Ant's *Vive Le Rock* album) would write songs about him – but Penniman was the one who would become a musical legend and influence legions of musicians.

Both Thornton and Penniman had to be toned down for mainstream success, something that many recent LGBTQ+ musicians are familiar with. Jerry Leiber and Mike Stoller, the songwriters of 'Hound Dog', argued over Leiber's insistence that the chorus should say, "You ain't nothing but a *motherfucker*", while Dorothy LaBostrie was given the job of taming Little Richard's 'Tutti Frutti'. There are differing accounts of the original lyric, which began, "Tutti frutti / good booty" and then was either, "If it don't fit, force it / you can grease it, make it easy" or, "If it's tight, it's all right / and if it's greasy, it makes it easy". Either way, it's safe to say the 1950s America that lost its shit over a straight white man wiggling his hips wasn't quite ready for *that*.

Even in their bowdlerised form, 'Hound Dog' and 'Tutti Frutti' are among the most lewd, lascivious and life-affirming songs ever recorded – and among the most important and influential too.

Those songs and their creators inspired everybody from The Beatles to David Bowie. If it weren't for 'Hound Dog' we might never have heard of Elvis and the future of pop could have turned out very differently; and if it weren't for Sister Rosetta and Little Richard, we may never have had anybody else. Ringo Starr was in the audience for Tharpe's English shows and describes Little Richard as his hero; the other Beatles adored Little Richard too, with John Lennon teaching Paul McCartney how to emulate Richard's trademark howl. "It blew my mind," Lennon recalled.[6] "We'd never heard anybody sing like that in our lives."

Lou Reed was a Little Richard fan,[7] as was David Bowie. Speaking in 1991 about Richard, Bowie said, "Without him, I think myself and half my contemporaries wouldn't be playing music."[8] Richard was also a formative influence on The Who's Pete Townshend, who has described himself as pansexual. Speaking about his 1966 song 'I'm a Boy', he said that at the time he had to couch songs of queerness and gender confusion "in vignettes of humour and irony."[9] Townshend, the Little Richard-loving Beatles and the gender-bending, bisexual Bowie would prove to be just as influential as their heroes, and had a huge impact on many of the musicians you'll read about in these pages.

That impact was more than musical. The Beatles may not have been queer – according to Yoko Ono, John Lennon believed we're all "born bisexual"[10] although he never experimented – but their image was considered to be unacceptably so by many conservatives. That image, shaped largely by their gay manager Brian Epstein, was scandalously androgynous by the standards of the time. Feminist writer Betty Friedan described it as a rejection of, "that brutal, sadistic, tight-lipped, crew-cut, Prussian, big-muscle, Ernest Hemingway"[11] machismo particularly prevalent in the US, while one US Pentecostal writer was so furious about their apparent femininity that he took to his typewriter to exclaim, "No matter how popular the Beatles become, American girls still like boys to look like boys."[12]

LGBTQ+ people were just as influential offstage. In the 1950s Larry Parnes, a gay man, created the first British rock star, Tommy Steele, and transformed multiple boys-next-door into pop stars with a change of name and some better clothes: Steele was born Thomas Hicks, Ronald Wycherley became Billy Fury and Clive Powell became Georgie Fame. Parnes also invented the rock concert tour, where a bus full of bands travelled the country to play just one night in each town. Parnes' uncanny ability to spot the stars of the future – he was the most successful British music manager of the 1950s and 1960s – only failed once, in May 1960. Parnes had given a young band called The Silver Beats the job of supporting Johnny Gentle at dates in Alloa, Inverness, Fraserburgh, Keith, Forres, Nairn, and Peterhead. They performed as The Johnny Gentle Band and adopted stage names: Paul Ramon, Stuart de Staël, Carl Harrison, and Long John. However, despite their excitement, their first "showbiz" adventure was short-lived: Parnes decided not to continue working with them. The band went back to their given names: Paul McCartney, John Lennon, George Harrison, and Stuart Sutcliffe, and The Silver Beats became The Beatles.

Parnes was the first of what would later be dubbed the "velvet mafia", the gay managers, producers and music moguls of the late twentieth century who knew exactly what and who would sell to teenage girls. They shaped the careers and images of artists ranging from Billy Fury, Marc Bolan, The Beatles, and The Bee Gees to Wham! and The Who, effectively inventing pop culture as we know it today.

That culture may have tried to hide its queer roots – and in those much less enlightened times, many artists certainly had to hide their love away. But you can't hide your love forever, and queerness came swaggering and strutting out of clubs in the 1970s to take its place not just in disco, but also in US punk and new wave. Disco would fuel dance, electronic and pop music forever, and the punk music – named after a term originally used by Shakespeare to describe sex workers of any gender, but more usually used for men – of Lou Reed's Velvet Underground and of The New York Dolls would influence rock and indie musicians from The Sex Pistols to The Smiths, Green Day to Guns'n'Roses, Misfits to The Manic Street Preachers. On this side of the Atlantic, the fuse of the UK punk explosion was lit in the gay clubs of London.

By now you're probably thinking: *This is a book about Scottish music. What does any of this have to do with Scotland?*

Music is a story, and we Scots are among the world's finest storytellers. We tell our children tales of selkies and kelpies, supernatural and shape-shifting creatures of magic and mystery, so it's only natural that our music would be full of magic and mystery and shapeshifters too.

Scots have a long history of moving things and people around the world; if England is a nation of shopkeepers, Scotland is a nation of shipbuilders. And when you move people and things around the world their music – our music – moves with them. When music moves, it finds new shapes to take, new songs to sing and new voices to sing them.

Today, beats made in Bellshill bedrooms can be trending on TikTok by teatime. But while that speed is new, the motion isn't. My kids' music travels at the speed of light through fibre-optic cables, but my music travelled too: it came to me on cover-mounted cassette tapes and over the airwaves from far away and fading FM stations. For the generations before, music travelled from the other side of the world, on shellac and vinyl discs brought to Britain in the cavernous cargo holds of giant ships.

When music travelled by ship and by sea, the songs of innovators would be inhaled by imitators across the water and sometimes exhaled in whole new shapes. Those shapes would then make the return trip and influence the influencers, setting the next stage in motion.

Much of that music came through Scotland, often on Scottish-made ships: in the 1900s, one-fifth of the world's shipping fleet was built by Clydesiders. Glasgow in particular was one of the world's busiest ports, dubbed the "second city of the British Empire", and as products and people moved through Glasgow, music moved with them.

That imperial history is not without its horrors. Many Scots emigrants would become slave owners, and Glasgow merchants grew obscenely rich on the backs of the Black slaves who harvested tobacco and sugar in distant plantations. Major Glaswegian streets bear those merchants' names today, a history Glasgow is only just starting to face up to.

But there are happier stories too. For example, if you've ever wondered why US country music is so incredibly popular in Scotland, and in the west of Scotland in particular, it's because we helped invent it.

US country is the music of the melting pot, and Scots were a key ingredient: in our many decades of emigration to North America, with more than 360,000 Scots boarding Clyde-built ships to travel to the US and Canada in the 1920s alone, we took our folk music across the Atlantic. There, it joined hands with other forms of music including Irish and German folk music and Black spirituals, creating a style that would bring us artists ranging from Charley Pride and Johnny Cash to Lil Nas X and Jimmy Shand.

According to US academic and musician Dr Willie Ruff, those Black spirituals may have incorporated Scottish influences too: the "lining out" singing style of nineteenth-century Black slaves is sonically very similar to the "presenting the line" hymns of Hebridean Scots, thousands of whom emigrated to the US in the eighteenth and nineteenth centuries.

As for the self-proclaimed King of Country, Johnny Cash, perhaps the Man in Black could have been The Man in Black Watch: Cash believed his family originally hailed from the Kingdom of Fife.

As you've probably guessed from the weight of the paper, the size of the e-book or the time markers on the audiobook, *Small Town Joy* isn't going to tell the entire story of Scots music. Instead, I want to tell you *a* story: one of music loved by and made by LGBTQ+ Scots that queered the mainstream, influencing generations of musicians and music fans both here and all around the world.

I've experienced Scotland's music scene in two different roles (as a musician and as a music fan), in two different time periods (the late nineties/early aughts and today) and two different genders (man and woman). I've seen big changes in LGBTQ+ acceptance and visibility in that time, and today's scene is a very different place for women and LGBTQ+ people than it was in previous decades. That difference isn't just in my favourite genres, pop and rock. It's in everything from trad to techno. That's something I find absolutely fascinating, and I hope you will too.

What I've come to understand is that in music, queerness is like glitter. It makes everything sparkle, and it gets *everywhere*.

I started work on *Small Town Joy* while promoting my trans memoir, *Carrie Kills a Man*. In that book I say that the recipe for people is like the recipe for minestrone: apparently simple, but capable of almost infinite variation. I think you can say the same about music.

Almost all music can be boiled down to just three crucial ingredients: rhythm, melody and harmony. Yet, in musicians' hands it becomes so much more. Especially when those musicians are queer.

Queer music is outsider music, and outsider music comes bearing more than just melody on the back of its beats. Outsider music is music with baggage, with bruises, with battle scars. Those are its base metals, and queer musicians somehow manage to turn those metals into gold.

The joy of queer music is all the more remarkable when it's so often forged in the most terrible fires. But that's what makes it so powerful too, why its love and its lust, its defiance and its desire, its escapism and its euphoria feel so transcendent and so vital.

What queer music tells you is the most important thing of all:

You are not alone.

For a book about joy, there are a lot of tears in *Small Town Joy*. But they're mostly the tears I cry at the back of the Barrowlands when the emotion overwhelms me, the tears I cry when Kim Carnie sings so beautifully about her "walking disaster" of a girlfriend in 'She Moves Me', the tears I cry when Man of the Minch sings mournfully in 'Mountains', the tears I cry when SOPHIE tells me that 'It's Okay to Cry'.

They're the tears I feel starting to well up when the glassy notes of a DX7 synth tell me that Jimmy Somerville is going to make me cry myself inside out all over again.

I'll come back to Jimmy shortly, and to all these other incredible musicians. But first we need to go to a much darker place.

CHAPTER 1:
CALL ME A SIN

F or many queer Scots in the 1970s, the best thing about the country was the railway tracks leading out of it.

Scotland may have been voted the best place for LGBTQ+ people to live in 2015 and 2016[13] – an accolade it has shamefully lost in recent years, falling to seventeenth place in 2023 – but in the decades and even centuries before, Scotland was definitely not glad to be gay.

We like to joke about members of the Wee Frees chaining up swings on a Sunday, but Scotland has long been a very religious country with a distinctly puritan streak on both Presbyterian and Catholic pews.

Scotland is now officially a secular country. The 2022 Scottish Census found that 51.1 percent of Scots had no religion, up from 36.7 percent in 2011, and the numbers of people who practice religion of any kind is much smaller. Christian church attendance has been in decline for many years – so much so that since 2023 the Church of Scotland has been selling off hundreds of churches, manses, halls, and cottages as attendance falls. Its membership declined from over 900,000 people in 1982 to just over 270,000 in the early 2020s and the average age of a congregant is 62. The Catholic Church is in decline too: in 1982 it had 273 men in training for the priesthood; in 2022 it had just twelve. Despite a recent boom in the number of Scots getting married, religious marriages now account for fewer than one-third of Scots marriages. We're far more likely to have, or attend, a humanist or civil ceremony.

This change has been slow, though, and slower than in England; Scotland's move towards secularism didn't really accelerate until the late 1960s and into the 1970s when multiple civil rights movements – notably feminism and gay rights – and technologies such as the contraceptive pill challenged the churches' grip. But the grip remained strong for a long time, and even today Scottish councils must by law have three religious representatives on their education committees, including one from the Church of Scotland and one from the Catholic Church. These unelected figures get a say in policies such as relationship and sex education in non-religious schools, and in which schools councils decide to save or shutter. Eight Scottish councils have removed religious representatives' voting rights since the controversial closure of Blairingone Primary School in Kinross-shire in 2019, when the committee's two religious representatives swung the vote from save to shut. 24 councils haven't.

Religion's hold on Scotland's society, politics and press perhaps helps to explain why it took us fourteen years longer than England to decriminalise consensual sex between two men, which England and Wales did in 1967 but Scotland didn't do until 1980.[14]

Lesbians were never criminalised by anti-gay legislation – in 1921 the House of Lords rejected calls to prohibit any "act of gross indecency between female persons" for fear of giving women ideas: "The more you advertise vice by prohibiting it the more you will increase it"; peers also suggested that such prohibition would be unfair because "women are by nature much more gregarious"[15] – but man-on-man action was outlawed during the reign of Henry VIII in 1533 and remained punishable by death in England until 1861. Scotland took even longer to change the law, becoming the very last part of Europe to abolish the death penalty for gay sex, which it finally did in 1889. And even when execution was off the menu throughout Britain, gay men could still be imprisoned – as Oscar Wilde was in 1895 – or subjected to chemical castration, as computer pioneer Alan Turing was in 1952.

The legal climate began to change in the late 1950s when, after three years of investigation, the Wolfenden Report recommended that the government should decriminalise homosexual activity. That was in 1957. It took another decade for England to act on that recommendation and another two decades for Scotland to follow suit. Gay sex wasn't decriminalised here until the Criminal Justice (Scotland) Act, which became law in 1980 but didn't take effect until February 1981.

Even then, Scotland didn't fully decriminalise gays having fun. We kept the same caveats as the English decriminalisation of the 1960s: gay sex remained illegal for men under twenty-one, for men who had sex in a hotel room or for men who had sex when a third person was present or participating. The age of consent wasn't lowered until 1994, but even then it was only lowered to eighteen. Full equality didn't happen until 2001, and equal marriage didn't hit the statute books until 2014.

Some of our politicians, such as Scotland's current Deputy First Minister Kate Forbes, say they would have voted against Scotland's equal marriage legislation;[16] others, such as Tory leadership candidate Murdo Fraser, was one of eighteen MSPs who did vote against it and says today that he is still opposed to it.[17] The SNP-led Scottish government resisted calls for equal marriage legislation for many years, arguing that the civil partnerships introduced in 2005 were enough, and equal marriage only became law in Scotland after David Cameron's Tories introduced equal marriage legislation for England and Wales in 2013. Even then, both the Catholic Church and Church of Scotland were in opposition and David Robertson, minister of St Peter's Free Church in Dundee, told the BBC, "We will now be discriminated against when we do not bow down to the new State absolutist morality... this will be detrimental to the people of Scotland, especially the poor and marginalised."[18]

That was in supposedly progressive 2014. Imagine what 1974 must have been like.

For queer musicians in the 1970s, the safest place in Scotland may have been the closet. The culture offered at best smirking homophobia and at worst serious danger.

There were a number of gay clubs, most notably in Edinburgh where the city's pioneering gay disco, at Nicky Tams on Victoria Street, became so busy that the scene moved to much larger venues such as Tiffany's on St Stephen Street. However, some people in their late teens who were below the then-unequal age of consent say they were made to feel distinctly unwelcome by the older patrons. Queer people of all ages seeking company faced multiple dangers, including entrapment by plainclothes policemen and violence in the streets.[19]

It's hardly surprising that, in this climate, few if any LGBTQ+ musicians were willing to go public about their sexuality. Billy Lyall, the multi-instrumentalist who was an early member of The Bay City Rollers and who co-wrote Pilot's first hit single, 'Magic', was gay, but kept his sexuality quiet; he was outed a decade after his death from an AIDS-related illness by his former manager, Thomas Dougal "Tam" Paton.

As with K-pop bands in the early 2000s, The Bay City Rollers had a frequently changing lineup of young, good-looking, supposedly virginal musicians whose squeaky-clean image was so crucial and so controlled that even having girlfriends was banned. Paton wouldn't have dreamed of outing Lyall or any other Roller in the 1970s: in the Rollers' world, all the boys were perfectly pure and as straight as straight can be.

But Paton's Rollers also featured at least one other closeted LGBTQ+ person, lead singer and teen girls' heartthrob Les McKeown. McKeown stayed in the closet until Paton's death in 2009, after which he publicly came out as bisexual and started talking about what had happened to him in the band.

Young closeted LGBTQ+ people can be very vulnerable, and that attracts predators – predators like Paton. He used his power and status to abuse multiple young men including teenage runaways, boys who'd been placed in care, would-be pop stars, and some of his charges, who he plied with alcohol and drugs to make more receptive. Three of the Rollers – McKeown, guitarist Pat McGlynn and original singer Nobby Clark – have said they were among his victims. In a 2023 documentary about the band and their manager, McGlynn said that Paton was "a monster... in the seventies, there were people who had the right to do what they wanted with you."[20]

Les McKeown died in 2021. In her report, senior coroner Mary Hassell noted that the singer had a markedly heavy heart,[21] and said damage from his lifelong struggles with alcohol and drug abuse were significant factors in his death. Those struggles dated back to McKeown's days as a Bay City Roller; he was abusing alcohol and cocaine while teen magazines reassured their readers that the strongest substance their idols enjoyed was milk.

It seems that many LGBTQ+ musicians of the era faced Hobson's choice: come out and say goodbye to your career and possibly your safety; stay in the closet and risk blackmail or worse.

That was definitely something Wendy Carlos believed. Carlos introduced the world to (and contributed to the development of) the Moog synthesiser, had a huge global hit with her 1968 album *Switched-On Bach*, and was also an early proponent of what we now know as ambient music. Her soundtracks for *A Clockwork Orange*, *The Shining* and *Tron* were critically acclaimed, musically stunning and hugely influential.

Carlos was a huge influence on other important figures including John Carpenter – "That's where I think it started,"[22] Carpenter said, crediting *Switched-On Bach* with fuelling his love of synth music – and Giorgio Moroder. The godfather of modern dance music, Moroder was inspired by Carlos to pick up a synthesiser, and without Carlos' influence there would have been no 'I Feel Love', no 'Love to Love You Baby', no 'Call Me', no 'Number One Song in Heaven'. It's not hyperbole to say that without Carlos, electronic music – especially pop and dance music – and movie soundtracks would be very different. CHVRCHES albums would certainly be a lot shorter.

Carlos is a trans woman who transitioned in 1972, but like other trans people of that era – such as the Emmy award-winning conductor and *Watership Down* composer Angela Morley, who transitioned the same year and decided she was no longer willing to appear on TV for fear of a negative reaction – she spent many years avoiding the spotlight. She would later say that she lost an entire decade hiding her true self from fame, refusing visits from famous fans including George Harrison and Stevie Wonder for fear of public ridicule. This was so strong that before what would be her final live concert, she decided that she wanted the audience to think she was a cisgender man. Carlos applied fake sideburns and drew on fake stubble, crying in her hotel room as she donned her disguise.

"There had never been any need of this charade to have taken place," she would later recall. "The public turned out to be amazingly tolerant or, if you wish, indifferent [...] It had proven a monstrous waste of years of my life." [23] But there were still many indignities, accidental or otherwise, because of her trans status; the 2001 rerelease of her *Clockwork Orange* soundtrack credits her under her deadname.

The electronic instruments that Carlos loved would play an important part in one of the three key musical movements of the 1970s, two of which rejected the largely macho swagger of what we'd now call classic rock. That movement was disco, which emerged in New York from the Black and gay rights movements and which mixed R&B, soul, synthesisers, and propulsive four-to-the-floor beats to thrilling effect.

The other standout anti-macho musical movement was UK punk, which took the Marlon Brando attitude to rebellion: when asked, "What are you rebelling against?" the reply would be, "What've you got?" Punk wanted to get drunk and destroy everything about the status quo from the po-faced proficiency of Pink Floyd to the patriarchy.

Last but not least, there was hard rock, which was transitioning to become heavy metal.

There's some distance musically between 'Rock the Boat' and *Combat Rock*. But disco and punk had a lot in common. While both scenes would ultimately be colonised and homogenised by very different demographics, they both initially emerged from disenfranchised communities: Black, LGBTQ+ and Latin groups in the US, and poor, working-class areas in the UK. Both scenes rejected the often oppressive societal and musical norms of the time and cast their nets widely: the foundational track of disco, 'Soul Makossa', was an import from Cameroon, and much of UK punk was heavily influenced by Jamaican reggae and dub. Both scenes faced significant opposition from the establishment. And both would be enormously influential for decades to come.

As Darryl W Bullock writes in his superb book *Pride, Pop and Politics*,

"The birth of British punk rock (as opposed to the American version) is inextricably linked to London's gay scene. When no venue would consider hosting punk bands or allowing them to practice there, it was the underground gay clubs of Covent Garden and Soho that provided space. When every other public house refused to serve these weird-looking kids with their spiky hair, outrageous make-up, torn clothing and safety-pin jewellery, it was London's gay clubs [that] embraced them. And when they needed a hangout of their own, it was a gay club, Chaguaramas, that became The Roxy, London's premier punk venue."[24]

One of the most infamous groups of English punks was The Bromley Contingent, followers of The Sex Pistols whose numbers included Billy Idol, Siouxsie Sioux and Steve Severin, later of Siouxsie and The Banshees. Many of the contingent were gay, and, as Siouxsie recalls, the period was "a club for misfits, almost. Anyone that didn't conform to any mass Mecca to belong to, it was waifs, there was male gays, female gays, bisexuals, non-sexuals, everything. No one was criticised for their sexual preferences. The only thing that was looked down on was being plain boring."[25]

After disco and punk, the third genre was heavy metal, which in the early seventies was moving away from its blues-rock

CARRIE MARSHALL

roots into something much harder. That was largely down to Judas Priest, the band credited with inventing the genre as we know it, thanks to their use of double-pedalled kick drums, Rob Halford's distinctive, octave-spanning vocal style and their then-blasphemous use of synthesisers. From Metallica to Slipknot and even the parodic Spinal Tap, if it's metal or one of metal's many subgenres, it owes a debt to Priest.

Judas Priest's influence wasn't just musical. Halford made the leather, spikes and studs of the gay and BDSM scenes his stagewear, a look that was widely copied by many macho men of glam rock and metal on both sides of the Atlantic. Halford wouldn't come out until 1998, but it's fair to say he was dropping some pretty big hints during the two decades prior.

It's said that everybody who saw The Sex Pistols play Manchester's Lesser Free Trade Hall in the summer of 1976 formed a band. For many Scots musicians, their year zero came slightly later in May 1977 when The Clash came to the Edinburgh Playhouse on the White Riot tour. As Vic Galloway writes in his book *Rip It Up*, the show would "instigate a Scottish post-punk revolution in its grand surroundings. Members of Orange Juice, Josef K and The Fire Engines were all in attendance and experienced an epiphany."[26] While the bill also featured The Jam and Subway Sect, it seems that the two acts with the biggest impact were Buzzcocks and The Slits.

Buzzcocks' *Spiral Scratch* EP, recorded with original singer Howard Devoto, is one of the most important records of what came to be called post-punk. But Buzzcocks' imperial phase began when Devoto quit in the spring of 1977 after fewer than a dozen gigs and was replaced by Pete Shelley (born Peter McNeish; Shelley was the name his mum would have called him were he born a girl).

Shelley, who was bisexual, wrote songs that were impishly playful, sometimes hilariously sexual and always incredibly relatable – and while he didn't release anything openly queer until his solo record 'Homosapien' in 1981 (featuring the wonderful couplet 'Homo superior / in my interior'), his sexuality was hardly hidden. When the band appeared on *Top of the Pops* in 1978 to perform 'Love You More', Shelley's guitar strap bore a large badge emblazoned with the words "I LIKE BOYS". More eagle-eyed viewers might also have spotted another, which read, "How dare you presume I'm heterosexual?"

Buzzcocks' 'Ever Fallen in Love (With Someone You Shouldn't've)' is rightly regarded as one of the greatest pop singles ever recorded. It's queer as hell, the LGBTQ+ 'Teenage Kicks'. Inspired by the Marlon Brando movie *Guys and Dolls*, which Shelley saw while relaxing post-gig in Edinburgh's Blenheim Guest House in late 1977, the song is about Shelley's relationship with Francis Cookson, the man he lived with for seven years. Viewed through a queer lens, the chorus is even more poignant: which queer person *hasn't* fallen in love with someone who couldn't or wouldn't love them back? I'm usually in double figures by lunchtime.

Shelley didn't hide his bisexuality, but I think he encrypted it: queer musicians, like other marginalised artists, often hide their selves in plain sight for mainstream listeners to ignore and queer folks like me to overanalyse. It's there if you know to look for it. Among the lists of masturbatory subjects in 'Orgasm Addict' there are "butcher's assistants and bellhops", and I've laughed a lot at online analyses of 'Why Can't I Touch It?' that talk about its lyrical explorations of existentialism and philosophy, when I'm pretty sure it's The Beatles' 'I Want to Hold Your Hand' rewritten with a very different appendage in mind.

Introducing his interview with Shelley in 1994, Matt Wobensmith of *Outpunk* fanzine noted, "Of all the British punk bands, the Buzzcocks were perhaps the most obviously open to gay sexuality. That they enjoyed all types of sex was well known, and in his liner notes to the Buzzcocks box set *Product*, Jon Savage (himself one the queerest of critics) makes a big point of noting that the Buzzcocks were a gay positive band."[27] Asked whether the early punk scene was more inclusive, Shelley replied,

> "It didn't really matter what you were, what sexual persuasion you were from or what gender you were. It was just a chance for everyone to do things, because lots of people were stretching the boundaries of what it was possible to do. So it didn't really matter, it didn't raise eyebrows if someone was gay… [gay clubs] were the freer places where you could actually hang out and dress like you wanted and it was ok. If you went to straight clubs, then you got odd looks."[28]

I think one of the things that punk offered queer people, as goth and emo would do in the decades following, was a place where you could hide in plain sight by being outrageous: punk was supposed to be provocative and shocking, a rebellion against whatever the older generations had. Queer people were part of that rebellion and queerness was part of that provocation: one of the most famous products ever sold by Sex, the shop run by Vivienne Westwood and Malcolm McLaren that spawned The Sex Pistols, was Westwood's "Two Cowboys" T-shirt, which reproduced an erotic illustration by Jim French of two very friendly cowboys. The first person to wear it in public was immediately arrested on grounds of obscenity, which of course was the whole point.

One of the key venues for Manchester's burgeoning punk movement was The Ranch, which Shelley recalled "was a gay bar really [...] gay bars were the places you could go and be outlandish with your dress, and not get beaten up. You could almost get into cross-dressing, without it being a big hassle. People were bohemian, while everybody was trying to conform. Your sexuality wasn't an issue."[29]

Buzzcocks' influence was immediate and long-lasting, not just musically but in Shelley's distinctly un-macho stage persona. The Slits' legacy was a slower burn.

The four women in the band – the classic lineup of Ari Up, Viv Albertine, Tessa Pollitt and Palmolive – were radical enough by simply being four feminists in a punk band. But they also claimed *Dionne Warwick Sings Burt Bacharach* as their favourite album, and their own debut LP was produced by reggae and lovers rock legend Dennis Bovell. Their extraordinary sound and rejection of gender stereotypes would prove to be enormously influential in queer punk of the 1980s and beyond.

The Slits' legacy was perhaps at its clearest in the 1990s Riot grrrl movement, whose Scottish contingent included the critically lauded Lung Leg, who split in 1999 before reforming in 2023, as well as more recent Riot grrrls of the 2020s including Tomintoul's sibling duo Bratakus and Glaswegian quartet Brat Coven. Both bands are fiercely feminist, proudly political and avowedly LGBTQ+ inclusive, and Bratakus have also helped inspire the next generation of grrrls of every gender through their work with Girls Rock Glasgow.

Punk enthused an astonishing group of Scottish artists including Edinburgh's The Rezillos (who were also strongly influenced by the energetically camp alt-pop of The B-52's), Scars, The

Prats, The Fire Engines, The Flowers, Dunfermline's Skids and The Exploited – whose Big John Duncan would later play in Goodbye Mr Mackenzie alongside the young Shirley Manson. The scene wasn't always quite as inclusive as Pete Shelley recalls – Scars would incite a furious response from crowds when singer Robert King took to the stage wearing heels and earrings – but the bands and fans of the time describe it as a golden age of creativity and experimentation.

While the pop fans of East Lothian and Fife scoffed at their big brothers' prog rock records and embraced punk's DIY ethic, Glaswegian punks weren't so fortunate.

Following a riotous show at Dundee Technical College's student union in early 1976, The Sex Pistols were due to bring their Anarchy tour to the Glasgow Apollo and the Caird Hall in Dundee later that year. Both shows were cancelled as threats to public order; Dundee's Lord Provost, Chic Farquhar, claimed at the time, "We have enough hooligans of our own without importing them from England."[30]

Some members of Glasgow's licensing committee also wanted to cancel the planned Stranglers show in the City Halls scheduled for June 1977. The show wasn't banned, but some members, including the Conservative licensing committee chairman Bill Aitken, went along and didn't like what they saw. As Glasgow's Lord Provost, David Hodge, put it, "If these people with their depraved minds want to hear this kind of thing, fair enough. But let them do it in private."[31]

It's been widely reported that in 1976/77, Glasgow councillors banned punk rock from Glasgow but, like a lot of stories around punk, it has been exaggerated: there was a short-lived ban, but only in venues that were licensed as theatres such as the Apollo and the City Halls.[32] The Burns Howff in West Regent Street and the Mars Bar in Howard Street, among others, put on punk bands such as The Jolts and

Johnny & The Self Abusers, who would later become Simple Minds. According to journalist Simon Goddard, "The stark reality of the risk [from putting on The Sex Pistols] was more depressing than terrifying. Before being cancelled, the Apollo had sold less than a hundred tickets. All the punks in Glasgow could barely fill a double-decker bus."[33]

The licensing committee may have put pressure on Glasgow's pubs to not host punk gigs, but it didn't ban them from doing so. However, for some venues, they didn't need to.

Many Glasgow venues had enough to deal with without adding punk rock to an already volatile mix. Glasgow was no longer the Mean City of the 1930s razor gangs, but it was still a tough town – and the dancehalls and clubs were notoriously violent from the late 1960s and throughout the 1970s. This was the Glasgow of the Maryhill Fleeto, the Yoker Toi and the Ibrox Tongs, teenage gangs who used the city centre and several of its venues as their battlegrounds.

As if that wasn't enough trouble, some venues had even more violent patrons: the Barrowland Ballroom, which everybody calls The Barras, became the stalking ground of serial killer Bible John, who murdered three women on their way home from nights out at the venue in 1968 and 1969. These killings were partly responsible for the venue closing in the early 1970s. It reopened as a roller disco and didn't become a significant venue again until 1983 when Simple Minds used it for their 'Waterfront' music video.

While the music scene in Edinburgh was energised by punk rock, the punks of the west mostly had to either head east to the capital or go outside the city boundaries to nearby Paisley, whose Silver Thread Hotel and Bungalow Bar became the focus of the DIY music revolution. The Silver Thread is long gone and the Bungalow has moved from its original home in

Renfrew Road, but it's still a busy live music venue, although these days you're more likely to see tribute bands than the original punks that made its seventies heyday so exciting.

The inclusiveness of early punk couldn't last. As Jon Savage writes in *The Secret Public*, the influence of gay men and lesbian women meant that punk initially rejected gender stereotypes and fuelled the rise of powerful women by creating "new templates for performers which included the strong, assertive personae adopted by The Slits or Siouxsie and the Banshees"[34] as well as the un-macho personae of Pete Shelley. What began as punk, a relatively open-minded movement, started to become punk *rock*.

We've seen this again and again: cultural movements go from underground to overground, and when they do they become assimilated and diluted and homogenised. What starts with Nirvana leads to Nickelback, and The Slits end up making room for Sham 69. The huge impact of The Sex Pistols in particular saw an influx of bandwagon jumpers as pub rock bands cut their hair and learnt to sneer so that they could try and ride the punk rock wave.

That's not to say there weren't some great punk rock bands. But for every Clash or Crass there were countless Sex Pistols copyists and bands like The Stranglers, whose 1977 album *Rattus Norvegicus* was horrifically brutal and misogynistic even by the subterranean standards of seventies rock.

Think of a punk rock band now and I bet you're envisaging four skinny, straight white boys in black jeans, not the bi-coded Buzzcocks or the lesbian-feminist Au Pairs. But those bands would leave a more substantial legacy than the legions of phlegm-flecked hooligans that rejected femininity, flamboyance and fun. As punk's horizons narrowed, new wave and post-punk would soar high above them.

Two Scottish labels would take this new energy and use it to release some of the most important, if not necessarily the best-selling, records by Scots artists and labels. It's said that Glasgow's Postcard was better at hype and that Edinburgh's Fast Product was better at the art, but both labels were hotbeds of unconventional creativity a world away from the macho, cishet bluster of the US rock and pub rock punk of the era.

As we'll discover, both labels produced some of the most famous and gorgeous music ever recorded, but queer-adjacent pop wasn't just happening in Scotland's two central cities. Some of the most extraordinary, beautiful, genre- and gender-bending music ever to come from Scotland was birthed somewhere between Bridge of Allan and Dundee.

CHAPTER 2:
A MATTER OF GENDER

I heard 'Party Fears Two' for the first time during one of those west of Scotland Saturdays where the sky and the M8 motorway are the same shade of grey, raindrops falling like wet hammers. I was in the back of my dad's powder-blue Ford Sierra and we were driving back to Ayrshire after an afternoon shopping in Glasgow. My dad turned on the radio to drown out the sound of the windscreen wipers and I had one of those *Wizard of Oz* moments where everything goes from black-and-white to Technicolor. Even now, 'Party Fears Two' sounds like it came from another universe.

'Party Fears Two' was the big single from *Sulk*, The Associates' second album, although it was written years before in 1977. The core of The Associates was founding duo William "Billy" Mackenzie, a singer from Dundee, and guitarist Alan Rankine from Bridge of Allan. The two met in Edinburgh in 1976 and discovered a shared love of David Bowie, pop and disco, and occasionally played together in cover bands before collaborating as part of a short-lived cabaret troupe. That gave way to the slightly more conventional Mental Torture, whose idiosyncratic and unlicensed cover of Bowie's 'Boys Keep Swinging' managed to get airplay on John Peel's Radio 1 show as an impressive piece of profile-raising trouble-making. But it was as The Associates that Mackenzie and Rankine would make magic.

Billy Mackenzie was a free spirit, which is often a euphemism for a huge pain in the arse. He could certainly be that: in his later career he was infamous for expensive pranks, spending binges and wilful behaviour, but he was also a warm, fascinating, funny, and very beautiful man with an astonishing talent and an even more astonishing voice, a four-octave tenor capable of operatic highs and subterranean lows.

Mackenzie was also gay or bi, although the definitive biography of his life, Tom Doyle's 1998 *The Glamour Chase*, skips over this until near the end of the book – a strange decision considering its clear relevance to his early life in Dundee and his later life as a pop star in what were still extremely homophobic times.

Speaking to *The Herald*, Rankine said that from the outset "it was fairly obvious that Bill was gay or bisexual or whatever, but it wasn't part of our vocabulary."[35] Mackenzie didn't really try to keep his sexuality secret, but he didn't talk about it publicly until an awkward *Time Out* interview in 1994 in which he said that he didn't really see gender when he was attracted to someone.

Like many LGBTQ+ people, Billy was picked on for being different – "Bill hadn't had a good time of it being gay in Dundee and not being really able to come out," Rankine said[36] – and like so many other LGBTQ+ musicians, he found a safe space in music. And what music he would make.

One of the things I like about many Scots bands of the early eighties is the lack of "Scottish Cringe", a term that initially described Scots politically, the idea that Scotland was "too wee, too poor, too stupid" for self-government. But it's a cultural phenomenon too. These are records made with wide-screen vision, drawing as much from the motorised rhythms of German electronic music as they do from more traditional pop and made to sound absolutely massive. Bowie's Berlin trilogy (*Low*, *Heroes* and *Lodger*) were clear influences on bands such as The Associates and peers such as Simple Minds. But the Minds' Jim Kerr never sang like this.

Listening to it now, The Associates' debut album *The Affectionate Punch* still sounds fresh and new. Sure, there are a few gated drums that haven't aged well. But it's a lovely, luminous thing that mixes angular guitar pop with lush instrumentation and Mackenzie's often astonishing vocals to create music that feels timeless. It's also fun to play spot-the-legacy; for example, among the pulsing beats and jittery piano of the title track there's a guitar riff that would fit beautifully on Franz Ferdinand's 'Take Me Out'.

NME's Paul Morley was one of several journalists to hail *The Affectionate Punch* a masterpiece. Like many reviewers, he found their music to be theatrical, but, "their sense of theatre is natural, even profound, not the usual pop flash-trivia."[37] One of the songs Morley singled out was 'A Matter of Gender', which he described as "a lush example of The Associates' private desperation and public drama."[38] Gender was something Mackenzie clearly liked to write and sing about. As Rankine recalled, "A lot of his songs are about his struggling with his gender and his sexuality."[39]

I don't know if Mackenzie would consider himself non-binary if he had been born twenty years later, but he was sometimes gender non-conforming and often provocative: in 1983, the *NME* reported that he'd been spotted in the foyer of a fancy hotel, his whippets howling and pissing on the legs of businessmen, while Mackenzie himself was in full drag.

"I can swing with the best of them," Mackenzie later said. "I'm the type of person who sees beyond genders."[40]

One of Mackenzie's haunts was the Hoochie Coochie Club in Edinburgh's Tollcross, where artists such as Soft Cell and Bronski Beat would perform. It was also home to local acts such as Goodbye Mr Mackenzie, whose keyboard player Shirley Manson would later become a star in her own right.

It's a long way from Tollcross in the late seventies to Los Angeles today, but when Manson calls me from the LA studio where she's currently recording Garbage's eighth studio album, the miles and the years disappear. "The Hoochie Coochie Club was the centre of my world," Manson says. "It was where I got exposed to a lot of amazing music, and it was the first time I had been immersed in club life. I came from a pretty conventional family, a very nice family, and finally getting in through the doors and being exposed to a counterculture, a subculture, was thrilling."

It was more than just music. "Being exposed to different expressions of gender, different expressions of sexuality and different expressions of identity all happened in that club," she adds. "I found it exciting, inspiring, and I felt for the first time ever I belonged somewhere."

Manson was introduced to Billy Mackenzie there. "He was delightful, and I was crazy about him," she recalls. "I can't even remember who introduced us because everything just went into slow motion and soft focus."

Mackenzie is "one of the greatest Scottish vocalists of all time," Manson says. "He's one of the great vocalists full stop, and definitely one of our greatest artists. To have spent even a tiny moment in his world is something I've never forgotten. He's deeply important to me."

Mackenzie wasn't just important to Manson because of

his musical talent and his charisma. He also mattered because of what he represented: a pop star who was one of us. "I don't think people who don't come from Scotland can fully understand what it was like growing up in the 1970s and into the 1980s," Manson says. "There were very few figures in popular culture that came from Scotland. Sean Connery was one, Annie Lennox was another, and then there was Billy Mackenzie." Seeing Mackenzie on *Top of the Pops* "felt empowering and unlimiting."

"I think that's one of the great things about pop stars," Manson says. "We identify with their ability to break free. And they become our kind of superheroes."

Sulk made Billy Mackenzie a pop star, which was quite something for a record that was described by one reviewer as "one of the most extreme demonstrations of emotional bloodletting ever recorded",[41] and that Mackenzie himself said was "a big moaning album, moaning about this, moaning about that."[42]

Mackenzie wasn't cut out for pop stardom. He started spending impulsively and extravagantly, flamboyantly and foolishly, blowing record company advances – each one a very large loan to which he'd keep adding more expenses – on his friends, his family and his beloved whippets. His extravagance, wilfulness and perfectionism were a record company's worst nightmare, but it was one they were willing to put up with while The Associates made great music. Mackenzie couldn't stop himself from pushing things too far.

In August 1982, the band were scheduled to play some UK dates before heading to the US for a tour and to sign a multi-million US record deal. There were also plans to record the next album in Robert Palmer's studio in Nassau. But at the very last moment Mackenzie decided he didn't want to do any of it. He wanted to stay home.

Rankine tried to talk him out of it. But with somewhat convenient timing the very next day Mackenzie contracted pharyngitis, a throat inflammation that can often be caused by the heavy consumption of spirits. The UK dates were pulled.

The US tour didn't happen either. A month later, on the night before the band were due to travel to the US, Mackenzie announced that the US tour couldn't go ahead because the band wasn't good enough. The US tour and record deal were history.

Mackenzie and Rankine officially parted company in 1983, with Mackenzie keeping the band name and Rankine continuing to make music. "I wish it could have lasted a bit longer, but it couldn't have been any other way," Rankine said. "Bill went on using the name, but I don't think he should have because it wasn't the same animal."[43]

The Associates returned in 1994 only for Mackenzie to be saboteur again: invited on *Top of the Pops* despite a low chart placing, Mackenzie deliberately sang the wrong melody.

As Mackenzie's money dwindled alongside his fame, it was reported that he was living in a squat, a consequence of what he called "the carnage of the *Trainspotting* heroin trip" of his London life.[44]

There was more music – the *Perhaps* LP of 1985, a hi-NRG cover of Blondie's 'Heart of Glass' in 1988 – and a scrapped album, *The Glamour Chase*, which was rejected because the label felt it wasn't commercially viable.

Mackenzie hopped from project to project until finally reuniting with Rankine in 1993 to record some new demos, but the much-hoped-for Associates reunion never left the studio. Mackenzie had no interest in touring and apparently lost interest in the project too. "Billy wanted a different route,"

Rankine recalled in *Herald Scotland*. "He wanted to play in gay discos! Because rock'n'roll is a very macho thing, and that whole iconography turned him off. If you said, 'Let's go on a forty-eight-date tour,' he'd say, 'Nah!' When you start to say this is your next eight months mapped in front of you, I think Bill just said, 'I can't do that'."[45]

Grieving the death of his mother and battling depression, Billy Mackenzie took his own life in 1997, overdosing on prescription medicine and paracetamol in his father's garden shed. He was thirty-nine.

After leaving The Associates, Rankine charted a new career direction. In 1994 he became a lecturer in music at Glasgow's Stow College. Along with Ken McCluskey of The Bluebells and Douglas MacIntyre of the Creeping Bent label, Rankine managed Kelvin College's student-run Electric Honey label, which released early music by upcoming artists including Belle and Sebastian, Biffy Clyro and Snow Patrol and is still going strong today.

Rankine continued to make music and inspire musicians until he died peacefully in 2023 aged sixty-four. Tributes poured in from across the world of music: Duglas T. Stewart of BMX Bandits; Gary Clark of Danny Wilson; The Trashcan Sinatras; Finitribe; and Belle and Sebastian. Responding to the news of Rankine's passing, Ladytron wrote simply, "No Associates = No Ladytron", adding that Rankine was the "creator of amongst the most joyous, magnificent pop music of all time." [46] Tim London, co-producer of Young Fathers, agrees. "The Associates and Billy Mackenzie made the perfect pop single."[47]

Billy Mackenzie wasn't the only person experimenting with gender in the 1980s. Horse McDonald, who we'll meet in the next chapter, rejected stereotypical femininity, embracing a much more masculine presentation that, like her extraordinary voice, crossed the gender binary. And when Annie Lennox of Eurythmics pulled off her long blonde wig in the video for 'Love Is a Stranger' to reveal her close-cropped hair, someone at MTV panicked and pulled the video mid-broadcast, fearing that the station had accidentally showed a video promoting homosexuality and transvestism.

Reassured that Lennox wasn't a cross-dressing man, the industry gave her a new label: gender-bender.

"I remember thinking, Gender-bender? What does that mean?" Lennox told *The Advocate*. "I haven't got a clue, because I was simply expressing myself, and I knew very well what my gender was. However, I think the bigger question became, Was I bending my sexuality? Well, I wasn't, because I'm not gay, but everybody sort of latched on to this notion that I would be gay and some people were disappointed that I wasn't or thought I was in denial."[48]

She adds: "It's so interesting because when you put something out that is strong and provocative in a way, people respond to it. They have their notion of what that is. But I wasn't thinking about any of that at the time."

Gender-bending, adopting the clothes associated with the opposite gender, was hardly new: Marlene Dietrich did it beautifully in the 1940s and the bulldaggers of Harlem did it two decades previously. But it enjoyed something of a renaissance in the early eighties with the provocative feminism of Lennox; the dad-confusing femininity of Pete Burns, Marilyn and Boy George; and entire volumes of *Now That's What I Call Music!* compilations featuring boys in blouses and borrowed blusher.

Like the hair metal or glam metal of 1980s, US bands such as Mötley Crüe, Poison and Warrant, the New Romantic style borrowed heavily from the glam rock of the seventies. Although the bisexual David Bowie and Marc Bolan were the key influences for the UK contingent, most of the glammed-up bands were like the bandwagon-jumping "brickies in eyeliner" of seventies glam, straight men embracing dandyism to impress girls. But the backlash against more macho stereotypes didn't just create a golden age of shiny pop. It also helped open doors for bands who weren't straight: bands such as Frankie Goes To Hollywood, Soft Cell and Bronski Beat.

CHAPTER 3:
THE HEATHER'S ON FIRE

T he Associates weren't alone in their magpie mixing of musical genres. Many early post-punk Scots bands took liberally from punk as well as Motown and disco. Buzzcocks, The Velvet Underground, The Slits, and Nile Rodgers' disco sensations Chic were particularly strong influences on Orange Juice, whose glorious 'Rip It Up' owes a deliberate debt to both the Velvets and to Chic's 'Good Times'. Chic were also a big influence on Orange Juice's sonically darker post-punk labelmates, Josef K.

Orange Juice began in Glaswegian suburb Bearsden as the Nu-Sonics in 1976, and the star quality of singer Edwyn Collins impressed would-be pop impresario Alan Horne so much in 1978 that he decided he'd start a label to put out the band's records. That label, Postcard Records, cheekily promoted itself as The Sound of Young Scotland – an homage to Motown's Sound of Young America – and would be influential not just because of the music it released, but also as a template for the many indie labels that sprung up in the UK in the 1980s and beyond.

Horne was very much in the mould of a Brian Epstein or a Larry Parnes, a Babycham-sipping, obsessive pop scholar with big ambitions. Horne's own musical career was short-lived – his band, Oscar Wild, didn't exactly set the heather on fire despite having some of the best names in pop, Brian Superstar and Miss Janice Fuck, in its lineup. According to Postcard biographer Simon Goddard, "Oscar Wild's concert career began and ended in a village hall in Troon, trembling before a local chapter of Hells Angels which, by the time Edwyn got hold of the story and inflated it into the weather balloon-sized farce he desired, ended in something approaching Altamont on the South Ayrshire coast."[49]

Horne's creative partnership with Orange Juice would be much more fruitful, although they too would find themselves hiding from angry audiences – most notably a truly terrifying tanked-up crowd in Glasgow's Maryhill demanding they play some Showaddywaddy.

Although they didn't know one another at the time, both Horne and Collins had been in the crowd at The Clash's White Riot show in Edinburgh. Neither was particularly enthused by the headliners – Horne was more taken by The Slits, while Collins' and the other Nu-Sonics' attempts to befriend The Clash by offering to help load their gear resulted in drummer Topper Headon throwing badges at them. For Collins, the real stars of the show were Buzzcocks, whose Pete Shelley let him and his bandmates sit in on a fanzine interview. Collins would write Orange Juice's second single, 'Blue Boy', about the meeting.

The story of Postcard records is essentially a sitcom featuring two larger-than-life wind-up merchants, a bromance between Horne and Collins who, according to Goddard, "took to Alan like a dog to a frisbee."[50] And unfortunately for the other bands signed to the label, such as Josef K, Aztec Camera and The Go-Betweens, that didn't leave much room for anybody else. Postcard really just had one goal: to make Orange Juice into pop stars.

As Robert Forster of The Go-Betweens later said, "Every couple of years I go back and listen to the first four Orange Juice singles. They are just amazing […] Whenever anyone's writing any sort of rock history, these four records, in terms of their influence, their beauty and their brilliance, are never really recorded."[51]

Orange Juice made a very different kind of guitar music, mixing disco-inspired bass and drums with Velvet Underground guitars, punkish attitude and a clear love of the supposedly "hippy" music punk rock had railed against. And in Collins they also set the template for a generation of indie band frontmen: pale, bookish, slightly camp and waspish, both in person and in song.

The straight boys of Orange Juice's affinity with queer music such as disco was musical rather than personal, but no less genuine – original drummer Steven Daly says, "We weren't being arch; it was just love of music that didn't recognise any boundaries"[52] – but their anti-macho style and personas occasionally attracted homophobia nevertheless. And that was deliberate. Glasgow at the time was a city with a hard-man image, but Orange Juice wore their hair long, their jeans tight and their heels high. Their Davy Crockett hats, cravats and even schoolboy-style shorts couldn't have been more camp.

As Collins recalled, "In 1981, we went on tour with The Undertones. There was a load of skinheads, and the minute we'd come onstage they'd shout 'Poofs!' And we'd shout back: 'Hare Krishna.' Rather than go into denial, we'd camp it up, just to annoy people. Of course, later, once we were preaching to the converted, it was time to change course."[53] Among others, Stephen Patrick Morrissey, who would form The Smiths with Johnny Marr the following year, was clearly taking notes.

Something that's very apparent in Orange Juice, Josef K and in much of the post-punk from Scotland that came in their wake is a particular sonic style: where traditional rock would put guitars front and centre, post-punk often used the bass as the key instrument with the guitar adding shapes and colour rather than being the main attraction.

There was a particular focus on sound rather than on showing off, so while there's a guitar solo in Orange Juice's 'Rip It Up', it's short, choppy and discordant, with guitars played through a phaser pedal over looped drums (originally played live, but cut up in the studio by producer Martin Hayles[54]) and water-drop sound effects that Edwyn Collins created by combining a flanger pedal with the sound of him tapping a guitar cable against a metal doorstop.

That kind of playfulness and experimentation would go on to influence a diverse range of bands from Primal Scream, The Smiths and Altered Images – whose Clare Grogan cites "Orange Juice, Simple Minds, Berlin Blondes [and] Josef K" as her band's most significant influences[55] – to Belle and Sebastian and Franz Ferdinand. And it owed a great debt to the 1960s work of troubled gay producer Joe Meek, who was Britain's very own Phil Spector.

Spector and Meek changed the way music sounded, pioneering the use of the recording studio as an instrument long before The Beatles or The Beach Boys would be praised for their sonic experiments. But while both men created a wall of sound that turned teen tragedies of living fast and dying young into almost supernaturally atmospheric experiences, there was a distinct difference in their output: where Spector productions were typically warm and luxurious, Meek's were colder, darker and cut from considerably cheaper cloth. Listening to his best-known tracks – the Tornados' instrumental 'Telstar', John Leyton's death disc 'Johnny Remember

Me', the Richie Blackmore-featuring 'Just Like Eddie' by Heinz, and Screaming Lord Sutch & The Savages' 'Jack the Ripper' – is to hear the bones of post-punk, of sci-fi pop and of garage rock.

Meek worked with Bowie and a teenage Marc Bolan, Ray Davies and Gene Vincent, Jimmy Page and Rod Stewart, among many more. He experimented with huge reverbs and dissonant feedback, and pioneered the use of tape loops and overdubbing decades before they became common in hip-hop, electronic music and experimental music. He pushed levels so hard and deliberately ran mixes so hot that the instruments distorted. He sent entire mixes through an echo chamber and delay to produce a distinctly eerie sound. These are commonplace today but were groundbreaking at the time.

Whenever you hear a recording that adds effects or that pushes the needle into the red, you're hearing an echo of Joe Meek's work. He's in the sci-fi pop of The B-52's and the scuzz rock of The Cramps, in Martin Hannett's spectral productions for Buzzcocks, Joy Division, Magazine, and Happy Mondays, in Edwyn Collins' solo records and – via Hannett's Joy Division productions and alongside a Velvet Underground infatuation, a splash of Spector and a whole shoulder full of chips – he's in the reverb-drenched fuzz of East Kilbride's The Jesus and Mary Chain.

The Mary Chain would go on to influence generations of guitar bands including Dalmarnock's Glasvegas as well as UK and US groups such as My Bloody Valentine and Black Rebel Motorcycle Club. And it's possible that if it weren't for the commercial success of their 1984 single, 'Upside Down', Creation Records wouldn't have survived long enough to bring us Teenage Fanclub, Primal Scream or Oasis.

As for Joe Meek, he died in 1967 in an apparent murder-suicide after arguing with his downstairs landlady Violet

Shelton, who he believed was spying on him by listening through the fireplace. Meek shot her dead before reloading and turning the shotgun on himself. Or at least, that's the official version of events. Some people believe that Meek was the victim of a gangland hit and Shelton was simply in the wrong place at the wrong time.

Meek's final chart hit was the beautifully melancholic 'Please Stay', a cover of the Drifters song – written by Burt Bacharach and Bob Hilliard – by The Cryin' Shames. The song would become the last dance soundtrack for dancehalls in Glasgow and Edinburgh, and later would lend its name to a nostalgic mid-2000s play set in Glasgow's Locarno during the mid-sixties.

'Please Stay' was based around an arrangement by Ivor Raymonde, who also wrote Dusty Springfield's glorious 'I Only Want to Be with You'. Two decades later his son, Simon, would create his own wall of sound as one-third of dream pop and shoegaze pioneers Cocteau Twins.

The music coming from Glasgow's thriving mid-eighties indie scene was a powerful magnet for pop fans like Mitch Katrina Mitchell, who moved from Fife to Glasgow to be closer to the city's music and who would soon become one of the people contributing to its soundtrack. Mitchell has long been drawn to some of pop's more interesting music and musicians – their teen loves included Soft Cell, Culture Club, Orange Juice, Marc Bolan, and David Bowie – and the combination of Kirkcaldy's sole record shop *Sleeves*, John Peel's radio show and the weekly music press introduced them to Scots indie and a band called The Pastels in particular.

The Pastels are one of Scotland's most interesting and important bands. Like their peers Orange Juice, they have a playfulness, an open-mindedness and an evident love of

CARRIE MARSHALL

all kinds of genres. Like Orange Juice, they got a lot of stick for their distinctly un-macho persona. Mitch laughs when I suggest that thoughtful and quietly spoken singer Stephen Pastel is perhaps the Scot least likely to jump on stage with a Flying V guitar and bellow "Hello Cleveland!" But that doesn't mean The Pastels can't rock: songs such as 1984's pounding 'Baby Honey' or their celebratory 2001 cover of Daniel Johnson's 'Speeding Motorcycle' are eminently danceable and enormous fun.

The Pastels formed in 1981, inspired by the Velvet Underground and Television Personalities, and played their first gig that year in Edwyn Collins' hometown of Bearsden. Stephen Pastel was a friend of Horne's flatmate and Oscar Wild guitarist Brian "Superstar" Taylor – according to legend, Horne would write incredibly libellous things about him in his fanzine, *Swankers*[56] – and Taylor was one of the first people to spot their potential. He would soon become the band's guitarist. Years later, a smiling Stephen Pastel would tell a Glasgow crowd that "Alan Horne suggested we be a synth-pop group."

When mainstream success came calling in the mid-eighties, they decided not to follow the well-worn path to London fame and maybe fortune too: The Pastels were determined to stay in Glasgow. That probably limited their commercial potential, but the band clearly love the city and have been a music-scene stalwart for five decades. In their early days they were a key part of Scotland's fanzine culture, and they have since collaborated with a who's who of Scots musicians. Stephen set up and co-runs one of the UK's best-loved record shops, Monorail Music, and he and Mitch also run the label Geographic Music, part of Domino Records.

Mitch joined The Pastels in 1989 on keyboards, guitar, bass and viola before becoming The Pastels' drummer. The legend says that they didn't know how to play and learnt as they went along, but that's untrue: Mitchell was already in a band, Melody Dog, and was a multi-instrumentalist across guitar, piano, vocals, and drums. As was often the case with the music press, the legend fitted the narrative better – and for many parts of the press, the narrative for The Pastels was a dismissive one. They were variously called "anorak pop", "shambolic" or, worst of all, "twee" – a word Mitchell clearly still finds irritating, and with good reason. Twee is an infantilising term also deployed against other mixed-gender pop bands such as Belle and Sebastian no matter how muscular their music, but it's rarely used against similar bands with all-male lineups.

While The Pastels would never become household names, they had a brief but enjoyable spell as pop stars in Japan and they've had enormous influence not just locally – bands such as Primal Scream and The Jesus and Mary Chain are among their famous fans – but worldwide, with artists such as Yo La Tengo, Sonic Youth and Kurt Cobain singing The Pastels' praises.

The Pastels continue to work with a range of musical collaborators, most recently Jarvis Cocker and Japanese pop duo Tenniscoats, and they release records at a relaxed pace. The Pastels' most recent album, 2013's critically acclaimed *Slow Summits*, was their first new album in sixteen years. That makes 2024's rather lovely Go! Team cover, 'Hold Yr Terror Close', almost rushed.

Today Mitch and Stephen remain at the core of the band alongside Tom Crossley, Alison Mitchell, John Hogarty and bassist Suse Bear, a queer artist who also records as Susan Bear and whose former band, the fuzz-pop duo Tuff Love, supported Grace Jones at Glasgow's Bellahouston Park.

In addition to their musical career, Mitch has worked for many years in a role supporting the LGBTQ+ community; I first met them not at a gig, but at a support group they ran for trans and non-binary people. In that role Mitchell has seen a noticeable change in the visibility of LGBTQ+ people, and I ask them if they've seen similar shifts in the music scene. "Oh, definitely," Mitch says. "There have always been queer people on the scene, but many weren't open about it. That's changed; there are so many more openly LGBTQ+ people in music now."

CHAPTER 4:
I FEEL LOVE

'**S**malltown Boy' may be one of the strangest singles ever to top the charts, peaking at number three in the UK and charting for twenty weeks in 1984. Where other artists took a kitchen-sink approach, throwing everything they could into their production, 'Smalltown Boy' is more minimal, centring those glacial synth notes and Jimmy Somerville's beautiful, soaring countertenor, a voice that announces its presence with a note so high it could be a scream. 'Smalltown Boy' sounds like what it is: a song of sadness, of escape, of hoping for something better. Somerville's backing vocals sound like ghosts.

Jimmy prefers not to do press interviews any more, but he's talked about his love of music and of his songs many times. As he told *The Quietus* on the release of his disco album *Homage* in 2015, he spent his childhood in Glasgow's Ruchill either watching *Top of the Pops* "religiously" or being glued to the radio. Disco was huge at the time and he found himself drawn to it. "I think when I look back at all of those songs there would be a celebration and something positive in the sound," he says.[57]

Although the teenage Somerville visited Glasgow's gay

45

where disco was the soundtrack, he really made a ound connection with the music in his bedroom. Short, 1-haired and looking "like a little girl", as he described 1mself, Somerville was experiencing the "shame and guilt and real anxiety" that so many LGBTQ+ people experience – but then "I would look in the mirror and pretend to sing like a Black man," he says. "It was my escape and my freedom."

His primary gay club was Shuffles, in Glasgow city centre. "I first went on my own and I was completely shitting myself. I think I was so scared, I threw up on the bus on the way." But when he got to the club, Giorgio Moroder-flavoured magic was waiting. "The first thing I ever danced to in a grown-up club was fifteen minutes of *Love Trilogy* by Donna Summer," he says. "By the time it had finished I remember thinking: this is it. This is what it is all about and what I am all about."

Like so many queer musicians, Somerville discovered a safe space in music – "I found a freedom on the dancefloor and also found a place to be on my own. I was in my own little world and I didn't need to deal with anything else […] everything I have ever done has been to get to a club in order to dance."

And he found something more. "Looking back at the history of the politics of disco, it was about gay men, Black men and also women having an uplifting celebration in the face of adversity and discrimination," he recalls. "While it's easy to dismiss disco as a throwaway genre – stuff like The Bee Gees and *Saturday Night Fever* – it is actually about a whole movement of emancipated people seeking liberation."[58]

Disco happened a long time ago and it's been endlessly parodied ever since, so what tends to stick in our mind is the worst of it from its final days, a time of novelty records, cynical cash-ins and even more cynical bandwagon jumping. Its modern-day incarnation as the sound of pink prosecco-fuelled hen nights and bad karaoke hasn't helped either. But disco was much more than the two-dimensional caricature that persists in popular culture. Before it became commercialised and diluted, it was celebratory and defiant and *dangerous* – joy as an act of resistance.

It's not a coincidence that disco started just after the bricks were thrown at Stonewall. That happened in the summer of 1969 after one heavy-handed police raid too many on the mafia-owned gay bar; one of the most influential disco clubs, The Loft, hosted its first party on Valentine's Day 1970. The host was David Mancuso, whose house parties had already provided a safe space for his gay, Black and Latino friends to dance without fear of police harassment, and The Loft would continue that tradition. Regulars would soon be pivotal in creating hi-NRG and house music via their own nights, such as Larry Levan's Paradise Garage and Frankie Knuckles' warehouse parties in Chicago.

Denied safety and dignity by the outside world and by the US cops in particular, marginalised people found safe spaces to celebrate their lives, their love and their joy – and they did so at a time when the civil rights and gay rights movements in the US were moving away from a deferential, don't-rock-the-boat kind of politics to something much more visible, vocal and vital. Disco was the soundtrack to a post-Stonewall world.

Inevitably, there was a backlash. Disco was too flamboyant, too decadent, too Black, too queer; *Time* magazine called it a "diabolical thump-and-shriek".[59] And perhaps the most visible example of the backlash was Disco Demolition, the "disco sucks" event in the summer of 1979 that saw disco records smashed and scratched by a very white, very cis, very straight, and very male crowd in a Chicagoan baseball stadium. Instead of the expected crowd of 20,000, slightly more than the usual crowd for the White Sox, more than 50,000 people turned up and thousands more sneaked in after the gates had closed. The event ended in a white riot with an estimated five to seven thousand people invading the pitch, causing so much damage that the White Sox couldn't play.

The parallels between the "disco sucks" crowd and today's self-proclaimed anti-"woke" warriors aren't hard to draw, and while those involved in the event have long denied racism or homophobia, it's hard to be charitable about a movement primarily made of straight, white young men who described disco as a "musical disease" destroying art primarily made and enjoyed by Black and Latino people, gay people and by women. Attendees noted that the records some of those young men brought to smash weren't even disco records, but albums in other genres by Black artists such as Marvin Gaye, Stevie Wonder and Curtis Mayfield. As White Sox pitcher Rich Wortham put it, "This wouldn't have happened if they had country and western night."[60] At the end of 1979, Dave Marsh wrote in *Rolling Stone*, "White males, eighteen to thirty-four, are the most likely to see disco as the product of homosexuals, blacks and latins, and therefore they're most likely to respond to appeals to wipe out such threats to their security. It goes almost without saying that such appeals are racist and sexist."[61]

Between "disco sucks", novelty records such as Rick Dees' quack-packed 'Disco Duck' – voted the worst song of the 1970s by *Rolling Stone* readers – and the inevitable commercialisation and dilution that ruins any successful musical movement, disco's imperial phase was over. But while the reactionaries may have won the battle, they lost the war. Forced back underground, disco would be instrumental in the birth of house music, the New York clubs that would so inspire Madonna and a generation of pop idols, and the clubs in Europe that would create Eurodance. What had become tired and formulaic in the charts would return triumphant in a galaxy of new genres.

All that was far in the future and a world away from Glasgow's sprawling housing estates in the summer of 1979. When Jimmy Somerville turned eighteen that June, he headed to London. "I had to," he told *Electronic Beats'* Max Dax. "I was openly gay and skinheads who hated homosexuals ruled the streets [...] They would have beaten me to pieces."[62] There he would meet another displaced Scot, Castlemilk exile Steve Forrest.

Forrest changed his name to Steve Bronski and, along with Londoner Larry Steinbachek, formed Bronski Beat in 1983. Perhaps inevitably for three gay artists in London during the anti-gay panic of the early eighties, they became involved in gay activism and set out to create avowedly political music. "I was involved in a whole underground movement of gay politics, radicalism and direct action," Jimmy says.[63]

As Somerville would later explain, "We took over a pub in Islington and formed a club called Movement in the basement. It was on a Saturday night, and it was the first time Gay and Lesbian people could break away from a growing commercial scene... [it] became this cultural hotspot for ideas: social politics, music, and the politics of sexuality. So from this little club called Movement a whole fashion change started to happen within the gay and lesbian subculture."[64]

As Somerville recalls, "'Smalltown Boy' was coming from a political ideal I had, and it was a narrative of social realism. Also it was one of the first pop videos ever to be made that was telling a story in three minutes, like a socio-documentary, drama narrative in the essence of British filmmaking, about social pop. That was kind of groundbreaking; and the fact I had this voice that was countertenor with these synthesisers."[65]

The video for 'Smalltown Boy' was revolutionary in another key way: the band looked absolutely unremarkable. They weren't Elton Johns or karma chameleons; they were just ordinary, the Bronski boys next door.

I don't think you can overstate the importance of that. If you're a smalltown boy, girl or non-binary person it can perhaps be hard to see yourself in the more fabulous aspects of queer celebrity. I know I didn't recognise myself in any of the very limited trans representation of the time, and it wasn't until I started seeing ordinary people just like me many years later that my trans egg finally cracked. And that representation is important in the wider culture too: bigotry depends in very large part on seeing marginalised people as different from you, as a strange and frightening other rather than people just like you. That's one of the reasons why the bigots were, and are, so keen on banning books, music and art about or by LGBTQ+ people.

Speaking to *The Observer* in 2006 about the song and the video, Somerville explained, "It was an amazing time because gay men and lesbians had just found their voice and we could introduce the idea that homosexuality wasn't just about what you did behind closed doors. It wasn't about 'the twilight world of the homosexual', or whatever the press used to call it; it was about gay people doing their food shopping in Sainsbury's. It's ridiculous to think about this now, but that hadn't been addressed in pop music at the time."[66]

"The thing about 'Smalltown Boy' is that it comes from the heart – and that's why I think it resonates with people," Somerville says.[67] "People tap into the emotion of the song, and it was a real cry and that's why I think it's so powerful. The whole history of the song is that it comes from a passion for change in politics and society. It's real heartfelt stuff."

Somerville was influenced by jazz and blues singers and by the women of the 1960s British pop explosion, as well as by hi-NRG and iconic artists such as Sylvester. Those influences helped him sing some of the best pop songs of the era, songs with heart and soul as well as epic hooks. Jimmy sang those songs in a way that very few men could sing: his countertenor voice is the rarest of adult voice types, more powerful than any falsetto and inhabiting the same register as female contraltos or mezzo-sopranos. Jimmy broke the vocal binary; he may have been a Smalltown Boy, but he didn't sing like one.

One of Jimmy's biggest hits was his cover of Sylvester's 'You Make Me Feel (Mighty Real)', the original of which was a huge club and chart hit in 1978 and was notable for Sylvester's stellar falsetto.

There's a lot of falsetto in disco, so much so that cultural commentator Anne-Lise François wrote an entire thesis, *Fakin' It/Makin' It*, about it. According to François, Sylvester's skyscraping voice "makes the point most obviously about falsetto as a gender-bending device."[68] In *Turn the Beat Around: The Secret History of Disco*, Peter Shapiro wrote that Sylvester's "use of his gospel trained falsetto in the service of gay desire and pleasure is surely the most radical rewrite of pop's lingua franca ever attempted."[69]

Sylvester, dubbed The Queen of Disco, was a fascinating character, proudly gay and fabulously genderqueer despite his record label's attempts to get him to tone things down a bit. As Sylvester told *The Village Voice*, that suggestion didn't go down too well. "You can try to change my image, but I ain't changing shit! So I went to the office in a negligee and a blonde wig and ran up and down the halls. Then I terrorised their studio until they had to give up."[70]

Sylvester was friends with Harvey Milk, the first openly gay man to be elected in California and a crucial figure in the gay rights movement. 'Mighty Real' was still in the charts when Milk was assassinated in San Francisco in November 1978, and it became an anthem for gay men and for the men of

California in particular.

Sylvester would continue to thrill music fans and pack dancefloors – his 1982 hi-NRG track 'Do Ya Wanna Funk' was a global hit – as well as being a very visible LGBTQ+ person. In 1986 he appeared on the New Year edition of Joan Rivers' *The Late Show*, angrily corrected her description of him as a "drag queen" by proclaiming "I'm Sylvester!" and talked openly about his marriage to his husband Rick Cranmer. As far as I can tell, that was the first time a celebrity had talked about equal marriage on US TV.

Cranmer died of AIDS just months later, and Sylvester was diagnosed the following year. He spoke openly of his diagnosis, telling *NME*, "I don't believe AIDS is the wrath of God"[71] and making arrangements for his posthumous royalties to go to AIDS charities.

As Broadway and television star Billy Porter said in the documentary *Love Me Like You Should: The Brave and Bold Sylvester*, "He crossed over. He was a gender-fluid Black man in mainstream music. My life has changed for the better as a Black, queer man. Any glimmer of seeing one's self reflected back at them through our culture changes lives."[72]

Bronski Beat were determined to use their profile politically. Second single 'Why?', dedicated to the memory of murdered gay playwright Drew Griffiths, was an incandescent indictment of homophobia over a Sylvester-style synth throb, the lyric based on a friend who'd been hounded out of the country by his boyfriend's violently homophobic parents. The album the songs featured on, *The Age of Consent*, listed the gay age of consent for countries around the world – listings that would be removed from the US release for fear of upsetting retailers.

Bronski Beat's imperial phase was short. Somerville left the band after just two years in 1985 to form The Communards before going solo in 1988. But their effect, especially on LGBTQ+ listeners, was seismic.

In May 2024, Jimmy took to his Facebook to celebrate the fortieth anniversary of 'Small Town Boy's release. He began with an impression of the synth riff and then broke into *that* note, the skyscraping high note that's been the undoing of many a karaoke singer, before reminiscing about "doing our first *Top of the Pops*, beamed into the nation's front rooms and then all over Europe on pop shows. We were three young gay men, out, proud and in your face."[73]

"We had a message," Somerville said. "And that message still resonates now, forty years later. We seem to be regressing in so many places, in so many countries, our rights being chipped away at. There's a real surge of homophobia, aggression and discrimination towards anyone who wants to be themselves and love who they choose. And you know what? Piss off! Just get on with your own life and let everyone else live theirs."

CHAPTER 5:
COMING DOWN THE LINE

T he night before Hallowe'en in 1986, one of Scotland's best bands played one of their worst gigs. The band was Edinburgh's Goodbye Mr Mackenzie, and the gig was in front of half the record industry at Fury Murry's in Glasgow. Singer Martin Metcalfe claimed there were twenty-nine record company scouts there and no actual fans; as the A&R men stayed at the bar, the band died on their collective arses. Thankfully, later gigs would be more successful.

Goodbye Mr Mackenzie were formed in Bathgate in 1984 by Metcalfe, the band's songwriter and driving force. The early lineup also included a young singer and keyboard player, Shirley Manson. Metcalfe recalls that he first met Manson when she was in a play about a mediaeval Scottish town ruled by the Devil.

The band first emerged via the government-funded Youth Training Scheme (YTS), one of many schemes used to reduce the number of people officially unemployed. The scheme, alongside similar initiatives such as the Enterprise Allowance Scheme, didn't have music or musicians in mind but would help finance the early careers of many indie musicians and labels who were able to exist, albeit frugally, without being forced into dead-end jobs.

In Bathgate, the YTS helped fund a music industry class for would-be record producers and label creators at the local college. As part of that class, the students were charged with discovering local talent, creating a record label – which they called Scruples Records – and releasing a single. They chose two local artists, Lindy Bergman and Goodbye Mr Mackenzie, and released a double A-side record in 1984.

The same model would later be adopted by other institutions such as Glasgow's Stow College, which helped launch the careers of Snow Patrol, Biffy Clyro and Belle and Sebastian. But as far as Metcalfe can ascertain, this was the first time it had been tried in Scotland – and the 100 copies of the split 7" double A-sided single, featuring Mackenzie's 'Death of a Salesman' and Bergman's 'Locked Inside Your Prison', all sold out. If you fancy a copy, expect to dig deep: at the time of writing, it's being listed for sale on Discogs.com for £150 plus postage.

Goodbye Mr Mackenzie's side of the single got airplay on Radio 1 by Janice Long and attracted the attention of Elliot Davis, whose Precious Organisation was already managing Wet Wet Wet. Davis released the band's next single, 'The Rattler', on Precious's own label, and it reached number eight in the indie chart. Not only that, but it got the band on music show *The Tube* and twenty-nine record label executives on the train to Glasgow.

All bar one of the record label men headed back to London with contracts un-inked. But Capitol Records, already wowed by 'The Rattler', signed the band.

'The Rattler' is one of the great Scots rock songs, and it went top forty when it was rereleased on the label; the band's 1989 debut album, *Good Deeds and Dirty Rags*, was a top thirty hit. 'The Rattler' would turn out to be the band's only UK top

40 single; its sound, and in particular its distinctive overlapping male and female vocals, would be deployed with much more commercial success by Deacon Blue.

Despite great songs, equally great reviews and successful US and European tours with new guitarist Big John Duncan, formerly of The Exploited, Goodbye Mr Mackenzie fell victim to record company shenanigans.

"Mackenzie was a wild band," Manson tells me. "I think when we got signed they knew we were wild – we had that reputation – [and] Mackenzie were given free reign up to a certain point until we didn't perform as well as they would have hoped."

Manson laughs. "And then we just got royally dumped."

The band's contract was taken over by Parlophone, a sibling label under the EMI umbrella, and when the band's next two singles didn't chart the label decided not to release their second album. Their contract was bought out by Talking Heads and Debbie Harry manager Gary Kurfirst, who put *Hammer and Tongs* out on his own Radioactive label, a subsidiary of MCA Records, but the momentum was gone: the two-year delay had delivered a fatal blow from which the band wouldn't recover.

The lack of momentum had a terrible effect on the band members too, some of whom were having problems with drink, drugs or both. The band split in 1993.

That wasn't quite the end, though. Radioactive re-signed Shirley Manson, with Metcalfe, Big John Duncan and Fin Wilson as her band. The project was called Angelfish.

Manson wasn't a songwriter or a focal point in Goodbye Mr Mackenzie, although before the band split there had been plans to have her sing lead on some of the third album's songs. But in Angelfish she found herself centre stage.

"Everything changes when you're up front," Manson told me. "I knew that I really shouldn't have been in the lead singer position. It should really have been Martin Metcalfe, who was just incredibly creative. But because I kept my shit together, I became the racehorse that everybody started to bet on."

They weren't public about it at the time, but two of the Mackenzies' escapees, Manson and Duncan, were queer: Duncan is gay and had allegedly been kicked out of The Exploited because of it (a rumour that persists despite the lack of any evidence I can find to support it), and Manson has since talked openly about identifying with "the idea of non-binary".

Angelfish released their first single in 1993, but the band was short-lived and ended in 1995. Duncan went on to become friends, guitar tech and occasional extra guitarist on stage with Kurt Cobain of Nirvana; rumour had it the band was considering making him a permanent member, although sadly the death of Cobain meant this never happened. Duncan would also work with Foo Fighters, Ministry and Twisted Sister.

As for Manson, she joined a new band where her songs of queerness and gender fluidity would make her an icon for a generation of music fans.

CHAPTER 6:
AND SHE SMILED

t's a frosty night in late November and there's the smell of wood smoke in the air over Cowcaddens, which either means someone's having a bonfire or the council just refused planning permission to turn another listed building into flats. Whatever the source, the all-ages crowd filing into the King's Theatre Royal is here for a different kind of fire: a passionate and ecstatic show by Horse.

Support act (and later, additional singer) Kirsten Adamson gets the show on the road with a set of quiet Americana, and it's clear her references to her late dad Stuart Adamson of Big Country don't land with the crowd until she covers one of his songs, 'In a Big Country'. That's when the realisation hits, and when it does the middle-aged man next to me bursts into tears.

Always a sharp dresser, Horse bounds on stage tonight in a very Vegas red diamond sequin-studded suit that lights up the room like a mirror ball. Her band, almost all women or female-presenting, have dressed up for the occasion too.

Horse is incredible. I already knew her voice on record was extraordinary, but live she's even more remarkable, her multi-octave range effortlessly encompassing notes that many singers could only dream of. Horse is clearly energised by the audience, telling self-deprecating stories and beaming with evident joy at her equally delighted band throughout. I discover later via the *Somewhere: For Us* podcast that the glee visibly radiating from bassist Lorna Thomas is because she's living her teenage dream: as a questioning teen, Horse was Thomas's first LGBTQ+ role model and Horse's music has been her constant companion ever since.

Thomas's fingers fly in the final section, a joyful and faithful cover of Sylvester's 'You Make Me Feel (Mighty Real)' segueing into Horse's own disco anthem 'Celebrate'. The entire crowd is on their feet, dancing like it's 1978.

I meet Horse in the lull between a polar frost and a Biblical storm early in 2023. There's no sequinned suit today – both of us are in the big jackets and jumpers that Scottish winters mandate – but Horse is just as charismatic and compelling in person as she is on stage.

Horse was born in Fife and lived briefly in Crail and Anstruther, but her family moved to Lanark when she was very young and spent her childhood there. The teenage Horse knew she was gay, but early 1970s Lanark was not a good place to be an androgynous-presenting lesbian woman.

"Lanark could have been Dennistoun, could have been Sighthill, could have been Edinburgh, could have been anywhere," she tells me. "There were no phones, there was no internet, I had no awareness of gay performers." Would things have been different if she had had such representation? She nods. "I think that makes a big difference. If we think we're not alone, that we're not carving this path ourselves, [that] someone else is going through what you're going through, it's a great comfort."

Horse tells me about a blog post she was sent a couple of

years ago, written by a gay woman who had been at the same school at the same time as her: "I think I was in fifth or sixth year at this point and she was just starting school […] she just knew she was the same as me." The writer chose not to come out at the time – "She said that she saw what happened to me, because I was chased by people and attacked and all sorts" – but simply knowing there were other people like her was life-changing. "I'm so grateful she wrote about it," Horse says. "It made me think about what a difference you can make in somebody's life without even being aware of it."

Horse's musical education came from her parents: her dad's love of opera, and her mum – "when my dad was out", because he loathed pop music – playing the radio. "So, there was a clash of Dusty Springfield, Shirley Bassey, Herman's Hermits, opera, Beethoven… the music in my life was very eclectic."

"There's a term in opera, *Sturm und Drang*, which means huge bursts of energy," she says. "I liked that. I like a bit of Gene Pitney, a bit of Scott Walker. I was brought up with that stuff in the background, but I never mimicked it." Horse refused to wear girls' or women's clothes and presented as a butch, cigarette-smoking, guitar-playing androgyne; were she a teenager today, she tells me, she might have considered herself non-binary. "I was the only [female] person that wore trousers at school," she says. "They just let me get on with it. I think they just thought there was no telling me."

Horse's presentation was almost a suit of armour. "I was trying to hide behind my clothes because I felt very vulnerable."

Being visibly non-conforming attracted negative attention, including physical attacks, and she experienced severe bullying at school and even harassment from the local police. When Horse talks about that time now, it's clear she still finds the memories upsetting.

When Horse began performing live, the suits were a crucial part of her on-stage persona. It was never about creating an image or following a trend – "I wore a suit before Annie Lennox," she says – but protection. "For a long time, wearing a suit and being androgynous was a way of protecting the person inside."

As someone living in a "small-minded town" where her androgyny made her a target, Horse wasn't too enamoured when pop stars began adopting a similar look from a position of relative safety.

"I went through that bloody struggle at school, through my teenage years, through university and college, studying, working, being who I was… I remember looking at Annie Lennox and thinking, 'But you're not gay. You can just step out of that suit.'" Horse is quick to add that she now understands that "she was probably doing the same thing: very dramatic, very theatrical, but she was hiding as well." At the time she felt that "it's alright for her because she can just walk away."

We've already read the response to Annie Lennox's gender expression, but I think Horse is describing a wider issue that many queer readers will understand: when you see someone metaphorically borrowing your clothes it can be hard not to see them as tourists, irrespective of the artist's intent.

There's often a chasm between artists and our perceptions of what they do. And there can be an even bigger chasm between the art and how it's processed by the wider culture. That's where things can get complicated. For example, when trans and non-binary people are so often demonised as tricksters, as deceivers, as people pretending to be someone they're not – one of the favourite anti-trans slurs from the genital-obsessed weirdo community is to accuse us of wearing "womanface" – then perhaps presenting gender transgression as a costume, a disguise, isn't exactly helpful. The fact that some of the most famous "gender-benders" such as Boy George have gone on to be so scathing about trans women and to post what some people interpret as biphobia too does add some weight to that argument.

The discourse is messy, it's been going on for decades – and it's not limited to pop music. Many TV shows and movies have been accused of flirting with LGBTQ+ viewers, adding a frisson of queerness to reel in younger, more enlightened audiences but nothing that might upset the most easily triggered conservatives. Authors have retrospectively claimed that characters in their books are queer, despite there being no reference to their queerness in any of the pages or in years of unchallenging author interviews. I know trans women who loathe drag despite its history and would rather it didn't exist because they don't want to be tarred with the same bronzing brush as the drag queens they fear people see them as. I'm writing this during what I really hope is a short-lived TikTok trend where pretty young cisgender women pretend to be trans for attention and advertising revenues, while trans and non-binary people's medical crowdfunders struggle to attract attention, let alone donations.

I'm quite sure the artists who transgress gender boundaries don't think as deeply about this as queer people do. But when you're starving for any kind of representation, as queer people were and still are, these things can become very important and take up a lot of room in your head – a head that's already full of self-doubt and sometimes self-loathing, especially if you're living in a culture and era where people like you are targeted for being people like you.

Horse didn't just try to hide herself. She also tried to masculinise her voice, to make it less feminine sounding. "I didn't want to have a high voice, so I deliberately pushed it lower," she says. "So much so that when we were recording the first album, I had to go and have an operation on my vocal cords. I didn't want to sound like a girly girl." The surgery changed her voice a little – she lost some of the lower notes and gained some new higher ones – and post recovery she learned to use all her voice, not just the lower registers. "Now I'm feeling and finding that when I sing in my higher voice, it's still just me."

Today, Horse is a national treasure: in 2020, Roxana Halls' portrait of her was acquired for the nation and it now hangs in the Scottish National Portrait Gallery. "I'm older, I'm a woman, I'm a lesbian and that portrait being in that gallery represents so much more than just me," Horse told *The National*.[74] "I never saw anyone who looked like I did when I was a child, but I hope that any wee girl or wee boy seeing that portrait will get a sense that they can be whoever they want to be." Horse was also the face of Glasgow's Pride festival in 2023.

Horse definitely didn't feel like a national treasure as a teenager but like many queer artists, she found a safe space in music: "Music saved my life."

"I think I was in a very lonely place," she says quietly. "I think that's when I began to talk with myself, began to let stuff out like a pressure valve [...] using my voice was the key for not totally spiralling into the darkest place. I think when things are difficult and hard, you bring it all back into your body and it gets trapped. And singing lets it all come out. I like to think that if I stand here and I sing for people, I think my joy, my pain, my passion... they feel it."

Writing songs in her small back bedroom enabled Horse to close the door on everything and escape to a better world. And what songs they were.

Her debut album, 1990's *The Same Sky*, was written with

songwriting partner Angela McAlinden, who Horse has called the Bernie Taupin to her Elton John and who she worked with for over fifteen years. It was groundbreaking not just for its music and Horse's extraordinary singing voice – her fans include B. B. King, Burt Bacharach, Pet Shop Boys, Bryan Ferry, and Tina Turner, and her songs have been covered by artists including Will Young and Jennifer Rush – but because of who was making it. "At that time there were no other out lesbians in the commercial music industry," Horse says: while Canadian folk-country singer k.d. lang is generally credited as the first mainstream artist to publicly identify as a lesbian, she didn't come out until 1992; Melissa Etheridge, another trailblazer, came out in 1993.

Faced with a toxic mix of sexism, homophobia and misogyny, Horse adopted what she calls a "genderless" image, "which meant I couldn't be controlled in a lot of ways."

Horse's refusal to play the game no doubt hindered her commercial prospects; faced with the task of marketing a hugely talented musician who didn't fit into neat boxes, Horse's record company decided to court controversy by dehumanising her. "On one tour, the publicity posters and flyers had the heading 'Horse: What is it? A man or a woman?'," she recalls. "I think that marketing was horrific, and I think that at that point in our journey it was the death knell: it was all about getting some controversy and the record company drove that as well as the press."[75]

Record companies have rarely given too much thought to their artists' mental health or safety when there's money to be made or controversy to be courted. Today, there are initiatives such as the industry-backed Help Musicians and the charity Music Minds Matter, and artist welfare is often discussed at industry events but in the late 1980s and 1990s there was no such support; artists were seen as commodities to be exploited, not artists to nurture. The issues Horse faced were sadly not unusual.

The problems facing women in music – not just women performers, but composers, producers, engineers, and others across all genres – are well documented, but lesbian and non-binary people have often experienced additional discrimination at every level of the music business. As Canadian indie duo Tegan and Sara, whose foundation aims to address inequality in music, told *Gay Times*, in their early career the homophobia and sexism they experienced was from "the press, the journalists, the radio station people, the club promoters; we were dealing on a daily basis with people who felt very comfortable asking inappropriate questions, talking about us in inappropriate ways, asking us for inappropriate things."[76] Open homophobia, often in the guise of being reasonable, wasn't just tolerated but ordinary: Horse was told by the producer of one Saturday morning kids' TV show that her videos weren't appropriate for broadcast to children simply because she appeared in them.

"All my life I've been silenced," Horse says. "Silencing myself, or other people silencing me. But when I sing, I find my voice and no one can stop me."

Horse may not have become the global pop megastar she deserved to be, but her distinctive vocals and emotionally vulnerable songs have thrilled audiences for more than thirty years and she's as creative as ever: in 2024, Horse released her eighth studio album, *The Road Less Travelled*, playing to theatres full of adoring fans.

"I always say to people, use your voice," she says. "It's never been about the money for me. It's the great joy I get from it, and the joy I see in other people's faces. It's incredible."

CHAPTER 7:
A JOCK WITH AN ACT

I 'm not the best person to talk to about clubbing; the one time a friend and young me went to the Metro nightclub in Saltcoats, people thought we were the drug squad. But even I was aware of Man 2 Man meets Man Parrish's 'Male Stripper', the hi-NRG track I've seen described – I think accurately – as "the gayest record ever". It's one of Scotland's most-loved dance tracks, with some Scots happily telling you that it's Scotland's best-selling twelve-inch of all time.

One of those Scots is Keith McIvor, better known as JD Twitch of dance legends Optimo (Espacio): posting on X (formerly Twitter), he said that 'Male Stripper' "has always had a v. special place in my heart & I'm always proud to tell people it is (possibly) the best-selling 12" of all time in Scotland".[77]

His post clearly brought back memories for many: Stuart Braithwaite of Mogwai recalled how the band's Barry Burns "thought the words were 'I was a male stripper in a local bar'"[78] (it's "go-go bar") while DJ and musician Alex Tronic said, "It never gets old… always reminds me of the waltzers at the shows."[79]

Dancing is in Scots' DNA. In the 1920s there were more dancehalls in Glasgow than anywhere else in Britain,[80] and our folk music has long been about filling floors. In the 1980s, Scots DJs started finding new sounds to get people moving, creating a love affair with dance music that's just as passionate today. That love affair began with hi-NRG.

Without hi-NRG artists such as Sylvester, we'd never had had 'Smalltown Boy' or The Shamen. You can hear its legacy in Scotland's unofficial national anthem 'Bits + Pieces' by Artemesia (aka Dutch DJ Patrick Prins) when it's played through the speakers at Hampden Park, over the airwaves by DJ George Bowie or as an encore at TRNSMT by Calvin Harris, and you can hear house everywhere.

Reaching number four in the UK charts, 'Male Stripper' was as big outside the clubs as it was in them, and at the end of the 1980s it seemed to be everywhere in my small North Ayrshire town: blaring out of Radio Clyde on bored petrol station attendants' FM radios; booming from boy racers' Golf GTIs, Mk2 Escorts and Peugeot 205s as they made endless passes of Fryer Tuck's Chippy; blasting from the speakers in the lounge bar of the Coach House pub on Friday nights.

Was it really the best-selling twelve-inch of all time in Scotland? I ask Keith McIvor, half-expecting it to be a wind-up. But no. "I can't prove it," McIvor says with a smile, "but I used to spend a lot of time in record shops where reps would come in from the independent distribution companies. They'd be selling the records to the shops, and because I spent so much time in those shops I got to know a lot of them. And one rep was saying that the number of copies of 'Male Stripper' they were shifting in Scotland and the north of England was 'insane'. They were selling nothing south of Birmingham; 99 percent of the sales were in the north of England and in Scotland. He said that the chart company thought there was something untoward going on because the sales were so high in Scotland." As a result, McIvor says, Scots sales were weighted and the track denied its rightful place at number one in the charts.

'Male Stripper' was a hit first and foremost because it's a great record but "the marketing of that record was insanely good," McIvor says. Today, we're used to artists releasing the same record across multiple formats – Taylor Swift is infamous for it – but at the time, 'Male Stripper's marketing was ground-breaking. "They pioneered releasing multiple versions, there were multiple remixes, there were picture discs..." McIvor recalls.

"People in Scotland were absolutely crazy for this record," he says. "But the vast majority of people buying it were probably straight men."

McIvor tells me about a friend of his wife who told him that he still had all the records he'd bought in the mid-to-late eighties. "Would I like to see it? And he brought around two hundred hi-NRG twelve-inch singles that he'd bought at the time, immaculately kept. And 99 percent of people who looked at that set of records would think, he's obviously a gay man but he was completely straight. He had no idea. [The gay aspect] was just going completely over his head because that was the sound of mainstream discos in Scotland at the time."

As McIvor explains, there were multiple factors in that. "Every town had its mainstream discos – Ayr would have one, Elgin would have one, and so on. And a lot of those DJs were probably gay, and they knew this music inside out and they were then playing it." There was also the power of pop music: PWL, the pop factory of Stock, Aitken and Waterman, "was the dominant soundtrack of the time [...] their music was a kind of diluted form of hi-NRG." And there was the late-night, post-pub viewing of *The Hitman and Her*, where Pete Waterman "would go around mainstream nightclubs, like the top forty nightclubs around the United Kingdom, filming people dancing and playing records." As Waterman travelled around the country, there was a noticeable shift when he took the camera crews north. "They'd go to, like, Elgin, and they're playing 'Male Stripper'," McIvor grins.

The appeal of hi-NRG and its offshoots isn't hard to see, or to hear. Like rock at its most primal, hi-NRG is music stripped down to its absolute essentials: the beat, the bass, the repeating refrain. It's up-tempo – typically 120 to 140bpm but sometimes even faster – anthemic, universal and euphoric. If you stick a personality on top, such as a Bonnie Tyler or a Pete Burns, you've got a massive chart smash on your hands. Burns' Dead or Alive gave Stock, Aitken and Waterman their first number one with the Burns-fronted 'You Spin Me Round (Like a Record)' in 1985 and the songwriting team's dance-pop dominated the UK charts and pop music from the mid-eighties well into the 1990s. When you're Rickrolled by 'Never Gonna Give You Up' or strutting your stuff to 'I Should Be So Lucky' or 'Relax', that's pop music with hi-NRG at its heart.

The contrast between the music and the culture couldn't have been more stark. This was Scotland in the 1980s, when we still had miners, shipbuilders and steelworkers; and yet for many straight Scots the soundtrack was straight out of America's gayest clubs. That probably wouldn't have happened if hi-NRG had kept its original name: as McIvor points out, "In the American clubs they called it Boystown, and it was very much in the hardcore gay clubs only." The music was rebranded as hi-NRG by a Northern Soul DJ called Ian Levine but "even he still thought that this was only going to be a gay club thing."

Scotland and the north of England had a real love of hi-NRG and Italo disco, and that love really was geographical:

the musical landscape changed dramatically once you headed south, and past Manchester it was transformed completely.

One of the reasons we loved hi-NRG so much is that, as McIvor says, Scots and northern English clubbers "liked any music with a lot of energy going back to Northern Soul, which was a very fast form of music; elsewhere in England music was a lot slower." It fit well with the most popular drugs of the time, which back then generally meant amphetamines but another key reason for the musical differences was that "back then, Scotland was not a very diverse place, racially," McIvor says. "If you go to clubs now it's much more mixed, and Scotland's ethnic make-up has changed so much for the better in the last thirty years." But back then Scotland, and clubbing, was "very white".

That lack of diversity was reflected in the music. In London, artists making jazz, funk and new soul were selling lots of records. "But they were selling nothing in Scotland," McIvor recalls. The mixing of musical genres that was so prevalent in the more multicultural London – not just in dance music, but also in other genres, such as the heavy dub influence on London-centred punk and post-punk – wasn't reflected in the music Scotland was dancing to.

"And then there was a tipping point," McIvor says. "Rave came in and it all changed very quickly."

McIvor was already DJing in the late eighties. "I was coming from a kind of Goth background, so I'd be playing things like Joy Division as well as Soft Cell and some hi-NRG," he says.

"In the early eighties I was a massive reader of music papers. I'd buy *Sounds* in particular, and *Melody Maker* if I could afford it. I'd read them cover to cover and absorb every bit of information."

I'm sure it sounds weird to anyone reading now, when almost all music ever recorded is a click away. But in many cases, McIvor was obsessed with bands he'd never heard. They weren't being played on the radio, let alone on *Top of the Pops*. "I had no money," he says, "so I couldn't buy their records. There was no way to hear them."

That was particularly true of the industrial music that McIvor found so exciting, with bands such as Throbbing Gristle and 23 Skidoo looming large in his imagination. "And then I inherited a small amount of money, and I was able to start buying all those records in places like Virgin Records in Edinburgh, where I'd buy Throbbing Gristle. I'd never heard them, and it just lived up to everything I had hoped for."

Throbbing Gristle would prove to be the gateway for McIvor's lifelong love of electronic music in all its forms, but one other people didn't necessarily understand. When McIvor played electronic music as a DJ in Edinburgh "people used to get really angry! 'Why are you playing this drum machine music?' And I'd say, 'Because I like it.' And then house came along and everything changed completely."

As McIvor recalls, the first house records started to filter through in around 1987. "There was a club in Edinburgh called Fire Island, which was a legendary gay club, and they did what I think was the first ever house music club. It was on a Thursday night, late '87 into '88, playing house music and that was very influential to me." McIvor got his first break from two gay DJs in the capital "who'd been on the alternative club scene there for many years [...] and the three of us tried to do something in Glasgow playing house music and acid house, but that never really worked. But then there was a sea change and house did take hold, and then after that rave music came in. A lot of the people who'd been involved in the hi-NRG scene before that became the first of the big rave DJs in Scotland."

One of the most important DJs in Scotland was Yogi Haughton, originally from Manchester but an early resident of Glasgow's Sub Club. Haughton ran Edinburgh's Hoochie Coochie Club and also DJed at Motherwell's Club 9; as he told *In the Beginning* in 2020, "If you ask a lot of original house heads where they first heard acid, techno and house, I'm sure they will say one of the clubs I played at."[81]

"There was a difference between Scotland and England," he recalled. "The Scottish scene was totally raw and cutting edge."

As Stuart McMillan of Glasgow DJ and production duo Slam told *Boiler Room*, one of the big changes in Scots dance music was a move away from just copying what was popular in London and turning to the US and Europe instead. "I was in a soul club that was on where the Sub Club is now. There was a DJ called Graham Wilson, he used to play, like, Luther Vandross records, and funk, and some hip-hop stuff, pretty much what was going on in London at that point, or anywhere. And one night he played this weird, strange record which later became this anthem. It was 'Nude Photo' by Derrick May. I ran up to the DJ booth and was like, 'What the fuck is this record, man!?' Looking back retrospectively that was a light bulb moment."[82]

That light bulb moment led to the creation of Slam in 1988, in the basement of the Tin Pan Alley club in Glasgow's Mitchell Lane. While the upstairs bar was full of "these gangsters [who] would wander in and be blasted by what, to them, must have been bizarre music", six months later, "these same people were probably right on one," McMillan says.

Keith McIvor was one of the attendees at Slam's huge Tramway Theatre event in 1989, which featured DJs from Manchester's Hacienda and artists such as 808 State, and which was one of the pivotal events in the emerging Scots techno culture. While his stints at The Backroom eventually stopped because "the crowd just hated it", McIvor would have much more success at the new UFO night in the capital. When football casuals caused so much trouble that UFO's club was shut down completely, McIvor and his DJ partner Andy Watson created Pure at The Venue. Pure in Edinburgh and Slam in Glasgow would help fuel an explosion of music in the two cities with DJs not just playing music, but making it too.

"My introduction to house was when I'd go to import record shops and these records started filtering through," McIvor says. "I didn't even really know what they were; they just seemed like a continuation of hi-NRG, and there was also Italo, a kind of Italian form of electronic disco. Some of those records were selling in such quantities that if Scotland had had more people, they would have been chart hits."

"The first place you would hear this music was in the gay clubs," he continues. "I used to go to Bennett's in Glasgow, and they had various Tuesday nights such as 'straight nights' that were semi-straight; you'd go and it would be mainly hi-NRG, but you'd also hear house music. Fire Island was another pioneering place. I'd say the most pioneering DJs were on the gay scene, and that was where you would go to hear what they used to call upfront music, which is music you're hearing before you'd hear it anywhere else. The gay DJs in Glasgow and Edinburgh were really leading the way. I was straight, but I'd go to Fire Island because it was so welcoming. That's where the music was."

The sound spread, with house becoming the sound not just of clubs in the central belt cities, but of Aberdeen (Fever), Dundee (Fat Sam's), Motherwell (The Garrion and Hattonrigg hotels) and boy racers everywhere.

Chicago House, of course, had its origins in the Black and

queer discos of the 1970s, but there was another deliciously queer twist: Marshall Jefferson, whose 1986 track 'Move Your Body' is widely credited with introducing the lead piano that would define the house sound, added piano because he was a huge fan of Elton John. As he put it, "Elton John, 'Benny [sic] and the Jets', man! [...] It was like straight out of a Black baptist church. He had so much soul he was on *Soul Train*!"[83]

House's influence on Scots music wasn't just one-way. Some Scots would have a huge influence on house, and on other electronic music too.

Like many bands, Finitribe formed when the members were still at school. But their trajectory would be very different from their peers. Finitribe were instrumental in the early days of acid house and had a huge impact on industrial music too.

As singer Chris Connelly told filmmaker Grant McPhee, "In 1984 the really exciting music of Edinburgh that we grew up with had grown to a kind of halt [...] the vibrancy of the early eighties had turned into people crawling to be signed to major labels, which is fine, but they were really blending out their sound."[84] Indie guitar rock wasn't really doing it for Connelly or his bandmates David Miller, Philip Pinsky, Simon McGlynn, and John Vick, and they found themselves out of step with the music around them. "We didn't have Beach Boys albums in our record collections," Davie Miller recalls. "We had lots of industrial records in our collections, and that's where we started."[85]

As the band moved further away from indie rock and into more industrial territory, they scraped together enough money to buy one of the earliest samplers, Ensoniq's Mirage. That was the hardware they used to sample the church bells that would end up as the signature of one of the key tracks in the early days of Balearic beats, 'Detestimony'. Released in

1986, the track became a hit in the clubs of Ibiza where DJs Danny Rampling, Pete Tong and Paul Oakenfold fell in love with it; they brought the song back to London with them and it became one of the pivotal tracks of the early acid house movement.

The song also travelled across the Atlantic to US label Wax Trax!, home of industrial bands such as Ministry and Revolting Cocks. It impressed Ministry's Al Jourgensen so much that he invited Connelly to sing for Revolting Cocks, a role that would soon become permanent with Connelly upping sticks to Chicago and leaving Finitribe behind.

Among many highlights in a long, eclectic and fascinating career, Connelly's 2017 project *Art & Gender* explored Connelly's feelings about gender; as he told music writer Meg Walters, "I consider my own work to be of both genders."[86] Connelly recalls his younger years as coming of age "in an environment where being gay, transgender, deviant or just different was accepted and celebrated, and I was able to relax. That's no longer there, or at least it's slipping away, and I can see so much negative energy coming forth from people… it's everywhere and it's horrifying and it's breaking my heart."

In addition to Connelly's work with Revolting Cocks, he was also one of the songwriters on Ministry's million-selling, hugely influential *Psalm 69* album and is a pivotal figure in US industrial music.

"Industrial music came from the UK band Throbbing Gristle, at least two of whom were in the LGBTQIA+ community," Luna Frighthouse of Scots industrial metal band Mrs Frighthouse tells me. The provocative, transgressive and sometimes deeply problematic TG, named after Yorkshire slang for an erect penis, had a genderqueer singer, Genesis P-Orridge, and the whole band engaged in relationships outwith heteronormative roles. TG would inspire not just the music that Connelly was listening to in Edinburgh and music fans such as Keith McIvor, but Connelly's future collaborators in the US too: Throbbing Gristle was a huge influence on Al Jourgensen, and Jourgensen and P-Orridge would later become friends. "We were on the same [musical] wavelength," Jourgensen recalled.[87] As Frighthouse points out, "Ministry took that sound and fused it with metal, and then Nine Inch Nails truly took it to the mainstream."

With Connelly stateside, the remaining members of Finitribe moved even further away from guitars – and they began turning their talents to producing other artists too. One was Aberdeen's Alone Again Or, named after the song on Love's *Forever Changes* album; the name is a good indicator of the psychedelic guitar music they were making. The band changed their name to The Shamen, and by 1987 band lynchpin Colin Angus was much more interested in the sounds of house than guitar rock; the records The Shamen made in that period would influence some of the era's most successful pop bands such as Jesus Jones and EMF.

One of the best-known records from what the press would soon dub "indie-dance" was 'Loaded', Andrew Weatherall's 1990 version of Primal Scream's 1989 'I'm Losing More Than I'll Ever Have'. It's not so much a remix as a musical *Jurassic Park*: like that film's scientists reconstituting dinosaurs from a single speck of DNA, the track is built around just seven seconds of the original record. But while 'Loaded' was a deserved smash hit, The Shamen got there years earlier – and they did it with significant input from Finitribe.

The Shamen began their imperial phase with the addition of Glasgow's Will Sinnott, aka Will Sin, who joined on keyboards and bass. He and Angus were passionately in love with acid house, but the other band members weren't so enamoured and left shortly after the release of 1989's *In Gorbachev We Trust*.

That album was made in collaboration with Finitribe, who helped move the band further away from their guitar roots and towards something more modern. It was a big success and got the band signed to One Little Indian records; one track, 'Synergy', gave its name to the band's Synergy shows, which were an attempt to unite rock and dance audiences and featured live performances and big-name DJs – something that's commonplace now but was incredibly exciting and innovative at the time. Their next release, 1989's mini-album *Phorward*, completed their transition from psych-rock to acid house.

Just as The Shamen's world domination seemed unstoppable, tragedy struck. While staying in Tenerife to film the video for what would become the huge hit 'Move Any Mountain', a remix of their 1990 track 'Pro-Gen', in the summer of 1991, Will Sin drowned.

The band changed significantly, with rapper Richard West, aka Mr C, taking a much more prominent role and effectively becoming the focal point of The Shamen on tracks such as the much-loved and loathed 1992 remix of 'Ebeneezer Goode'. The song's video featured controversial Scots comedian Jerry Sadowitz as the titular character and featured so many flashing images some TV channels prefaced it with epilepsy warnings; the BBC briefly banned the song over its very obvious ecstasy references before relenting and inviting the band to perform on *Top of The Pops* on condition they changed some of the lyrics. West agreed, changing "Got any salmon?" – rhyming slang for tobacco, aka snouts – to the even more baffling "Got any underlay?" As West later explained, it was a rug reference.

'Ebenezer Goode' reached number one and its parent album, *Boss Drum,* reached number three. But The Shamen never really escaped the novelty-record tag that 'Goode' saddled them with. They stopped releasing records in 1998.

As the sound of Scotland's clubs began to change, the drugs in the clubs changed too. Amphetamines gave way to ecstasy. "The very same people who six months previously would have gone, 'Why are you playing this drum machine shit?' suddenly – that's all they wanted to hear," McIvor says. "It was like a gateway. I think a lot of people needed that. They opened up their ears and their minds and they were hearing music in a different way."

"The whole dynamic changed," he recalls. "Previously, you'd go to mainstream clubs and guys would dance with their girlfriends or with other girls, and nobody else. Maybe in the cooler clubs they would, but not in the 'straight' clubs. And then the minute people started taking X, everyone's dancing with everyone."

McIvor didn't partake himself, but says, "Whatever you think about drugs, it was a positive thing that opened up a lot of people's minds. They were a lot more open to being with people from different backgrounds, from different sexualities, than they would have been prior to that. It really did knock down a lot of barriers."

It knocked down musical barriers too, with many rock fans – and musicians – discovering clubbing during this period in clubs such as McIvor's Optimo, which was famous for its open-minded booking policy that extended way beyond superstar DJs – partly because, as McIvor says with a smile, those DJs were far too expensive. Franz Ferdinand's original drummer Paul Thomson was one of the many musicians who loved the club, telling *The Guardian,* "There was no snobbery, they genuinely wanted to share information with as many people as possible. You went down with the intention of hearing something you'd never heard before [...] it broadened my understanding of what music could do to you physically and emotionally, and we brought a lot of that to

Franz Ferdinand. Even lyrically, the characters in the songs were all of that world."[88] Franz would return to Optimo as performers as well as punters, and the club also hosted the likes of Edinburgh's The Fire Engines and Glasgow's Bis.

"I've always been someone who goes to see bands," McIvor explains. "I was from a bands background and I knew lots of people who'd go out, but who wouldn't go to a dance club. I guess when Optimo started, I really wanted to bring that audience in. A lot of people who came to Optimo had probably never been to a dance club in their life – and conversely, a lot of people who came to Optimo were from a dance background and had maybe followed me and my DJing before that, and they'd never been to see a band before. It was really divided: you were into clubbing or you were into bands. Now everyone does everything. I wasn't that interested in DJs, so it became about booking bands, and eventually the two audiences kind of blended and fused into one. It's stayed that way ever since."

Did McIvor feel at the time that he was part of a generational shift? He nods. "It felt strangely – and naively, in hindsight – utopian," he says. "You really felt that you were this generation that was going to change everything, that all the old was going to be ripped down and we'd create a better society. And, of course, nothing really changed. But while it didn't change the world, I think it changed a lot of people's lives. It introduced a colour to people's lives, and I think a lot of people who felt trapped in dead-end, boring jobs started to become creative and find ways to make a living in a creative way."

It changed the culture for the better. "It definitely helped break down a lot of homophobia and racism," McIvor adds. "I mean, Edinburgh at that time was a violent city with, like, football gangs fighting one another. I had several friends that were savagely beaten up for holding hands or just expressing any kind of emotion. Now I constantly see gay couples holding hands, and I love that: even twenty years ago that would have been absolutely impossible."

CHAPTER 8:
THE PARTY'S OVER

N o party can last forever. While Scotland danced, dark forces were gathering.

AIDS arrived in Scotland in the early 1980s, with the first case of HIV in Edinburgh diagnosed in 1983. In the year from June 1987, reported cases of HIV infection in Edinburgh alone rose from 1,239 to 1,504.[89] Roughly one-half of cases were from drug use, one-quarter from contaminated blood and one-quarter from gay sex, with a significant number of cases transmitted by straight sex.

Drug use was instrumental in the rise of AIDS in Edinburgh, where cheap heroin from Afghanistan and Iran flooded schemes such as Pilton and Muirhouse. In a 1986 study by Muirhouse GP Roy Robertson, 51 percent of the 164 heroin users he tested had HIV, and he suspected the real figure could be as high as 85 percent. The police's so-called war on drugs was another contributing factor, with what Dr Robertson described as police "hostility" towards harm reduction causing a citywide needle shortage that led to multiple addicts sharing the same needles and spreading HIV further.[90]

In the eyes of the press, AIDS was a "gay plague", and their hateful reporting put acceptance of LGBTQ+ people into reverse.

If you haven't seen the 2021 drama *It's a Sin*, I'd encourage you to watch: it was created to show the reality of AIDS in the UK, its effects on queer communities and most of all, how its victims were treated. There are strong echoes of the ignorance and fear we experienced during the early parts of the COVID crisis – many AIDS sufferers were held in quarantine, food slid under doors by nursing staff too scared to come close; dead people's flats were left uncleared by their families for fear of infection – but there was one crucial difference: COVID victims weren't demonised by the press as deviants who had it coming or by politicians who wished them dead.

The native Scots press weren't as overtly vicious as the wider British tabloids with their tales of Tory councillors wanting gay men thrown into gas chambers or vicars who'd shoot their gay sons, but the *Daily Record* front page of January 6, 1989 is still telling. "You gave us AIDS!" it screamed. "Now innocents demand millions." The article was about "innocent AIDS victims", Scots haemophiliacs who contracted AIDS from contaminated blood, and the repeated dog whistle of "innocent" made it clear that in the eyes of the establishment, some people with AIDS deserved it.

AIDS took a terrible toll on queer communities, on queer artists and on queer music. It killed Jobriath, the first openly gay rock musician signed to a major label and a big influence on Morrissey, in 1983; Klaus Nomi, who so inspired David Bowie, also in 1983; The B-52's Ricky Wilson in 1985; Sylvester in 1988; The Bay City Rollers' and Pilot's Billy Lyall in 1989; and many more in a too-long list.

The mid-eighties was the era of music with a conscience, of Band Aid, Live Aid, Ferry Aid, Sport Aid, but there was no AIDS Aid: there was a benefit event, Stand By Me (aka The Party), at Wembley Arena in 1987, but it failed to attract the same kind of attention; as Smash Hits magazine reported, George Michael "was a mite cutting about 'the absence of some of his contemporaries from the present line-up' (i.e. other mega-stars who wouldn't commit themselves to an AIDS benefit... [some were] rather afraid of being associated with the event because it has to do with AIDS."[91] I think English anarcho-punks Chumbawamba may have hit the nail on the head with their 1986 response to pop star charity: *Pictures of Starving Children Sell Records*. Pictures of dying gay men, not so much.

The first UK single raising money for AIDS charities didn't feature any celebrities, although Soft Cell singer Marc Almond, a friend of the band, appeared in the video. The song was Coil's 1985 version of Gloria Jones' 'Tainted Love', the Northern Soul classic made famous by Soft Cell four years previously.

Coil were two gay men, graphic designer, photographer, filmmaker, and musician Peter "Sleazy" Christopherson, one of the founders of Throbbing Gristle, and poet, occultist and singer John Balance of the experimental Psychic TV. Together they turned the exuberant pop hit into something much darker and more terrifying. Their video matched the funereal music with a bleak, hospital-set narrative heavy on religious imagery, and was the first music video to go on permanent display at the Museum of Modern Art. Christopherson's directorial career would later include work with Ministry, Nine Inch Nails (including their infamous, unreleased horror short *Broken*) and, er, Hanson. Coil's support for the Terrence Higgins Trust – the charity their single raised money for – wasn't temporary; in 1992 they also soundtracked its educational documentary *The Gay Man's Guide to Safer Sex*.

Other charity singles seemed determined to avoid admitting what they were actually raising money for: Dionne

Warwick's 1985 'That's What Friends Are For', for example, featuring Gladys Night, Stevie Wonder and Elton John, was supposedly about raising AIDS awareness, but the lyrics were anodyne Live, Laugh, Love platitudes about keeping on smiling and shining, woah-oh-oh. The Justified Ancients of Mu-Mu's Beatles and Samantha Fox-sampling 1987 'All You Need Is Love', made by the pre-KLF Jimmy Cauty and Scots provocateur and former Echo and the Bunnymen manager Bill Drummond, made use of the terrifying John Hurt *Don't Die of Ignorance* public information films, but it was a chaotic, incoherent jumble: as *Underground* magazine said in its review, "It appears to be anti-AIDS but [...] it could be a piss-take."[92]

The first big-name UK artist to make an AIDS charity single was Elton John, whose 'Sacrifice/Healing Hands' was a UK number one in the summer of 1990. Again, though, the songs were incidental to the cause; both songs were about straight or straight-seeming relationships between men and women, although the proceeds were shared among four AIDS charities.

Sometimes it takes a Scot to speak plainly, and not for the first time that Scot was Jimmy Somerville. Fresh from his chart-topping celebration of Sylvester, his 1990 solo single 'Read My Lips (Enough Is Enough)' was explicit in its demands: what AIDS needed, Somerville sang, wasn't complacency. It was money.

One of the reasons so many people died from AIDS was politicians' refusal to take it seriously or to even care about the dead and the dying. In a shocking recording from 1982, when more than 1,000 people had already died, you can hear US president Ronald Reagan's press secretary Larry Speakes being asked about AIDS and responding with ignorance. When a journalist then explained that over one-third of new cases had died and that the disease was being called a "gay plague", the assembled press pool laughed. "I don't have it," Speakes responded to more laughter. "Do you?"

The UK was similarly heartless. There was little political will for saving the lives of gay men or drug users, and even providing potentially life-saving information had to be fought for: in an echo of the hostility that saw the police consider harm reduction as condoning and encouraging drug abuse, Prime Minister Margaret Thatcher believed that providing safe sex information would encourage unspeakable depravity.

As Lord Fowler, who launched the *Don't Die of Ignorance* campaign in 1986, recalled, "Right from the beginning Margaret was a sceptic about having this major campaign [...] on the dangers of contracting HIV and how you could avoid it."[93] Lord Fowler also recalls that there were calls for a "moral campaign" to make people change their "sexual habits" through complete abstinence, calls that he rejected.

Lord Fowler may have rejected those calls, but his party didn't. Far from supporting LGBTQ+ people, the Conservative government and the right-wing press colluded in the demonisation of them and of gay men in particular. Just months after Lord Fowler launched the UK AIDS awareness campaign, Margaret Thatcher made her infamous speech to the Conservative Party conference. "Children who need to be taught to respect traditional moral values are being taught that they have an inalienable right to be gay,"[94] she said, adding, "All of those children are being cheated of a sound start in life."

"Yes," she emphasised. "Cheated."

A few months later, the government introduced Section 28 (aka Clause 28; Clause 2A in Scotland) of the Local Government Act, which banned the "promotion" of homosexuality and "the acceptability of homosexuality as a pretended family relationship" in all local government, all education services and in the arts and library services of the UK. It stayed in force until 2000 in Scotland and until 2003 in England, Northern Ireland and Wales.

Nobody was prosecuted under Section 28, but it had the desired effect on LGBTQ+ people: fearing prosecution under an act that seemed deliberately open to the widest possible bad-faith interpretation, many local government employees from librarians to teachers chose to keep their heads down and to keep quiet.

As we saw then and as we're seeing now with anti-LGBTQ+ laws in the US, you don't need to actually prosecute librarians or teachers if you want certain books or conversations banned; all you need to do is scare them, or the schools and local authorities that employ them, into thinking that you might. Section 28 was worded so ambiguously that many people understandably believed that simply being openly LGBTQ+ or helping a pupil who was suffering homophobic abuse might count as "teaching the acceptance of homosexuality". It didn't just keep queerness out of schools; it kept pupils and teachers in the closet.

Section 28 and the moral panic that led to it did incredible damage: social attitudes surveys from the time showed anti-LGBTQ+ sentiment at record levels, with some 75 percent believing that same-sex relationships were wrong. As I wrote in my contribution to the book *Twenty-Eight*, an anthology of pieces about Section 28, "The chance of a teacher at my school coming out and keeping their windows unsmashed or a gay couple walking down the road arm in arm without violent objection was pretty much zero. Of course, I know now that I went to school with gay people, with ace people, with trans people. I just didn't know that at the time, let alone understand that I was one of them."[95]

Pop music's response was muted, perhaps fearing attack by the viciously homophobic press: this was a time when Piers Morgan wrote a *Sun* feature called "The poofs of pop" speculating on pop stars' sexuality, and the same paper libelled Elton John multiple times.

With some notable exceptions – Sinead O'Connor playing Gay Pride in London just a month after Section 28 came into force; Billy Bragg condemning Section 28 from the stage at his shows; Boy George's 'No Clause 28', an acid house track that sampled Public Enemy's 'Bring the Noise' and featured a guest rap by MC L-Dog that somehow managed to connect Section 28, NHS underfunding and, er, the clamping of cars; and Chumbawamba's 'Smash Clause 28', which raised money for the London Lesbian and Gay Switchboard – there was little in the way of popular protest music.

That was especially true in Scotland. The apparently straight, cisgender* Scots musicians who topped the charts in the year after Section 28's introduction offered escapism, not anger or allyship: Fairground Attraction's 'Perfect' and 'Find My Love'; Wet Wet Wet's 'With a Little Help from My Friends'; Aztec Camera's 'Somewhere in My Heart'; Deacon Blue's 'Real Gone Kid'.

That's not to say Scots musicians didn't make political stands or make political music in the late eighties. They did, but they were usually either focused on matters far from home – the only overtly political chart hit by a Scots act in 1988/9 was Simple Minds' *Ballad of the Streets* EP, with Jim Kerr singing about the Irish Troubles ('Belfast Child') and South African apartheid ('Mandela Day' and a cover of Peter Gabriel's 'Biko') – or had their songs' politics hidden so well that most listeners would be completely unaware of their subjects.

---

* If any of these artists were not straight or cis, they hadn't and haven't come out.

How many Wet Wet Wet fans heard 'Wishing I Was Lucky' as a scathing critique of Thatcherite economic policy, Hue and Cry's 'Labour of Love' as a song about the British public voting for a government that would actively work against them, or The Proclaimers' 'Letter from America' as an allegory with the Highland Clearances as a proxy for the destruction of Scotland's industrial base? Boy George's anti-Section 28 record might not have been very good, but at least it was clear what it was about.

CHAPTER 9:
DON'T BE AFRAID
OF YOUR FREEDOM

House music and ecstasy would have an incredible impact on all kinds of Scots musicians, propelling some – such as Primal Scream and The Shamen – to stardom and putting Bellshill's The Soup Dragons on *Top of the Pops*. For some musicians, though, the influence of queer dance music was perhaps a little less apparent, but no less significant. Take Simon Neil of Biffy Clyro: the affable rocker famed for his shirtless guitar heroics credits his time working in a Glaswegian gay bar during his 1990s university days as a crucial part of his musical education, much like Nirvana's Dave Grohl took inspiration from disco drummers including Chic's Tony Thompson and bands such as The B-52's, whose 'Rock Lobster' Grohl says "opened up a whole new world to me."[96]

"I learned a lot about dance music – quality dance music," Neil told US LGBTQ+ newspaper *Metro Weekly*. "At that point I was a big rocker – I only ever listened to metal and things that were written on guitars. As an 18-year-old, it opened my eyes to the world and to different cultures. It was exactly what I needed coming from a small town. It made me appreciate genres of music that I didn't know about."[97]

As the 1980s became the 1990s, many rock bands suddenly proclaimed a love of ecstasy and of dance music, releasing dance-tinged rock or, more cynically, getting their people to commission remixes by hot dance music producers, but The Soup Dragons were the real deal. Like Primal Scream and The Shamen, they were initially known as an indie guitar band – and like many of their contemporaries, they were heavily influenced by US psychedelia and garage rock and by Buzzcocks' lovelorn punk-pop.

Their enthusiasm for dance music was no affectation. The Soup Dragons' singer Sean Dickson has a lifelong love of electronic and dance music, so much so that his parents bought the young Sean a Roland 808 drum machine and SH-101 bass synth because of his obsession with Soft Cell. The fourteen-year-old Dickson produced an entire cassette album of electronic dance music in his Bellshill bedroom using the synth, a Casio mini keyboard and a friend's TR-808 drum machine; one of the songs, 'Waste Away', would become BMX Bandits' 'Strawberry Sunday'. The recordings, under the name Silent Industry, were thought lost, but by happy accident Dickson found the tape in a box in late 2023, shared it on social media and was approached by a label who wanted to release it; the vinyl run sold out immediately, but you can still get the album digitally online.[98]

Dickson laughs when I ask him if a new Silent Industry album is on the cards. "It sold out quicker than any other record I've ever made in my life," he says with evident amusement. But he agrees that there's a through-line between the electronic music he was making as a teen and the music he's making now. As Dickson recalls, when he rediscovered the tape, he asked his longtime friends and musical collaborators Duglas T Stewart (BMX Bandits) and Norman Blake

(Teenage Fanclub), "Do you remember me making this when we became friends? It was around the time when we all started hanging out together. And they were like, 'Oh God, yeah, you used to play us this stuff *all the time*'."

It's a sunny day in East London and we're chatting the day after *Daylight*, Dickson's latest album in his current and critically acclaimed HiFi Sean project, has been announced. Dickson is fun and funny company, and while our conversation goes to some dark places, he's joyful and enthusiastic not just about his own music, but about all music.

"The first music I wanted to make was electronic music," he says. "Of course, as I child I watched *Top of the Pops*, but I also watched *Tomorrow's World* – and I think that created a period where we were fascinated equally with music and with sci-fi."

Tomorrow's World was a show that brought cutting-edge and near-future technology to BBC viewers, introducing the nation to incredible concepts including the pocket calculator, the synthesiser, the digital watch, Kraftwerk's *Autobahn*, and the compact disc. The latter would have gone viral if we'd had the internet in 1981: to demonstrate that CDs would indeed provide the promised "perfect sound forever", presenter Kieran Prendiville cheerfully scratched the surface of a Bee Gees CD with a stone. Many people misremember this as him smearing a CD with jam, but that was Radio 1 DJ Peter Powell on a different programme. Prendiville didn't smear it with honey either; that was Radio 1 DJ Mike Read on yet another show. While Prendiville wasn't part of the strange preserve-based war that his BBC colleagues appeared to be waging on the new music format, the most important thing he didn't do was attempt to play the CD again – because of course, thanks to his efforts, the disc was now scratched to fuck.

Like Dickson, I was glued to the show and absolutely

convinced that by 2001 I'd be living in some kind of jetpack-powered, silver-trousered wonderland. "So, when music suddenly started getting sci-fi, when there were so many electronic acts, it was just so fascinating," Dickson continues. "I wanted to be in The Human League, I wanted to be in Soft Cell, I wanted to be in Depeche Mode. All that stuff to me just sounded like music from another planet."

As a teen, Dickson became friends with Blake, Stewart and others, and he and Blake used to share records. While the Bellshill scene was based around jangly guitar pop, the vinyl and cassettes they were exchanging were much more varied and included a lot of disco and dub reggae but as Dickson explains, guitar music was the part of the Venn diagram where everybody's musical tastes overlapped. "We all had our own inputs, different things we liked, but somewhere in the middle there were all these guitar bands. I think when you're that age it's just the easiest thing," he says. "It wasn't really about how it sounded; it was about the attitude of what we were doing."

Dickson and his friends were fans of Bowie and The Velvet Underground, but his biggest influence was much nearer. "My Sex Pistols were The Jesus and Mary Chain," he says. "To have them eight miles up the road from Bellshill [...] when I got 'Upside Down' it had their home address in East Kilbride and it was just, people can make music like this! As a sixteen-year-old that really blew my mind." From there, Dickson fell in love with bands such as The Pastels and "the whole Glasgow scene. I felt very connected to it."

That scene coalesced around the Splash One club in West George Street. "That was the club night that members of Primal Scream and others put together," Dickson says. "There were so many bands that were spun off from people who used to go along."

At the time, Dickson, Blake and Stewart would go into

Glasgow to busk in the hope of making money to buy records – "We'd stand outside Marks & Spencer doing The Velvets' 'Femme Fatale' for grans with their shopping," Dickson laughs – and met other Glaswegian musicians on the street. "People liked us," he says. "And that's how we started going to Splash One."

When Dickson talks about the Splash Club, I'm reminded of Shirley Manson's memories of Edinburgh's Hoochie Coochie club. As Dickson recalls, the club was "a huge community of people who suddenly realised, 'Oh my God, there are other weirdos like me.' It was a collective weirdo Sunday night. It felt like you were in a world that you didn't need to worry about the outside world."

"When you find like-minded people, you feel safe," he adds.

Another club would soon become even more important to Dickson. "The energy in the indie scene by about 1988 was getting really boring. Everybody was trying so hard to be cool that there was no life, no atmosphere in anything. I started going to an acid house rave in Glasgow called UFO, in a place called Tin Pan Alley," he says. "It just blew my mind. It was like walking into another planet, and it was everything I'd started making music for. It was like – *this* is where the energy is."

The Soup Dragons were enthusiastic regulars, visiting weekly, and Dickson felt his musical horizons expanding; for Dickson, acid house was the sci-fi psychedelic music he'd been longing for since his days watching *Tomorrow's World*. "It was like the energy of punk rock, but using machines," he says.

Dickson was fascinated by the overlap between apparently different genres, and was particularly interested in what he heard as similarities between 'Push It', the superb 1986 hit by US rappers Salt-N-Pepa, and the staccato guitars of The Kinks. "I was having a long conversation with somebody and

I said 'Push It' was The Kinks," he says. "They said, 'That's just bollocks' – but it does sound like 'All Day and All of the Night'. It's got a real rock'n'roll feel to it."

Intrigued, Dickson began "messing around with samplers and stuff"', took the beats from 'Push It' and put a Kinks-style guitar riff on top. The resulting song, 'Backwards Dog', is a great piece of pop – but most of the people who heard it were baffled. "Nobody got it," Dickson says. "Nobody got what I was trying to do."

But Dickson persevered, and the more acid-influenced 'Mother Universe' resulted in an unlikely gig: on stage at the UFO club "in the middle of an acid house set." Dickson wasn't sure whether to do it, but the offer of a huge bag of ecstasy – "that we gave to all our friends, and that lasted for months" – sealed the deal. The band mimed to the twelve-inch.

Ecstasy was a crucial character in the evolution of dance music in Scotland and beyond. It'd be convenient to claim it as another successful export from queer clubs, and one of the myths around the drug certainly fits that narrative: the story goes that ecstasy was first brought to the UK from the US via Manchester's gay club Stuffed Olives. Like all good myths there are many versions of this one, none of them the same; some say it came via English DJs returning from the clubs of Ibiza, and others credit criminal gangs who successfully connected Dutch chemists with UK clubbers via cheap flights on budget airlines. However it made its way to Scots clubs, its effects were earth-shattering.

Every scene has its drugs, whether those drugs are cigarettes and alcohol, weed, speed, cocaine or ketamine. For Chicago house and then dance music more widely, the key drug was ecstasy, aka MDMA, and while every substance can have negative effects (especially when it can't be obtained by legal means), ecstasy isn't like the other drugs mentioned here.

Part stimulant and part hallucinogen, ecstasy doesn't have the same effects as alcohol, weed, speed or cocaine; it doesn't usually make you want to fight people like alcohol can, leave your brain baked like weed can, make you frazzled and edgy like speed does or turn you into the insufferable arsehole that every coked-up person I've ever encountered appears to be. It's considered by most to be a positive drug, one that enhances how music and dancing makes you feel, a drug that means someone on it is more likely to hug you than hit you.

"That whole period of '88/89 was just […] you're messing around with these new synthetic drugs that made you feel on top of the world and opened your mind in a different way," Dickson explains. That wasn't just broadening musical horizons, but social ones too. "There was so much more community. I loved the fact that I was going to places where there were gay people, where there were people from every community, where you had people who loved Indian music, who loved rock music, who loved dance music. It broke down all barriers."

If this book were a movie, Dickson would pause at this bit and a bell would toll in the distance. "And that's where 'I'm Free' came from."

'I'm Free' was the making of The Soup Dragons and the breaking of them. It would turn the band into pop stars and turn the music press against them, and it would ultimately cause crises both personal and professional. Yet it was only ever intended as a bit of pop fun.

"I came back from UFO one night and put the TV on," Dickson tells me. "It was BBC Two, and The Rolling Stones at Hyde Park came on." Dickson, who was in the middle of coming down from whatever he'd ingested at UFO, parked himself on the sofa "and they played 'I'm Free'. I'd never heard the song before. I actually found out later that it was the first and only time they'd played it on stage." He grins. "Until we made 'I'm Free'. Then they started playing it again."

The following day, the band were messing around in the studio and Dickson persuaded them to play his half-remembered version of the song. "All I could remember were the 'I'm free to do what I want' bits, and I made the rest up," Dickson says. "And a few weeks later we went into the studio." The band partied during recording, and when they met Jamaican DJ Junior Reid at one of those parties, the band and the DJ became fast friends. "We hung out with him, had a laugh, and said, 'Do you want to come to the studio and sing on the record?'" He did, and the band then scoured *The Yellow Pages* to find a gospel choir to sing on the track because, well, why not? "It was that insane," Dickson says with a smile.

"And then suddenly you release the record and it's a worldwide hit, which you did not fucking expect at all."

A big hit changes the trajectory of bands – and their audience. Radiohead famously refused to play 'Creep' live for decades, and Nirvana were similarly dismissive of 'Smells Like Teen Spirit'. "You have all the new people that love you, and all the people who used to love you don't love you," Dickson says.

The music press weren't exactly big Soup Dragons fans to begin with and the success of 'I'm Free' painted a target on the band's back. Now signed to Universal and Mercury in the US, they were portrayed as bandwagon-jumpers and cynical careerists. At a time when "selling out" was considered to be the worst crime a band could commit and mixing indie rock with dance music was probably the second, that was devastating – and a misquote that Dickson suspects was intentional would prove to be the final nail hammered into The Soup Dragons' coffin.

In an interview, Dickson made a pretty unremarkable comment about his longtime love of electronic music, disco and dub: "There's always been a dance element to our record collections." But crucially the "collections" bit didn't make print, and the out-of-context misquote, "There's always been a dance element to our records", often misquoted further as, "There's always been a dance element to our music", became a stick the music press would use to beat the band with. The term became shorthand for a particular kind of indie-rock careerism practiced by bands who'd never stepped on a dance-floor in their lives – something that clearly wasn't true of Dickson's band, who'd been chewing their faces off for years in Glasgow clubs. But the press had made up its mind and found The Soup Dragons guilty with no right to appeal.

It was a horrible experience for the band and for Dickson in particular, who tells me, "It just completely demeaned me as an intelligent person. The demise of The Soup Dragons was from that point on, because we were struggling with that." The band broke up in 1995 and Dickson formed The High Fidelity, where his love of dance and electronic pop was even more apparent. He spent a lot of time in the New York club scene where he started to understand that he might not have been as straight as he'd previously believed. While he seemed to be doing just fine, internally Dickson was trying to deal with the cyclical depression he'd had throughout his adult life. As he tried to find his place in music and come to terms with his sexuality and what that meant for his marriage, years of stress and sadness reached a crisis point. In 2001, Dickson had a severe mental health crisis that saw him hospitalised.

"When someone takes your laces and belt off for your own safety, that's the point where you realise that you can't go any lower than this," Dickson says quietly.

It's a horrendous story, but Dickson still manages to find

humour in it: he tells me that at his lowest point he found himself becoming obsessed with the 1988 hit song by Yazz and the Plastic Population, 'The Only Way Is Up'. "For some reason I couldn't get it out of my head for a week, lying in this confined room," he says. "You're in a mental health institution, locked behind a key, and you're lying in bed singing, 'The only way is up, baby.' It's so pathetically crass that it's actually quite funny, but it saved me in a bad time." Thinking about it since, it's helped Dickson look at 'I'm Free' more fondly. "I get told all these stories about it," he says, about people who've contacted him to say the song helped them find the courage to leave abusive partners, people who tell him the song helped them through sad times, and people who've taken Dickson's line "Don't be afraid of your freedom" as their mantra.

Dickson would take his own song's advice in 2001, coming out as a gay man and later telling his story on BBC 6 Music in the hope of helping others. We talk about the pros and cons of going on air to talk about coming out, something I've done too. "It was quite difficult because I think my daughter heard some things that she didn't know, so there were conversations to be had about that. But it was important for me to tell my story because there wasn't the information or support that people have now."

This was still the era of Section 28, so much of the information and support for LGBTQ+ people that we take for granted today didn't exist. "I was phoning up the national AIDS helpline just to speak to somebody about how to deal with being a gay married man," Dickson says. "There was no one to talk to. I phoned the Samaritans, who said that the only people you can really talk to are the HIV helpline, and when I phoned them up they said, 'Are you HIV?' When I said 'no' they were like, 'Then why the hell are you phoning?'"

Thankfully this story has a happy ending. Dickson met the

man "who saved my life" and married him; today he makes music with a cast of collaborators including The B-52's and Bootsy Collins. HiFi Sean, as he's known now, seems much happier than Sean from The Soup Dragons, and makes beautiful records such as 'Love Is Love', which he describes as "a song about how I would feel as an eighteen-year-old, knowing that I'm now a gay man."

In late 2023, The Soup Dragons reformed for a triumphant, celebratory UK tour with some of their friends in tow: BMX Bandits, The Vaselines and in Glasgow, The Pastels doing a DJ set. These were the original lineup's first shows in over thirty years – and the first Soup Dragons shows that Dickson's husband had ever seen. His review? "He loved it," Dickson shared online.[99]

Dickson's current project is HiFi Sean and David McAlmont, a dance-pop collaboration with one of our generation's finest singers that began when Dickson asked McAlmont to sing on one of his songs for his album of collaborations, *Ft*. "We had a coffee, and then we started hanging out with each other and became friends, which is like how I started with The Soup Dragons," Dickson says. "He's an incredible talent. I've never worked with anybody who, every time I write a song with them, it completely blows me away. He's made me cry many times." Their debut *Happy Ending* album was critically acclaimed – *Louder Than War* called it "exotic, timeless and epic",[100] while *Mojo* said that Dickson is McAlmont's best foil since Bernard Butler "spinning a kaleidoscope of suave, modernist soul-pop."[101]

I catch HiFi Sean and David McAlmont live in a show that runs the gamut from subterranean EDM bass to sparkling Motown shuffles, Soft Cell synth stabs, acid squelches, propulsive dub, and, of course, house and disco. The show is in a former church, and while it's easy to make the link between religious and pop transcendence that doesn't make the beauty here any less real: if there's a heaven, I'm pretty sure it sounds like this.

Like Dickson, McAlmont first became a pop star in the 1990s: he sang in the short-lived band Thieves, releasing their ill-fated breakup album as a solo project before topping the charts alongside Bernard Butler with 1995's 'Yes', a song that led *Melody Maker* to predict, "One day he will open his mouth and a cathedral will fall out."[102]

In the 1990s, McAlmont looked like a very beautiful alien. Today's model is perhaps a little more fabulous gay uncle than man who fell to earth, but his voice and his charisma are undimmed. "He's the fucking British Marvin Gaye," the man in front of me yells to his pals.

Most of the songs played tonight are from *Daylight*, the first of two conceptual records the duo will release in 2024 and 2025. *Daylight* is themed around the warmth of summer and is intended for release on the first day of summer 2024, a date Dickson immediately regretted when he discovered how little time that left him to finish the record before the vinyl needed to be pressed, and its sibling, *Twilight*, will be released in the winter. Dickson kindly sends me a secret link so I can hear the first album in its entirety months before my pre-ordered copy arrives, and it's a beautiful, joyful collection that frequently makes me grin and brings the odd tear too.

My favourite part of the record is probably the closing trio of 'Living Things', 'Celebrate' and 'The Show', the latter of which closes the album on a euphoric note, but it's the penultimate 'Celebrate' that's in my head for days afterwards thanks to a single repeated line, beautifully sung over burbling ARP synths.

"My instinct for survival is to celebrate," McAlmont sings. "My instinct for survival is to celebrate, celebrate."

CHAPTER 10:
THE QUEEREST
OF THE QUEER

The 1990s rocked, but not always in a good way: both grunge and Britpop soon had their interesting edges filed off by more careerist bands who took the basic template but none of the nuance. Few of the Nirvana-alikes drew any inspiration from Kurt Cobain's own influences such as his beloved Vaselines, the Glasgow band that emerged from a short-lived group featuring Douglas T Stewart and Sean Dickson, and as a musician playing tiny venues around that time, I don't recall the Oasis-ification of the lower rungs of the live music ladder with much enthusiasm. It seemed like every second band was called The Shine, pronounced *she-eye-eye-unn*, with their frontmen – and they were *always* men – adopting Liam Gallagher's simian swagger and bringing back not just hackneyed chord progressions, but hackneyed sexism and homophobia too.

It all felt very... *straight*.

When Oasis reformed in 2024, endless middle-aged commentators chortled about the band's infamous banter. Few cared to recall the band's outspoken homophobia; as music journalist Simon Price wrote on Twitter years earlier, Liam Gallagher's choice of heckles for Kylie Minogue and Robbie Williams at the Q Awards were "lesbian!" and "queer!" respectively. "Two decades on, it's still his go-to insult," Price wrote, quote-tweeting Gallagher calling his brother's band "bum chums" in 2018.[103]

It wasn't just the music, but the media around it. The mid-nineties saw the rise of aggressively heterosexual lad culture via *Loaded* magazine, which launched in 1994, and the rebranded *FHM*, previously *For Him Magazine*. *FHM* was originally a stuffy men's shoes-and-watches periodical, but it went deliberately and dramatically downmarket in the early nineties with great success. By 1998, *FHM* and *Loaded* were shifting more than 1.2 million copies per month between them, nearly ten times the weekly sales of *NME* (90,626) and *Melody Maker* (40,349) combined.[104] Many even lower-rent imitators followed in their wake.

Under the false flag of irony, pretty much every -ism we thought we'd left behind was sold to young men – and men old enough to know better – as edgy rebellion by writers so conservative that some would later become right-wing politicians; *Loaded*'s Martin Daubney's post-magazine career included standing as an electoral candidate for the Brexit Party, becoming deputy leader of Laurence Fox's Reclaim Party, and in 2007, organising a "straight pride" march.[105]

Lad culture was the big cultural story of the 1990s but thankfully it wasn't the only one, and it certainly wasn't the most interesting.

I can't remember where I was the first time I heard 'Queer', but I remember what I thought: Garbage's 1995 debut single sounded like all of pop and rock music happening at once.

'Queer' mixed hazy hip-hop beats with walls of guitar, R&B rhythms and an extraordinary, beguiling vocal. It was one of the most exciting things I'd ever heard, and I'd later discover with some astonishment that the singer was Shirley Manson, formerly of Goodbye Mr Mackenzie.

Award-winning American writer Niko Stratis felt the same excitement from her own introduction to the band, their second single 'Only Happy When It Rains', writing:

> "Manson's voice was otherworldly in a way that felt removed from what I'd previously heard of women's singing on modern pop radio. She had an edge and a swagger that felt almost masculine to me, similar to the way that my older male coworkers moved through the world. Manson's style, the way she sang and carried herself with unbridled confidence, was the first time I understood something could be both male, female, and maybe something outside of the two."[106]

Stratis, like me, is trans. She, like me, hadn't quite come to terms with that in the mid-1990s, but something about Garbage, about Shirley Manson and her lyrics and her voice, connected with us in ways we weren't quite ready to understand. For both of us it would be a later Garbage song, 2001's 'Androgyny', that was "the crack that let the light in", as Stratis puts it. From the very beginning, Stratis and many other queer people understood something important about Manson's use of the Q-word, a word that for so many at the time was a shouted slur rather than a badge of pride:

When Shirley Manson sang the word "queer", she meant queer as in "fuck you".

Garbage were formed by producer and musician Steve Marker and his friend, drummer and producer Butch Vig, and from the outset they were determined to go against the grain. With the rock scene obsessing over authenticity and "real music" played on "real instruments" – a list that included many of the rock records Butch Vig had produced, such as Nirvana's *Nevermind* – they set out to make pop music that mixed heavily processed guitars with electronic beats and loops using technology that's the norm now, but was unusual in rock and would turn out to be a nightmare to tour with.

As *Sound On Sound* magazine put it, the production owed as much to Public Enemy as to Led Zeppelin: "It's a measure of their success that the once-radical techniques they used on their first two albums are now commonplace in mainstream rock music."[107]

Musical innovation doesn't sound shocking for long: from Hendrix's guitar pedals to the hyperpop of SOPHIE, it's quickly absorbed, emulated and evolved by other musicians until what once sounded electrifyingly new becomes the new normal. Garbage's use of Pro Tools as an instrument was as groundbreaking as the sonic studio experimentation of Joe Meek; the first time I heard the opening bars of 'Supervixen' with their complete, clinical, absolutely silent stops, I thought my CD player was broken.

To sing that unique music, Marker and Vig wanted a unique singer. They wanted somebody understated, somebody as distinct and as compelling as a Debbie Harry, a Patti Smith, a Chrissie Hynde or a Siouxsie Sioux. They found her in Manson, entirely by accident. The video for 'Suffocate Me', the first single from her post-Goodbye Mr Mackenzie band Angelfish, was only broadcast once on MTV's *120 Minutes*, but that broadcast was spotted by Marker, who thought Manson would be perfect for Garbage.

What really struck Marker and Vig was the way Shirley sang: where most female rock singers went high, Shirley went low; where many would grandstand, Shirley Manson growled.

While her first audition was disastrous, her ad-libbed lyrics for 'Vow', 'Stupid Girl' and 'Queer' – her first attempts at songwriting – and her almost genderless vocal delivery had the edge Garbage was hoping for. After a more successful second meeting, Manson joined the band.

Manson is one of the best rock stars, and her influence is enormous. Lauren Mayberry of CHVRCHES put it plainly: "I wouldn't be in a band if it weren't for Shirley Manson. I discovered Garbage at a pivotal time [and] Shirley's voice, heart and fearlessness inspire me to this day."[108]

Lzzy Hale of Halestorm is one of many other high-profile artists to cite Manson as an influence, posting praise on her Instagram: "One of the only women in the 90s that really cornered a sound all her own. Dripping with a unique, kind of brooding sass and catchy melodies. She could hang with the rock crowd and the pop crowd, no one can match her."[109]

Amy Lee of Evanescence is another fan – "I love the music, but also just her. Her personality and her strength. And being this powerful woman, like it wasn't even a thing"[110] – as are Florence Welch of Florence and the Machine (who called Manson her "heroine"[111]), Hayley Williams of Paramore, and Lady Gaga. In conversation with Debbie Harry, Gaga explained that as "*such* a huge Garbage fan" she would "put your albums and Garbage's albums [in] my Discman and walk around the block because my mom wouldn't let me walk more than one block by myself."[112]

"Shirley just has one of *those* voices," Lauren Mayberry tells me over email. "You know immediately who it is when you hear a song and it just has that certain something that is hard to quantify. Growing up, there really weren't many women taking up that much space in music, and especially not Scottish women."

Manson isn't just an icon. She's also fiercely supportive of her peers. "Shirley has always been incredibly kind to me," Mayberry says. "I think the hardest part of my work has often been the loneliness and lack of self-belief which I am sure I was just born with, but is definitely worsened by the isolation of being the only woman in a lot of the experiences CHVRCHES has had. Shirley was one of the first people to reach out to me when the band started doing well, and really validated a lot of those feelings. She always seemed like a real girl's-girl and it was reassuring as a fan to know how true that is, and I respect how much she has consciously and vocally made sure people know that Garbage and her feminism is intersectional on all levels."

Shirley Manson's taste in music has always been eclectic; while her first album was Bowie's *Ziggy Stardust* and Bowie was also the first artist she saw live, she had a teenage love of The Stray Cats and grew up listening to and playing classical music. "I was in a choir, I played in an orchestra, my mother exposed me to jazz music [...] but the thing that really imprinted on me was that it wasn't just music I loved," Manson told me. "It was the personas that carried the music. David Bowie just made an unbelievable impact on me, and the same with Siouxsie Sioux: she was equally as influential on me and completely changed my view of the world."

Manson has long had what she describes as "weird feelings about gender". "I was so tired of all the female tropes that I was surrounded by and didn't identify with at all. I never identified with the pretty girls or the very cis ideal of femininity," she explains. "And then when I saw Siouxsie, she didn't feel to me like anything I'd ever seen before."

Manson makes a good argument for including Siouxsie in the pantheon of queer artists "just by nature of not falling into all of these tropes, the traditional rules and regulations of femininity." While Siouxsie doesn't really talk about her private life very much, in 2007 she told *The Independent,* "I've never particularly said I'm hetero or a lesbian. I know there are people who are definitely one way, but that's not really me."[113]

"She was like a goddess to me," Manson says. "Like some genderless goddess. Her androgyny really spoke to me, excited me and empowered me."

Angelfish proved to be a false start, but Manson's low, binary-defying vocals on single 'Suffocate Me' brought her to Garbage. And in Garbage Manson became a global icon, a role that's often sat uneasily with her.

Becoming the frontperson of a multi-million album-selling band was a very different experience to Goodbye Mr Mackenzie, where Manson was "just happy to be in the gang [...] I think I enjoyed myself because I had so little skin in the game. Back then it was a riot for me." Manson became the figurehead of a global rock band, the pressures of which only added to the problems of body dysmorphia and depression she's had all her life.

"Because of the way I began in the music industry, I never thought I was an artist of any worth," she says. "I never even thought of myself as an artist until I was in my forties [...] because of all the things I'd been told when I was young that were wrong, I was deeply ashamed of things – I was embarrassed by my rage, but now I realise that if I hadn't had that rage I wouldn't be here today with a healthy career forty years on. You need some fucking rage."

It helps that these days, Manson really loves her job. "I think there are a lot of artists out there who don't enjoy being artists, who don't enjoy the workload, who don't thrive. They emerge, and they're beautiful and glorious, and then the industry destroys them."

From the beginning of Garbage, Manson has written about gender and queerness. The timing wasn't always the best: promotion of *Beautiful Garbage*, whose songs included 'Androgyny' and 'Cherry Lips' and which was arguably Garbage's queerest album to date, was halted in the aftermath of 9/11. Despite being a great pop record with an astonishing video, lead single 'Androgyny' didn't crack the UK top twenty and didn't break into the Billboard chart at all, but as people like Niko Stratis and I can attest, that didn't mean it didn't have an impact.

"I think they're incredible songs," Manson tells me today. "Every time we perform them, I'm proud that they're in our discography. To me, they're talking about things that are vitally important. People are talking about how relevant they are now and how ahead of the curve they were back then, which is lovely in retrospect. I'm glad we were talking about things that really needed to be discussed, particularly now when LGBTQ+ people are really up against it."

I tell Manson about my own epiphany with 'Androgyny' and she's audibly moved. "That makes me happy," she says. "I'm really proud that we have these songs. It makes me so happy that we are able to provide that kind of joy for people."

"Queer culture has had such a huge influence on music and on identity," she continues. "Music's glorious, but it needs a great translator – and the best, the greatest, are usually the genderless. Because it's about freedom. Freedom and expression."

CHAPTER 11:
IN THE BEGINNING THERE WERE ANSWERS

One of my very favourite pieces of music by anybody, Scottish or otherwise, is the song *In Remote Part / Scottish Fiction*, which closes Idlewild's 2002 album *The Remote Part*. The first half is a beautiful, fragile thing of friendship and maybe more with singer Roddy Woomble at his most vulnerable, and it then erupts in a storm of guitars with Scots Makar Edwin Morgan sounding like the voice of God: "it isn't in the castle / it isn't in the mist / it's in the calling of the waters as they break…" It's an astonishing, incendiary, beautiful meeting of minds.

I like that Idlewild chose Morgan for their song: the man who wrote that "Love rules. Love laughs. Love marches." was gay, although he didn't come out until he was 70: as a poet who lived in less enlightened times he felt compelled to hide his queerness behind genderless language in his love poems. In later life he was out and proud and beloved; Scotland's first Makar, our national poet.

Like all great rock bands, Idlewild are musical magpies with influences from everywhere – as you can see from the Spotify playlist they put together to mark twenty-five years of making music[114] and in Woomble's solo work, which shows his love of Scots and American folk music. There are three artists in particular I think made a huge impact on them, on many of their peers, and on many Scots rock bands since.

The first of those artists is Bob Mould of Hüsker Dü and later, Sugar. Idlewild weren't alone in their love of Hüsker Dü, the Minneapolis punk rock band famed for Mould's incendiary and extraordinarily fast guitar parts: his irresistible mix of melody and aggression – perfect pop played on chainsaws – was a huge influence on Pixies' Black Francis (the ad that led bassist Kim Deal to join said, "Band seeks bassist into Hüsker Dü and Peter, Paul & Mary") and Pixies were in turn a pivotal influence on Nirvana. Nirvana bassist Krist Novoselic said, "What Nirvana did was nothing new. Hüsker Dü did it before us",[115] while drummer and later Foo Fighter Dave Grohl would then say, "No Hüsker Dü, no Foo Fighters".[116] The band were also key influences on Dinosaur Jr. and Green Day, whose legacy is audible in Scots venues every weekend.

Although Hüsker Dü were a key part of the US hardcore punk scene, they weren't quite the same as their peers. Hardcore was an even more intense take on punk rock, with the same rejection of the status quo and the aggression turned up to eleven. While many of their peers rejected what we'd now term classic rock, Hüsker Dü happily stole from it. The first Hüsker Dü song I ever heard was their gleefully irreverent cover of The Byrds' 'Eight Miles High', a hazy, sixties classic reimagined as a high-speed sonic assault where the lyrics aren't so much sung as screamed. Even at its most abrasive it's still beautifully, emotionally melodic – and that same mix of beauty and ruin, as Mould would title a later solo album, was what made Hüsker Dü such a distinctive and influential band.

Bob Mould's influence on Idlewild pre-dated Idlewild. In

1989, Roddy Woomble's family moved to Greenville, South Carolina, for two years. During that time a school friend made Woomble mix tapes of US punk rock, and the young Woomble fell in love with The Replacements, Black Flag, Minor Threat, and Hüsker Dü. It "was unlike anything I'd heard," Woomble told journalist Nan Spowart many years later. "It was raw and exciting and full of ideas. It also seemed achievable to make music like this."[117] It inspired Woomble to form his first short-lived band in the US, and after a short time back home in Carnoustie he went to Edinburgh to study photography. There, he met Rod Jones and Colin Newton and formed Idlewild in 1995.

Bob Mould is gay and Hüsker Dü drummer Grant Hart was bisexual, although Mould didn't come out until later; as he recalled in 2020, there were very few openly gay musicians in the US hardcore punk scene of the early eighties. "The army's credo was, 'Don't ask, don't tell'; in hardcore, it was, 'Don't advertise, don't worry'."[118] Despite the scene being largely welcoming – Mould describes it as "a community of misfits" – some bands were extremely queerphobic. When the notoriously abrasive hardcore punk pioneers Bad Brains stayed over at Hart's parents' home, they left a note reading, "Die, faggots, die".

Mould didn't talk about his sexuality at the time, but it clearly fuelled his music, particularly the more relationship-focused songs of 1984's *Zen Arcade* and beyond. Mould was particularly influenced by Buzzcocks' Pete Shelley, whose 'I Don't Mind' Mould would later cover. "The way Pete wrote all the songs gender-neutral, that's where I was unconsciously connecting," he explained. "That was something that got into my songwriting. Now when I look back at the '80s, and I look back at people who were writing relationship songs that were gender-neutral, maybe more of them were LGBT than I knew at the time."[119]

Mould did hint about his sexuality; the video for Sugar's 1992 song 'If I Can't Change Your Mind' video featured same-gender relationships, including a blink-and-you'll-miss-it photo of Mould and his partner. The photo was flipped to say, "This is not your parents' world."

"I'm guessing some of my fans just thought it was some political statement, some unaffiliated political statement, because there was nothing super-gay about it," Mould says. "It was a subtle message; it was probably speaking in code maybe a little bit to people still."[120]

Mould wasn't out, and didn't plan to come out, but *SPIN* magazine had other plans and pressed him on his sexuality in a 1994 interview. The implications of that were difficult for Mould. "I wasn't Jimmy Somerville, or Tom Robinson, the guys who'd done the heavy lifting back then. I couldn't be a spokesperson for anything other than my music."[121]

The *SPIN* article that effectively outed him coincided with the launch of Sugar's *File Under: Easy Listening* album, and subsequent events appeared to confirm his fear that he might be pigeonholed as a gay musician rather than just a musician. Sugar's 1992 debut, *Copper Blue*, was *NME*'s album of the year, an MTV regular and a radio hit but *F.U.E.L.* received a cooler reception, especially from US radio stations. "I lost some fans, and I lost a little bit of support at commercial radio in the deep South," Mould told *Yahoo! Entertainment*.[122] "Maybe they didn't like the record, or maybe it coincided with the article. But the two happened together. I don't know."

Mould responded by stepping out of the spotlight to make electronic music and to DJ at techno clubs for several years before returning with more of the buzzsaw pop that's made him so influential. He's much more confident about being a gay man in rock music today, speaking out against the "evangelical ISIS" targeting queer people and trans people in particular. "Hats off to musicians these days and kids," he said. "I think over the decades, there's been some enlightenment. I hope."[123]

The second and third crucial bands are R.E.M., whose 'Gardening At Night' Woomble cites as one of the songs that changed his life, and The Smiths. "You can hear that all over Idlewild – the influence of punk rock, R.E.M. and The Smiths," Woomble told *The Line of Best Fit*. "Particularly early Idlewild, before we started putting our own personalities into the music. Michael Stipe and Morrissey were big influences in terms of how I thought about song words."[124]

As with Bob Mould, R.E.M. singer Michael Stipe preferred not to discuss his sexuality with the press – he didn't start describing himself as a queer artist until 2001, fourteen years after R.E.M.'s huge hit 'The One I Love' first made him famous – but when he did become more open about his sexuality it was hardly a surprise.

Stipe and his band were hugely influenced by their hometown's B-52's, a band with just one straight member and a wonderfully camp aesthetic. Guitarist Ricky Wilson cited influences including children's records and Esquerita, and Wilson's distinctive and unusual guitar style would influence R.E.M.'s Peter Buck who, in turn, would influence a generation of alternative rock guitarists. Wilson's guitars may have had six strings, but he often only played four or five of them, and those guitars were typically tuned to open tunings rather than the E-standard tuning of most rock and pop guitar. So, for example, instead of the traditional guitar tuning of E, A, D, G, B, and E, Wilson's guitar in 'Rock Lobster' and 'Dance This Mess Around' was C, F, skip two strings, F, F; for 'Private Idaho' his guitar was E, B, D, skip a string, B, B. By moving all the notes around and creating new resonances and interactions, such tunings take guitar players to unfamiliar places and help them map previously uncharted musical territories.

Wilson was friends with Holly Woodlawn, the trans actress Lou Reed sang about in 'Walk on the Wild Side' (also an inspiration to Frankie Goes To Hollywood's William "Holly" Johnson, who took her first name in tribute to her), and he was audibly influenced by Reed's Velvet Underground, a band who embodied and embraced queerness in many forms in some of their best-known songs such as 'Candy Says', 'Venus in Furs' and 'Sweet Jane'. Reed lived the life as well as singing about it and was a key figure in Andy Warhol's New York scene, which he'd later reference on his *Transformer* album – a must-have for pretty much any rock fan.

Lou Reed and the Velvet Underground were formative influences on Michael Stipe, too. In R.E.M., Stipe would echo Ziggy Stardust-era David Bowie in playing Velvet Underground covers to new audiences. Bowie had loved one Velvet Underground song, 'I'm Waiting for the Man', so much that it was a regular in his live performance across decades, and R.E.M. covered many Velvets songs during their career, including 'Femme Fatale', 'Pale Blue Eyes' and 'There She Goes Again', all of which were released on R.E.M.'s compilation album *Dead Letter Office*. 'After Hours' appeared on the CD of 'Losing My Religion' and Stipe would later cover 'Sunday Morning' as part of the Velvets tribute *I'll Be Your Mirror*.

Lyrically and vocally, I can see and hear a strong Buzzcocks influence in many R.E.M. songs: like Pete Shelley and Bob Mould, Michael Stipe would write about his personal life and his queerness in opaque ways.

I think you can hear a lot of Stipe's influence in Roddy

Woomble's vocal melodies and rhythms, especially on '100 Broken Windows', and you could see it in Woomble's stage persona: like Stipe, Woomble exuded a bookish, androgynous charisma that for me mixed the anti-macho stance of Orange Juice with Stipe's playfulness. Was Woomble gay, or bi or queer in any way? I had no idea, and it didn't really matter: he wasn't like the other boys, and that just added to his considerable charm. You could call it confusion in the best way possible.

The Smiths are arguably the most influential queer rock band of all time, despite three-quarters of them being straight. Influenced by sixties pop, Marc Bolan, The Velvet Underground, The New York Dolls, and (in Johnny Marr's case at least) Chic, The Smiths' career was relatively short – they were only together from 1982 to 1987 before imploding in acrimony – but their legacy has been huge. Johnny Marr is rightly regarded as one of the finest and most interesting guitar players of all time, and while these days Morrissey seems to have positioned himself as the Nigel Farage of indie rock, he was once one of the most excitingly queer singers in pop.

Morrissey didn't officially come out until he published his autobiography in 2013, in which he said he was "humasexual", and prior to that he spoke of himself as celibate or as a "prophet of the fourth gender",[125] but his songs and the iconography of the band's record sleeves made it very clear that Morrissey was anything but straight and far from uninterested, and he became even more open about his desires once The Smiths were over. His 1990 album *Bona Drag* took its title from the coded gay language of polari and included songs such as 'Piccadilly Palare', a celebration of gay sex workers. Earlier songs were just as queer, albeit less obviously so: 'These Things Take Time', 'Back to the Old House', 'What Difference Does It Make?' and 'Hand in Glove', among many others, are songs packed with queer longing. 'There Is a Light That Never Goes Out' is particularly devastating.

Not as devastating as Morrissey's decline into reactionary rabble-rousing, mind you. Since the demise of The Smiths, the same man who told *Rolling Stone,* "The sexes have been too easily defined. People are so rigidly locked into these two little categories [...] I think we should slap down those barriers,"[126] proved all too keen to erect barriers against other marginalised groups.

I think had Morrissey come to fame in today's era of social media, his views on race in particular would have been much more widely known and loudly condemned, but in the pre-internet era, fans wouldn't necessarily have seen him dismiss all,"Black modern music, which I detest"[127] or claim that there was a Black pop conspiracy to keep white artists down, as he told *Melody Maker* in the dying days of The Smiths. Even as he waved a Union Flag while singing his song 'The National Front Disco' – key line, "England for the English!" – on stage in 1992, many fans didn't want to face up to the fact that this didn't appear to be a persona.

To this queer Smiths fan, Morrissey's rightwards trajectory has been more devastating than any of his lyrics: by 2019, the Morrissey who wrote songs that made you feel welcome, and wanted, and understood, was appearing on TV wearing a badge showing support for For Britain, a far-right political party that even Nigel Farage dismissed as a bunch of "Nazis and racists."[128] Morrissey has also spoken against #MeToo and in support of the English Defence League founder Stephen "Tommy Robinson" Yaxley-Lennon.[129].

Like Bob Mould and Michael Stipe, Morrissey deliberately kept things opaque in his more confessional lyrics – so while they were often painfully specific in the situations and feelings they described, you could assign any gender or sexuality to the people in the songs. That was deliberate, as Morrissey told *Rolling Stone*. "It was very important for me to try and write for everybody," he said. "I find when people and things are entirely revealed in an obvious way, it freezes the imagination of the observer. There is nothing to probe for, nothing to dwell on or to try and unravel."[130] That mystery and non-specificity was part of The Smiths' genius. It meant their music was a safe space for people of all genders and sexualities, and of none.

The Smiths only visited Scotland a few times and broke up long before I was old enough to be a gig-goer. Their first Scots show was in 1983 ("It was in Sauchiehall Street and I remember it well," Marr told journalist John Dingwall. "I remember standing on the stage playing to that enormous audience of 11 people."[131]), they returned four times in 1984 and then came back for a proper tour in 1985 when they played Irvine, Edinburgh, Glasgow, Dundee, Lerwick, Aberdeen, and Inverness with support from Easterhouse, one of Scotland's great lost bands. The Smiths would return once more, to the Barrowlands in 1986, before breaking up the following year. Despite their relatively short career, their influence on Scots music fans and musicians has been long-lasting, both directly – it's particularly evident in the first few albums (and album cover photography) from Belle and Sebastian – and in Johnny Marr's elevation to godhood by musicians such as Radiohead, James and the guitar players of Britpop.

One of the things I love about Idlewild, and other Scots bands of a similar vintage and sensibility such as Frightened Rabbit and Franz Ferdinand, is that they don't bother with clichéd macho rock nonsense. Take Franz, for example. They're not a queer band, but the music they make is often queer or queer-adjacent – such as early hit 'Michael', a love song to another man that singer Alex Kapranos sings with infectious enthusiasm. Not everybody listening understood what or who it was about, however. As one commenter on the YouTube video for 'Michael' admits, "When I was around 12 and I used to listen to this song on *Gran Turismo 4*, I thought this song was about Michael Schumacher."[132]

Franz emerged from the thriving Glasgow scene of the mid-nineties, and each member already had quite the musical pedigree. In addition to being in what seemed like most of Glasgow's indie bands including The Yummy Fur, The Karelia, The Amphetameanies and Quinn, Alex Kapranos was also the band booker at the 13th Note venue. There he helped build the Note's reputation as the place where interesting, independent musicians came to play, one that continued thanks to subsequent bookers including Brendan O'Hare, formerly of Teenage Fanclub, and Kay Logan, aka composer and avant-prog musician Helena Celle.

The Note wasn't just open-minded. It was exceptionally affordable too, for both audiences and artists. The beer and food were cheap, and for as long as I've known the Note you could hire the whole venue, including its sound system, for just £50 – even at weekends.

That was a fraction of what other venues charged, and it was a real alternative to the "pay to play" approach of many cities' venues where bands would be handed a fistful of expensive tickets to sell. Under pay to play, which sadly still persists, musicians have to reach into their own pockets if they don't sell a minimum amount – a system that takes all the risk from the promoter and puts it onto the artist, removing any incentive for the promoter to do the slightest bit of promotion: their fee is always guaranteed.

The Note was a much better deal, and a much better place to play. Even if hardly anybody turned up you were unlikely to lose money, and that made it a haven for more obscure, interesting and experimental acts, and for marginalised musicians of all kinds.

That makes its loss all the more devastating. After years of under-investment – in the 2010s I returned to play there after more than a decade away and saw the same holes in the ceiling that bands put there in the 1990s and 2000s – in 2023 the Note's staff attempted to unionise after their complaints about unsafe working conditions, low wages and zero-hour contracts appeared to fall on deaf ears. Their complaints seemed to be valid and in the summer of 2023 the venue was shut down by environmental health officers who discovered a rodent infestation. When the Note's staff went on strike, they were immediately sacked and the venue went into voluntary liquidation. As I write this in late 2024, it's still empty, a blank and much-missed space where a vibrant cultural centre used to be.

Like many musicians of their generation, Franz were big fans of David Bowie and of The Velvet Underground, but their love of Chic, of Josef K and most of all, of the wonderfully flamboyant Sparks – a band whose catalogue ranges from the Associates-inspiring operatic pop of 'This Town Ain't Big Enough for Both of Us' to the Giorgio Moroder hi-NRG of 'The Number One Song in Heaven' – is clearly very significant too. Their admiration of Sparks turned into a full-blown collaboration with the synth-poppers under the name FFS, a collaboration that underlined just how much the band are pop fans as well as pop stars. Of course, Franz's music is a little bit queer: I'm sure that at least half of their record collections and the contents of their bookshelves are too.

CHAPTER 12:
A GENIE IN A BOTTLE

A s the 1990s made way for the early aughts, there were plenty of wins for LGBTQ+ people. Scotland repealed Section 28 in 2000 and England and Wales followed suit in 2003; the Gender Recognition Act was passed in 2004 (something the Labour Party likes to take credit for, although the reality is that the GRA was the result of the Tony Blair government being forced by the EU courts to stop depriving trans people of basic human rights), and the Civil Partnership Act came into force in 2005.

Queer representation was improving too. *Queer as Folk* in 1999 was a landmark for queer rep on UK televisions; Julie Hesmondhalgh played the first trans character in a British soap, in *Coronation Street*, from 1998 onwards; and US imports such as *Sex and the City* and *Will & Grace* showed LGBTQ+ people in a positive light.

There were countercurrents too. Lad culture infected mass culture, its not-really-ironic sexism and backlash to so-called "political correctness" – the 1990s equivalent of "woke" – saw Pot Noodles called "slags", chocolate bars branded "not for girls" and old prejudices and stereotypes returning under the guise of having a bit of fun.

This was a time of faux-lesbianism made for the male gaze, not just on the covers of lad mags but on TV too; the most talked-about moment of the 2003 MTV Video Music Awards was when Madonna spontaneously kissed both Britney Spears and Christina Aguilera. Of course there was nothing spontaneous about it; the kiss was planned as a watercooler moment and you can stream rehearsal footage showing the already well-practiced winching on YouTube.[133] While the kiss wasn't real, the predictable – and intended – outrage was: right-wing newspapers made it sound like MTV had televised five hours of fisting, and the channel's employees received death threats.

While many shows and films were LGBTQ+ friendly, some of the biggest still got it very wrong: for example, the smash-hit show *Friends* ran several episodes where transphobia and "gay panic" were played for laughs. One of the key characters, Chandler Bing, was frequently mocked for having a "gay dad", and the writers seemed unsure about whether said dad, Charles, was a drag queen or a trans woman: the character was played by cis actor Kathleen Turner. In season seven's 'The One With Monica and Chandler's Wedding', in which Chandler's dad was misgendered and deadnamed, one supposedly gut-busting gag featured Charles' ex-wife asking them, "Don't you have a little too much penis to be wearing a dress like that?"[134] *Friends* wasn't particularly homophobic or transphobic by the standards of the decade; despite the jokes, Chandler's dad wasn't portrayed as a victim or somebody who was, or should be, ashamed of who they were.

Much more unpleasant kinds of homophobia and transphobia were common in films, particularly those aimed at younger audiences. In *Ace Ventura: Pet Detective*, Jim Carrey's titular character discovers that the gorgeous woman he just kissed is trans; he vomits in the toilet, takes off all his clothes and burns them before climbing into the shower to weep,[135] a scene made all the more offensive by its deliberate invocation of women traumatised by sexual assault. In *Naked Gun 33⅓*, a trans-as-trickster joke reveals Anna Nicole Smith's character's penis – which, inevitably, is unnaturally bent – in silhouette, a reveal that leads to Leslie Nielsen spewing into a tuba.[136]

One of *Teen Wolf*'s big jokes is when Michael J. Fox's friend sputters, "Are you going to tell me you're a fag? Because if you're going to tell me you're a fag, I'm not going to be able to handle it," only to be reassured that, "I'm not a fag. I'm a werewolf."[137]

The *Police Academy* films featured recurring jokes about cops being sent to the Blue Oyster Bar, a leather bar where the patrons would force them to dance.[138] In *Crocodile Dundee*, the titular Australian chats up a very attractive woman in a New York bar. When another patron informs him that the woman is in fact a man, he turns to her, grabs her crotch and exclaims, "That was a guy! A guy dressed up like a Sheila! Look at that!" The humiliated woman leaves in tears, the other drinkers laughing and jeering, and it's clear we're expected to be laughing along with them.[139]

Even sympathetic queer characters in TV shows and films tended to have very short life expectancies, if they weren't already dead, as so many were in crime-themed TV dramas where queer people could only ever be victims or killers. The tendency to kill off queer characters is so common there's a name for it: Bury Your Gays. There's another term for it: Dead Lesbian Syndrome. When the character Lexa in cult TV show *The 100* suffered an untimely case of Dead Lesbian Syndrome in 2016, queer website Autostraddle decided to count the number of lesbian and bi characters killed off too soon. The total? Two hundred and thirty-five, across shows including *Prisoner: Cell Block H; Babylon 5; Brookside; Star Trek: Deep Space Nine; Bad Girls; Xena: Warrior Princess; Buffy the Vampire Slayer;*

NYPD Blue; Seinfeld; Queer as Folk; The L Word; Battlestar Galactica and many more.[140]

As Reise, author of the piece, pointed out, from the mid-1970s until well into the 2010s, "Lesbian and bisexual characters seemed entirely unable to date an actual woman or stay alive for more than three episodes, let alone an entire run, of a show." While some of the deaths were inevitable given the type of shows – *The Walking Dead* isn't exactly a safe space for anyone, queer or otherwise – Reise argues that, "We comprise such a teeny-tiny fraction of characters on television to begin with that killing us off so haphazardly feels especially cruel [...] they still add to the body count weighing down our history of misrepresentation."[141]

Stories matter; that's why almost every major religion relies on parables and allegories, and why every culture has its myths and legends. The advocacy group GLAAD argues that increasing queer visibility in TV shows and popular culture helped increase approval for marriage equality, and if that's true then the still comparatively low visibility of queer Scots in the run-up to the millennium left room for bad actors and bigotry.

It certainly seemed that way. Late-nineties Scotland saw a fierce anti-LGBTQ+ backlash that came to a horrific head in the Keep the Clause campaign of early 2000, which plastered Scotland with disgraceful anti-LGBTQ+ billboards demanding that the hated Section 28 remain law. The campaign, funded by evangelical Christian and Stagecoach bus millionaire Brian Souter, was as far from grassroots as it was possible to get: there were no members, no activists having meetings. What it did have was the *Daily Record*, Cardinal Winning of the Catholic Church and additional support from the *Scottish Daily Mail* and *Scottish Daily Mirror*. The campaign demonised LGBTQ+ people, accusing them of being a danger to children – a tactic that has since been enthusiastically revived against trans people.

For significant sections of the Scottish press – but not most of the Scottish public which, as now, was much more inclusive than the papers would have you believe – queerness was still something to be ashamed of. God help anybody with a public profile who wanted to keep their sexuality private.

If you're a queer music fan, you're likely to be drawn to queer artists: there's a power in being seen, and of hearing your own experiences in song. As a queer musician, I know there's a great joy in seeing queer people connect to your music, but if you haven't sought out that community, if queerness is a label that's been put on you rather than claimed by you, the attention can be suffocating. That's something Bob Mould feared when he was outed in the 1990s, and it's something Scotland's Jill Jackson experienced a decade after.

Today, Jackson is a successful and critically acclaimed Americana artist. In the early 2000s, she was the singer in short-lived Scots pop sensations Speedway. Speedway were briefly media darlings and had musicians such as Paisley's Paolo Nutini as their support acts. The band's big hit was a cheeky cash-in on an online smash: Freelance Hellraiser's mash-up of Christina Aguilera's 'Genie in a Bottle' and The Strokes' 'Hard to Explain' went viral, but the Hellraiser's record company refused to release it, so Speedway recorded an almost identical cover and took it to number ten in the UK pop charts.

The band's new profile made them a tabloid target, and when somebody tipped off *The Scottish Sun* that Jackson was in a lesbian relationship with Alex Parks, the winner of TV show *Fame Academy*, the newspaper went for her. Jackson was still married to her husband at the time and hadn't come out to her parents or to the wider world. *The Sun* didn't care.

As Jackson says, "*The Sun* called to say they were running

the story so I had no choice but to tell my family. It was such an invasion [...] no one knew I was gay, except my sisters [and] obviously the girls I'd been with. The record company didn't know."[142]

Speedway broke up shortly afterwards and Jackson began to focus on her real musical love, Americana. Her childhood had been soundtracked by Dolly Parton and Johnny Cash, and she later gravitated to Emmylou Harris and Patty Griffin. While she's become highly successful in her chosen genre, being an out gay woman has come with a price that's included not just media harassment but harassment and heckling at gigs and unwanted online attention.

Writing on her Facebook page in 2020, Jackson expressed her frustration at being objectified as a lesbian artist rather than admired as an artist who happens to be a lesbian. "Since I was outed on the front page of *The Sun* I have fought to have my musical voice heard over the 'gay singer/songwriter tag'" she wrote in response to being featured on what she described as "a gay playlist".[143]

Jackson isn't alone in this. Gay, lesbian, trans or queer aren't genres of music, and if you're identified and classified by your gender identity or your sexuality rather than your art, this is marginalising – even by people who mean well.

The most dramatic example I can think of wasn't about queerness, but it was Scottish and it did apply to marginalised genders. In 2018, the multi-million-pound successor to the T in the Park music festival, TRNSMT, was widely criticised by music fans, musicians and the Musicians Union for its very male lineup: out of twenty-three main-stage acts, only three of them featured women. The festival promised to do better, and the following year it created a separate stage for female artists, far from and much smaller than the main festival stage – so small and so far that some of the event security staff didn't even know where it was.[144] I'm reminded of Douglas Adams' description of a council document that was exhibited in a cellar, in the dark, under a missing staircase "in the bottom of a locked filing cabinet stuck in a disused lavatory with a sign on the door saying 'beware of the leopard'."[145]

For Jackson, and for some of the LGBTQ+ artists I've spoken to and/or interviewed, there's a genuine fear of being ghettoised, of being lumped in with artists with whom they have no musical common ground and of attracting an audience who isn't there for the music. As Jackson said, "I have worked so hard to engage with an audience that is made up of a wide range of people with the common thread of loving music, nothing more. So if you come to my show because I am gay, don't."[146]

Thankfully not all artists' experiences have been quite so toxic. For example, KT Tunstall has had an enthusiastic gay following from the very start of her career, one she's delighted to have and for whose rights she's been a very vocal ally despite considering herself mostly straight.

Many powerful and creative women have been assumed to be lesbian if they didn't perform simpering 1950s femininity – my very first crush, 1970s bass warrior Suzi Quatro, was presumed gay because she dressed in leather and, in her own words "never did gender"[147] – but Tunstall's gay following was in part because she sent out the lesbian equivalent of the bat signal.

As Tunstall tells it, the cover of her breakthrough hit *Eyes to the Telescope* in 2004 wasn't supposed to be signalling anything but her taste in culture; she was playing homage to Patti Smith's *Horses* and wore rainbow braces because she loved the Robin Williams TV show *Mork & Mindy*.

If that was how it was intended, it definitely wasn't how it was interpreted. As Tunstall would later recall, "It wasn't me pretending to be gay, but I'm on the front of my album with these bright rainbow suspenders on. All the gay community thought I was gay – and they still think I'm gay! They're just waiting for me to figure it out."[148]

Tunstall defines herself as mostly straight, but "not locked-down straight" and happily recalls encounters with other women.[149] When it comes to being attracted to other people, "I am absolutely all about no boundaries and no labels," she says. "I'm gender fluid."[150]

As the response to Tunstall's frankness in the mid-2010s onwards demonstrates, we have thankfully come a long way from the tabloid harassment of Jackson in the early 2000s, at least for gay, bi and lesbian artists; when Aberdeen soul queen Emeli Sandé came out as LGBTQ+ in 2022, the same *Scottish Sun* that made Jill Jackson's life miserable shared Sandé's "happy news" and "loved-up snaps".[151] Brighter Days indeed.

Brighter days kept on coming. The Equality Act (Sexual Orientation) Regulations 2007 made it illegal for providers of goods and services to discriminate on the grounds of sexual orientation; the UK appointed Carol Ann Duffy as the first ever Scots poet laureate as well as the first openly lesbian poet laureate in 2009; and Scotland saw its first openly gay political leader in the form of the Conservatives' Ruth Davidson in 2011. Scotland passed its equal marriage legislation, albeit with some get-out clauses for religious groups, in 2014.

While all this was happening, Scotland was undergoing another musical shift. The acid house generation was growing up, settling down, and playing their rave tapes on the school run.

CHAPTER 13:
IT'S OKAY TO CRY

When the girl who would become Sophie Xeon was growing up in Glasgow in the early 1990s, much of her musical education came from the rave tapes her dad played her in the car; he took her to her first rave aged ten. While Dad was introducing Sophie to rave, her mum was introducing her to disco; Sophie would later cite the energy of disco and house DJs such as Larry Levan of Paradise Garage and Chicago's Frankie Knuckles as key influences. By the age of ten, Sophie was telling people she wanted to quit school and make music full-time. Aged twelve she began DJing at family weddings.

Like many successful Scots musicians, she had to leave Scotland to find fame; Sophie went to Berlin and London in her teens, where her 2013 single 'BIPP' brought her to worldwide attention and she became a collaborator with London's PC Music. Her 2014 song 'Lemonade' was picked up for a McDonalds advert, and over the next few years she would work closely with artists including Charli XCX – who would later dedicate her album *Crash* to her – and Madonna, for whom she co-produced the single 'Bitch I'm Madonna'.

Sophie's sound was like nothing you'd ever heard before:

while house music was a clear influence she twisted dance and pop into entirely new shapes, creating extraordinary sounds and using digital effects to hyper-kinetic consequence with vocals pitch-shifted and chopped up and stretched almost beyond recognition. Her first band, the Berlin-based Motherland, is still on SoundCloud where you can hear her early experiments from 2012, but while they're fun and have barely dated they don't really prepare you for the astonishing things she would do with tunes and technology in the years that followed. On her later records the only organic thing you'll hear are the vocals, and even then they're processed to the point where they're often unrecognisable.

Listening to her songs now, what sounded impossibly alien a decade ago forms the template of much modern pop. It just took a while for pop to catch up.

In an interview with *The New York Times*, she explained that her focus was to "condense particular feelings down to the most concise, shortest form possible [...] to try and create this immediate feeling, through sound and lyrics, that communicates itself instantaneously."[152]

The newly capitalised SOPHIE was instrumental in creating and popularising hyperpop. The term was first used to describe Grangemouth's Cocteau Twins back in the 1980s, but in its current form it describes the hugely influential genre of electronic pop from the 2010s onwards characterised by a distinctly avant-garde sensibility, heavy use of digital effects and an everything-including-the-kitchen-sink approach to genre.

One of SOPHIE's key collaborators was London-based producer AG Cook of the PC Music collective, who met her in late 2012 after he discovered her SoundCloud demos. The two became fast friends. "SOPHIE had her way with people," Cook recalls. "She could be critical, demanding, laid-back and mischievous all at the same time, an approach that turned everything into a potential collaborator."[153] There were many collaborators. As SOPHIE's star rose ever higher she worked with Lady Gaga and Kim Petras, and her production work in particular was a huge influence on 100 gecs and Rina Sawayama.

For some years SOPHIE used her female name, but didn't discuss her gender and actively avoided the spotlight; at one infamous show in 2014 she stood at the side of the stage disguised as a security guard while drag performer Jesse Hoffman pretended to DJ in her place. That reticence – about which SOPHIE later said, "I think my intentions have been clear, but misinterpreted, maybe"[154] – caused some friction as her celebrity increased, with rivals such as Grimes accusing SOPHIE of "feminine appropriation": speaking to *The Guardian* in 2015, she said, "It's really fucked up to call yourself Sophie and pretend you're a girl when you're a male producer [and] there are so few female producers."[155] Grimes would later apologise.[156]

The year before, electronic music magazine *FADER* published a hit piece, now deleted, claiming that Sophie and other "men" from Cook's PC Music stable were "colonising the female body and using it as an instrument for projecting their own agenda." The accusations clearly stung, but she refused to respond in kind; speaking to *Teen Vogue*, she admitted, "I've found it difficult to accept the things people have said" but it was "not my vibe to call people out, because I speak through my music and that's all I need."[157]

SOPHIE's music was always clearly, exhilaratingly queer, but SOPHIE didn't come out as a trans woman until 2017. As Cook recalls, "She had an aversion to the whole notion of 'coming out' to describe a process that is more about actual-isation than transformation, but there was an honest pride in that particular moment. She talked about hormones, gender and her own experiences with a new lightness that I hadn't seen before."[158] When she did come out, she did it in some style, with her song 'It's Okay to Cry' and its accompanying video – the first time she'd used her own voice and image in any of her releases – introducing a whole new audience to what by now was a completely thrilling pop phenomenon.

SOPHIE was clearly delighted when *Teen Vogue* suggested that by embracing both unabashed pop and the avant-garde she was collapsing false binaries. "I love that," she says. "People do think in binaries, and when you confuse what those are, they're like, this is wrong. But this is what I'm here to do."[159]

Reviewing her London Fabric shows the following year, *NME* described her as "an unmissable live artist", a "masterful" live performer who delivered "something different, something you've probably never seen before and will never witness again", a show that "might fuck with your head, incense you or leave you feeling a near sexual level of euphoria."[160] You don't get that at a Gerry Cinnamon gig.

I'm not just dumping on Cinnamon here (although I am a little bit), but I think the comparison is illustrative, because there are two distinct kinds of artists. There are artists who comfort, and there are artists who challenge; artists who perfect styles we know very well, and artists who invent what's never been heard; artists who plunder pop's past, and artists who play its future to you. The singer-songwriter Cinnamon is very much the former, and SOPHIE was very much the latter.

And then she died.

She was just thirty-four.

SOPHIE's death was all the more tragic for the sheer randomness of it. This was no pop star death, no drugs overdose, no living fast and dying young. In 2021, she had been at home in Greece and climbed onto the roof to get a better view of the full moon; she slipped and fell to her death.

Tributes came from artists including Sam Smith, Peaches, Rihanna and Vince Staples; Redcar, the singer and musical driving force of Christine and the Queens, called her "a stellar producer, a visionary, a reference. She rebelled against the narrow, normative society by being an absolute triumph, both as an artist and as a woman."[161] When Kim Petras became the first trans person to win a Grammy for pop music, she said that SOPHIE had made her win possible; in 2021 the International Astronomical Union named an asteroid, Sophiexeon, after her.

In addition to dedicating her 2022 album *Crash* to her mentor, Charli XCX also dedicated the heartbroken 'So I' on her 2024 follow-up album *Brat* – "I was in awe of her and wanted to impress her [...] I didn't feel like I was magical enough for this unbelievably magic person," she told *The Face*.[162] SOPHIE was also the inspiration for 'Sweetest Fruit' on St. Vincent's 2024 album *All Born Screaming*, and Caroline Polachek's 'I Believe' (2023).

SOPHIE was always incredibly ambitious about her music. Speaking about her collaboration with former Motherland bandmate Matthew Lutz-Kinoy, with whom she created a performance for New York's New Museum in 2016, she explained the kind of music she wanted to make. "I think it would be extremely exciting if music could take you on the same sort of high-thrill 3-minute ride as a theme park roller coaster. Where it spins you upside down, dips you in water, flashes strobe lights at you, takes you on a slow incline to the peak, and then drops you vertically down a smokey tunnel, then stops with a jerk, and your hair is all messed up, and some people feel sick, and others are laughing—then you buy a key ring," she said.[163]

There are endless examples of SOPHIE delivering just that. 'Whole New World/Pretend New World', the nine-minute epic that closes her 2018 album *Oil of Every Pearl's Un-Insides*, is one of them. It begins with stabbing synths and single looped syllables, and then it builds and builds until a mid-song drop that's teasingly, almost unbearably long before the pummelling, mechanical beats arrive to rearrange your ribcage. The final third of the song changes once more to deliver a musical *Wizard of Oz* moment as it becomes widescreen and Technicolor.

SOPHIE's music casts a long shadow, with many contemporary artists – particularly female or female-presenting ones – citing her as an influence. Edinburgh's Sound of Young Scotland award winner Rachel Lu, aka singer and producer LVRA (pronounced "lu-rah") is one of them, and her debut *Soft Like Steel* EP mixed hyperpop, happy hardcore, trance, and even samples from traditional Chinese music to thrilling effect.

One of LVRA's most compelling songs is the shuddering, bass-heavy 'Venom', a collaboration with the queer Glasgow-based visual artist, singer and sound designer Spent and the boundary-breaking DJ and producer TAAHLIAH.

Originally from Kilmarnock, TAAHLIAH was the first Black trans artist to be nominated for a Scottish Album of the Year Award and for Scotland's other prestigious music awards, the Scottish Alternative Music Awards (SAMAs for short). Not only that, but she was the first artist to be nominated for and to win two SAMAs in the same year. The Association of Independent Music gave her the coveted One To Watch award in 2022, and in her acceptance speech she told the audience that she hoped the award "also shines a light on how important it is for our marginalised identities to be recorded, cherished, and recognised. I have no doubt that there will be people in this room that believe I shouldn't be here."[164]

Like SOPHIE, TAAHLIAH's early musical education came from her trance-loving dad. She also listened to a lot of hardcore at school, but her musical vocabulary really exploded when she moved to Glasgow in 2017 to attend the Glasgow School of Art.

Speaking to music writer Jim Ottewill in 2023, TAAHLIAH explained that in Glasgow she "spent time in open spaces where they would play pop one night, techno the next and experimental or jazzy the one after." She never set out to be an artist: her main goal was to be able to be herself among the Glaswegian queer club scene. "Accessing this community can be hard and the easiest way to do it is to go out," she said.[165]

TAAHLIAH had already taught herself to paint, and in Glasgow she taught herself to DJ. When she moved to Berlin in 2019, she taught herself to make electronic music. "I really find solace in making mistakes and being really shit at stuff," she told *Mixmag*. Electronic music "made the most sense to me, because it allowed me to open up my practice and never feel constrained by anything. With electronic music you can basically do anything."[166]

TAAHLIAH has said that we're experiencing a culture shift, an unravelling of gender, and that it's particularly prominent in electronic music. "Even though electronic music is a very white, male, straight, cis dominated industry, I think when you take away the industry and you look at electronic music at its fundamental basics, it's genderless at the end of the day," she said. "When you think about people like Wendy Carlos, the real pioneers of electronic music, and you look back at its history, how can gender not influence it when it was in the hands of gender non-conforming people all along?"[167]

Like many queer artists, TAAHLIAH considers herself an artist who happens to be trans, not a trans artist, but she's very aware of the power of representation. In addition to making her friends and family proud, she also wants other Black trans people "to know that this can happen: we are here and we exist and people can take us seriously. We don't need to be XYX, we don't need to look a certain way, and we don't need to portray a certain kind of archaic image of ultra-femininity. We can just exist and make really fun music."[168]

When we lose musical innovators at any age, we mourn what's been lost and I think when those innovators leave too soon, we also mourn what we never heard. One of the reasons SOPHIE is so missed is because she gave the impression that she was only getting started; the release of 2024's *Sophie*, the album she was working on when she died, illustrates that. It's the most accessible music she'd made, packed with glorious pop and the obligatory dancefloor fillers, but it's also wide-ranging in its influences and inspirations, which vary from movie soundtracks to trap beats, and in its creation, which mixes live performance and collaboration with SOPHIE's trademark synthetic sounds.

It's a fascinating record, an artefact, a snapshot, a moment preserved in amber. It tells us everything about where SOPHIE's head was when she was recording it in 2021, but nothing about where she could have taken pop next.

The first single from the album, 'Reason Why', is built around a vocal hook by Kim Petras. SOPHIE was "the first trans artist friend I've ever had" Petras says in *The New York Times*. "I think we both really related to the alienation that you face, especially in the music industry, and people's perception of you, and talking about it behind your back, and not knowing how to deal with trans people. SOPHIE was just really radical – and not afraid to put that into the music."[169]

The album also features vocals by SOPHIE's friend and fellow PC Music alumni Hannah Diamond, who has previously said that she feels her biggest accomplishment is, alongside her PC Music peers, creating a space in dance music for the LGBTQ+ community. For Diamond, the electronic music community she first encountered didn't feel very welcoming to LGBTQ+ people; "I know I didn't feel particularly comfy or safe in those music spheres."[170]

As Diamond recalls, SOPHIE was a crucial part of changing that: when stage fright nearly derailed Hannah's first performance, SOPHIE was the one who gave her a pat on the back and pushed her out on stage. "SOPHIE would encourage people to be the biggest, brightest form of themselves," she says. "With SOPHIE it was always like, 'If I'm winning, everybody's winning. We're all going to win together and we uplift each other.'"[171]

CHAPTER 14:
REBEL GIRLS

I n 2003, *The Scotsman* published a list of "The 100 Best Scottish Albums Of All Time". It features a lot of wonderful records, but very few by female or queer artists; the list includes four Teenage Fanclub albums, three Simple Minds albums and three by Primal Scream, with the Scream's *Screamadelica* taking the top spot.

The Scotsman had another go in 2024, this time limiting the number to twenty. *Screamadelica* topped that chart too, and once again it featured familiar names such as Frankie Miller, Teenage Fanclub, Simple Minds, The Blue Nile, The Proclaimers and Runrig. Previously listed artists such as The Associates, Billy Mackenzie (as a solo artist) and Garbage didn't make the cut this time around and there were no queer artists at all, despite multiple LGBTQ+ Scots making a big impact in the previous five years. There was apparently no room for the critically acclaimed and musically fascinating Sacred Paws, who won the Scottish Album of the Year Award in 2019; no room for the big-hearted pop of Joesef, shortlisted for the same award in 2021; no space for queer punks Comfort, short-listed in 2020; no room for TAAHLIAH, or for C Duncan, or for SOPHIE, or...

All these lists are completely subjective, of course, although they're usually presented as definitive. Sometimes they're the work of a single writer picking their personal favourites. Sometimes they're clickbait, intended to get people arguing in the comments section to drive up advertising views. In the case of *The Scotsman*'s most recent chart, it was based on an online poll of readers – and as we've known since Belle and Sebastian fans swamped voting for The Brit Awards in 1999, such polls are easily rigged. Whatever the intention, they don't exist in isolation, and when you look at them collectively – as the website BestEverAlbums does, aggregating some 60,000 such lists – a very clear pattern emerges. When you create a best of the best-of lists, you'll discover the best album of all time is Radiohead's *OK Computer*; the remaining top nine are two more Radiohead albums, two by Pink Floyd, three by The Beatles, plus *Ziggy Stardust* and *The Velvet Underground & Nico*.

Whether it's *The Scotsman*'s top twenty, *NME*'s top 100 or an online list, the canon they typically describe and reinforce contains no alarms and no surprises. That's a problem because it tells us what kinds of music supposedly matter – and through omission, what kinds of music don't.

Musicologists Ralf Von Appen and André Doehring analysed thirty-four different lists purporting to list the best 100 albums of all time.[172] Of the top thirty albums from their meta-analysis, nearly all were by white men from either the US (43 percent) or the UK (52 percent); that reflected the fact that the people making the lists were "predominantly white males from the western hemisphere."[173] The lists largely ignored Black and female musicians and non-rock genres, and while it wasn't part of their analysis it's safe to say queer musicians didn't feature too prominently either.

As Von Appen and Doehring explained, when the cultural conversation is dominated by a particular demographic, in this case straight white guys who like traditional rock music, you end up focusing on a lot of straight white guys who play traditional rock music. That, they suggest, "reduces the unimaginable versatility of popular musics from all over the world to a small collection of albums within very narrow stylistic bounds, and defines pop and rock music by the standards of late 1960s rock."[174]

All too often, best-of lists reflect the priorities and preoccupations of decades of music journalism that lionised music that's mostly white, mostly male, mostly straight, and mostly rock, and that affects much more than sales of "classic" albums and their vinyl reissues. It tells musicians that some of them are welcome, and that many of them are not.

It's late summer in Scotland, so of course it's chucking it down, but it'll take more than the Scottish weather to dampen the enthusiasm of the young people heading into the Queen Margaret Union in Glasgow. Forty-six kids aged from eight to nearly seventeen are here for the first day of Girls Rock Glasgow, a "rock 'n'roll summer camp for girls+" that's now in its ninth year.

Girls Rock is proudly inclusive and extremely affordable: through a combination of fundraising gigs and support from established musicians, it's able to offer a full programme for a very low cost. Over the years the camp has been supported by a who's who of Scots musicians including The Pastels, Honeyblood and Emma Pollock; it was also where sibling punk duo Bratakus played their very first gig.

Girls Rock exists in part to address a structural problem with music outwith chart pop: it's very much a straight man's world, and the same narrow horizons of the best-albums lists are reflected in who gets to play and who doesn't. As previously mentioned, of the twenty-three main stage acts at 2019's

TRNSMT festival, there were just three women; of the first twenty-one acts the festival announced for 2024, only six contained female or non-binary musicians. The BBC reported in 2023 that for the fifty biggest festivals in the UK, 74.5 percent of the headline acts were all-male, 12 percent mixed, 13 percent all-female and 0.5 percent non-binary.

Yet Fender, the guitar company, told me that half of its new and aspiring guitar-playing customers are young women (it doesn't record non-binary genders). Their research found that the barriers to marginalised musicians start early: as Fender CEO Andy Mooney explained, Fender's young women buyers preferred to buy online "because the intimidation factor in a brick-and-mortar store was rather high."

The barriers to women and non-binary people go up before they've even played a note. Girls Rock is designed to help them fight back.

By the end of this first day, the participants will have discovered artists such as Shirley Manson and Lauren Mayberry – whose band, CHVRCHES, helped dig Girls Rock out of a financial hole in the late 2010s, and who along with The Pastels' Mitch Mitchell donated instruments for the very first Girls Rock summer school – and they will have learnt how to play some Bikini Kill on guitar. Over the next eight days the girls, grrrls and non-binary kids will write zines; make posters and T-shirts; take part in workshops about consent, LGBTQ+ rights and body positivity; and best of all, form multiple bands and put on a gig in Glasgow's Mono.

Bikini Kill was an early influence on what would become GRG: doing the publicity round for the first GRG in 2015, co-founder Jude Stewart explained, "It's like the Bikini Kill song 'Rebel Girl' – we all have crushes on girls, we have girls we want to be and try their look on… [we need] female role models, but actually we can find them in ourselves too."[175]

GRG also took some inspiration from the other side of the central belt: the Edinburgh Schools Rock Ensemble (ESRE), a band with a constantly changing lineup of school-aged musicians that's been running for more than twenty years with members including Chris Bainbridge of Man of Moon and Stina Tweeddale of Honeyblood.

Girls Rock Glasgow is part of the wider Girls Rock universe, a worldwide movement to encourage young people to express themselves through music. GRG is powered by dozens of volunteers, many of them working musicians, and its two co-directors are musician and producer Alice Black (who plays in Venus in the Lake, aka VITL, and Sister Ghost) and musician and educator beth black (whose musical CV includes flinch and Slowlight). Like many arts organisations, Girls Rock is a Community Interest Company (CIC), a kind of private company whose goal is to contribute to the community rather than to make money for shareholders. "We've got so many plans," Alice tells me with infectious enthusiasm.

I've arranged to meet Alice in Glasgow's Cottiers bar, a converted church that's usually pretty quiet on weeknights, but when I arrive I find myself walking into what looks like a rowdy convention of hip librarians; they're here to see Carla J Easton and Teenage Fanclub's Norman Blake play acoustic sets in the venue next door, a gig I didn't know about. The combination of their pre-show conversations and the building's high echoing ceilings sends us scurrying outside into the unseasonably warm October evening so we can speak without shouting.

Just describing Alice's schedule is exhausting: in addition to working in live TV with its early starts and long hours, they have been playing a flurry of gigs and, with beth black, exploring fundraising ideas, applying for funding and researching places that could become a permanent home for Girls Rock.

I ask Alice about their own Girls Rock journey. "I really loved music as a kid and started playing guitar at high school," Alice says, recalling that she quickly abandoned the school-mandated classical guitar lessons for something more entertaining. That love of music took them into youth music education in Edinburgh's The BIG Project and working with youth groups in collaboration with musicians such as Karine Polwart and Kim Edgar, but in high school and beyond Alice found the music scene stifling. "It was just, like, a bunch of guys soloing over each other," they say. "They were all nice enough, but I had the perception that it didn't really feel like my space. I didn't feel welcome. So it didn't really feel like it was the kind of thing I wanted to be doing." Feeling doubly excluded as a woman and as an LGBTQ+ person, Alice continued doing youth work but drifted away from making music in their local scene. "It didn't feel like fun anymore," Alice says. "I was constantly feeling that I had to prove myself. And I didn't know how to get into it – I wanted to be in a band, but I couldn't really find people I felt comfortable playing with, I didn't know how to put on a gig. Other people knew how to do it, but it was like a secret I didn't really know about."

Alice's world changed when one of their friends volunteered for Girls Rock and urged them to come to a fundraiser. "She said, 'You need to come along. You'll love this. It's right up your street.'" That friend was proved right almost immediately. "The first band was these kids in corpse paint, just screaming into the microphone, not really playing chords – just slamming their instruments and screaming." Alice grins. "I was like: I love this. This is it. This is what I want it to be."

As Alice explains, Girls Rock isn't like other music-based organisations; music isn't so much the end goal as a means to an end, a way to help participants gain confidence and experience. "That's what I loved. Seeing these kids expressing themselves however they wanted, without inhibition. I was in love with it from that point."

Alice sought out Girls Rock founder Jude Stewart and became part of the Girls Rock family as an enthusiastic volunteer. As they recall, "I think the biggest thing for me was meeting all the other volunteers. I'd never been in a room with so many women who were doing music and who were saying, 'Yeah, we're making it happen.' There was no gatekeeping; everyone was so supportive. It was really inspiring being in that environment."

"For the first year I didn't teach any music; I did more of the extracurriculars," Alice says. "Jude asked, 'Can you do a history of women in music?' So I researched it and learned so much myself. I'd studied Higher and Advanced Higher music, but nobody had ever sat me down and talked about the women. I knew all about the guys, but this whole world opened up for me."

We're both using the word "women" as shorthand: Girls Rock is proudly inclusive of marginalised genders and sexualities, and while there's an ongoing debate over the best language to use – the Californian branch of Girls Rock has changed its name to Amplify Sleep Away Camp to better reflect the diversity of its participants and counsellors – the Girls Rock summer school is emphatically open to straight, queer, cisgender, trans, and non-binary people. "If you feel like this is a space for you, then this is your space," Alice says.

That inclusivity is reflected in the Girls Rock curriculum. "We talk about LGBTQ+ people and trans people because they've been such a huge part of music and culture," Alice says. "It's shaped so much of the rock we teach about."

We talk about music as a safe space for people, a way for people to be themselves in a supportive environment, and

Alice tells me about some of the Girls Rock moments that made their heart three sizes bigger. "There was one kid at the beginning of the summer who was just sitting on the steps saying, 'I don't want to be here,' and their mum eventually persuaded them to stay. By the end of the week, this kid was up there on stage shredding guitar, having the best time. And we had one kid who was non-verbal, their mum stayed with them the whole time in the background because they couldn't be separated. But by the end they were up there screaming death metal vocals into the mic."

"I think having this safe space where there's no judgement, where it's accepting of everyone and it's all about supporting people, that's the main thing," Alice says. "When you see a kid being able to have the confidence or the space to be themselves without judgement, that's a big thing. I think it's really cool, and it's something I never experienced when I was younger. To say, 'This isn't anyone judging you. This is you expressing yourself and having fun, and everyone's here to support you.' I think that's what makes it really special."

One of the regular Girls Rock helpers is Jen O'Brien, who's been volunteering there since 2018. Jen also runs Music Broth, aka "Scotland's loudest library": a musical instrument lending library which provided more than sixty instruments for this year's participants. Jen is a member of the Scottish Parliament Cross-Party Group on Music, and she is the singer and main songwriter in Steeljoy, an all-female and non-binary band whose live shows feature eclectic line-ups of musicians from marginalised groups. "Queer people and allies have always been at the forefront of music and movements," O'Brien says. "We're here to stay and be loud."

We meet surrounded by guitars, synths and sample controllers in the upstairs of Music Broth's space in Glasgow's Southside, as heavy dub bass comes from below us. Tonight is the regular Trans Jam, where a loose collective of trans and non-binary people come together each week for the joy of making music. There are seven musicians this evening, with not just guitar and drums but also some more unusual instrument choices: melodica and saxophone. As Jen and I talk, the soundtrack they provide spans dub, spiky Joy Division-esque post-punk and jazz-flavoured pop, all played with evident enthusiasm and the kind of good humour you don't always get when multiple musicians share the same space and songs.

As O'Brien explains, Music Broth began "to fill a gap around affordability, accessibility and use of musical instruments and equipment." Marginalised people are often economically marginalised too, and that was something Music Broth aimed to address. "We recognised that it's not a level playing field in terms of everyone being able to access music-making due to the costs of instruments, equipment for bands starting out, and availability in different communities and family backgrounds."

The move into helping people play as well as providing instruments came naturally. "When people were taking instruments out, they were saying, 'Can you teach me how to play it?', and then when we got a space it was like, 'Can we come and jam?', so it grew from there."

Music Broth has been inclusive from the outset – "I've experienced it myself; the music industry is still a bit white, male and stale" – and its Shift The Power workshops and events are an attempt to address that by supporting female, non-binary and gender-expansive people. "I wanted people to have a safe space where they could express themselves," Jen says. "I think there's a different kind of music that happens when you don't have someone in the room judging you."

Jen is quick to praise other organisations and collectives such as Hen Hoose, Queenz Sounds, Slay Sessions and LGBT

Youth Scotland. She also praises Creative Scotland, the organisation that helps fund many arts projects in Scotland, although she believes there's still plenty of work to be done at a governmental level to address some of the structural issues that persist – for example, the difficulties arts organisations have finding affordable places to operate in towns of ever-rising rents while "there are buildings left empty and landlords holding on to them until they fall apart."

Jen would like to see politicians "valuing creativity as a human right as opposed to a luxury", pointing out that during the COVID lockdowns, it was art that kept so many of us going. "That's how we come together as a community," she says. Organisations such as Music Broth and their peers were created to fill a gap. "We've proven we're needed," she says. But without government support many of these organisations' existences are precarious.

Does Jen feel like Music Broth is winning? She laughs. "I have good days and bad days," she says. "When I see people coming together and they're happy and enjoying themselves and they're feeling creative, or when I see them playing on stage for the first time, or if I just see them get that spark where they're like, 'I can do this!', that's winning for me."

I'm reminded of the first time I got to see and hear Girls Rock Glasgow in action, at a showcase gig in Glasgow's School of Art. What struck me about the newly formed bands wasn't just their youth. It was their volume, and their rage, and their joy. In a very short time – just one week – GRG had given them permission to be bold, to be loud, to take up space. Of course, those are the very things marginalised people are often discouraged from doing. It was, as Jude Stewart once said, very much like the Bikini Kill song 'Rebel Girl'.

CHAPTER 15:
THE TIDE IS AT
THE TURNING

I t's a humid Friday in July and I have been crying for twelve days. I've been spending every day in hospital visiting my mum, who is dying. Tonight's tears are different, because my brother has swapped visiting times with me so I can have a couple of hours crying along to some of the most beautiful music I've ever heard.

The event is Ceòl is Craic: Sradagan na Sràide; in English, Street Sparks. It's a five-year project that brings artists and writers together to reflect the lives of urban Gaels: while a lot of Scots folk music is about wide-open spaces far from the cities, one-tenth of Scotland's 65,000 Gaelic speakers live in Glasgow. The city has the highest concentration of Gaelic speakers outwith the Western Isles and the Highlands. Street Sparks is all about creating music to reflect that.

I had long assumed that folk music was small-c conservative and probably pretty reactionary too, but I was very wrong: folk music is often outsider music and at its best, Scots folk is gleefully inclusive in both the influences it absorbs and the people who perform it.

Tonight's performers include Josie Duncan and Pedro Cameron, who are gay, and author and singer Maya Evan MacGregor, who is agender. The compere talks about their queer activism and Cameron plays his haunting and beautiful song 'Sgùrr Alasdair', which he explains to a hushed crowd is about the victims of the AIDS crisis.

All of tonight's music is new to me, and as I don't have any Gaelic the lyrics to most of the songs are a mystery, but, of course, music is a universal language and you don't need a lyric sheet to feel the emotion here. When MacGregor dedicates a particularly beautiful song to their friend, who has just passed away after a long illness, my composure cracks. The combination of MacGregor's singing and my frazzled emotional state means I don't so much cry as eject water like a New York fire hydrant in a heatwave.

Two weeks later, MacGregor and I talk about love, loss and mourning as we sit under a thundery sky in Glasgow's Victoria Park, watching the swans protecting their cygnets. MacGregor and I have more in common than just our queerness and our shared love of making music; they and I are neurodivergent, MacGregor with autism and me with ADHD. We talk about the sadness and joy of discovering who you really are relatively late in life and of mourning lives not lived, and about how music can be a safe space for queer and neurodivergent people.

As MacGregor explains, LGBTQ+ music was there all their life – first in the US, where they grew up, and later in Scotland, their chosen home. "I grew up with the Alaskan and Pacific Northwest lesbian community," they tell me, smiling. "So, like the Indigo Girls, k.d. Lang […] there's a lot of folk influences in a lot of their music, and that was a really powerful thing. And then there was Gaelic folk and Gaelic music. As I was getting to know the community there were lots of queer people who were out and performing, and that really helped me to see myself."

Although MacGregor has had a lifelong love of singing, they didn't perform live for most of their twenties – "I'd only sing in the shower or in the car, or occasionally in places where I didn't know anyone and I'd do karaoke." MacGregor worked as a bartender, and sometimes after closing time when there was nobody else around, they'd sing to the empty bar.

The combination of a move to Glasgow and making sense of their gender would change MacGregor's stage shyness, albeit slowly: in Glasgow, they joined a folk choir.

Although MacGregor by then understood themself to be agender, they didn't talk about it to the other choir members and they continued to use their given first name. "I found so much of myself within the Gaelic community and within the choir, a level of acceptance that I was absolutely terrified of losing," they explain.

MacGregor had good reasons to fear the worst; at their school in Montana in the 1990s queer people were targeted, "and the teachers didn't do anything about it. I was really heavily ostracised and dealt with a lot of really vitriolic homophobia as a kid., It's really hard to go from that to expecting safety when you have been conditioned to know that you're not safe."

After quietly coming out to a few of the younger members, it became very clear that the choir was a safe space. "They've been really phenomenal," MacGregor says. They're not the only queer chorister, and the choir has renamed its sections to soprano and tenor rather than men and women.

"Something I started to see was that not only were queer people present, but some of them were leading it," continues MacGregor, on discovering the Gaelic and traditional folk community. "I felt like I had a place to belong there, a place where I could be safe."

One of the people making musicians like MacGregor feel more safe was the aforementioned Pedro Cameron, whose musical CV includes bluegrass band The Dirty Beggars, electro-trad duo Valtos and his own project Man of the Minch, in which he mixes anthemic electro-pop with more traditional Scots music. We arrange to meet for a drink and a chat on a chilly February evening in Glasgow's West End, not far from SWG3, where a fortnight previously Pedro joined Valtos on stage for a triumphant Celtic Connections show.

Like MacGregor, Cameron's home was largely filled with country music and some folk: "John Martyn and Steve Earle and Johnny Cash and bands like that," although his parents also listened to a lot of experimental seventies and eighties bands, such as Pink Floyd and Genesis.

Cameron played fiddle from the age of seven, and even then he was mixing up genres. "My dad used to play Rolling Stones or Johnny Cash songs on guitar in the kitchen, and I would make up parts to go along with them."

Although his first live concert was Capercaillie, the teenage Cameron was obsessed with the Spice Girls ("I had a shrine to them on my wall"), before moving on to Alanis Morissette, Avril Lavigne and Michelle Branch. After that he fell in love with emo metal before he was given three country and bluegrass records for Christmas: Alison Krauss & Union Station's *So Long So Wrong*, Gillian Welch's *Time (The Revelator)* and Nickel Creek's greatest hits album. "I was like, 'Whoa... this is what – this is what I really love'," Cameron recalls. "Sad songs, harmonies and acoustic instrumentation."

At the same time, though, Cameron was also loving, "trance pop songs – 'Toca's Miracle', ATB, Chicane and Sarah McLachlan's 'Silence'. I just love good songs, good melodies and when melodies make you feel something. It doesn't have to be too highbrow; I love pop music, I love country music, I love dance music, I love pop-country."

"I think it's interesting that none of these musicians were queer," Cameron tells me. "I wasn't really identifying with queer music, or at least picking up on it. I didn't hear 'Smalltown Boy' until I was in my twenties. I can't think of a single queer musician that I felt I had some sort of affinity with or identified with."

Cameron came out when he was nineteen. "I think I was in quite a lot of denial about my queerness until quite late on," he says. "It wasn't until my late twenties that I was like, 'Wait a minute, my music and my queerness aren't sitting together.'" It wasn't until Cameron first saw Brothers Osborne "who are very pop, very country – very masculine, macho country" that things started to fall into place. "Their singer came out as gay a few years ago and he's got this big baritone voice and he's a masculine man. I think that was the first time that I was really like, 'Oh my god.' I wish I'd known about him when I was growing up. I just loved that this was some guy who just turned out to be gay."

Cameron's experience with representation chimes with mine: we both took a while to work out who we were because we didn't see much representation of queer people who were just like us. Cameron felt that lack of representation, that isolation, more keenly when he began to perform live. Talking about touring the US with The Dirty Beggars, he says, "I never really felt safe, I never really felt that I could totally be myself in crowds." When Cameron began performing solo as Man of the Minch, he wanted to find his musical tribe. "I hadn't been around [LGBTQ+] people that love folk music like me, or that love country music like me, so I felt that I needed to create that space," he says.

That space was Bogha-Frois, which is Gaelic for rainbow.

155

"The dancer Nic Gareiss once said to me that someone told him there were no gay people in Scottish folk music," Pedro says with a smile. "They couldn't have been more wrong. They're some of the best musicians on the scene."

Bogha-Frois began as a conversation between Cameron and fiddle player Laura Wilkie, and that conversation became a folk music workshop for LGBTQ+ musicians at the Scottish Storytelling Centre. Led by Cameron, Wilkie, Rachel Sermanni, Josie Duncan, Grant McFarlane and Marit Falt, the workshop would lead to more events including an extraordinary evening performing at the 2019 Celtic Connections festival. "I was just trying to make music and hang out with people," Cameron says. "It ended up being this massive night with about forty musicians playing. In all my years of playing traditional music I've never felt so much love and so much community on stage, both from other musicians and from the audience."

Afterwards, Cameron received messages from other musicians who told him that they were no longer afraid to be themselves, or afraid to come out to their musical and queer communities. That's something Cameron could relate to; before Bogha-Frois, Cameron had "always felt like an island" as a gay folk musician.

Bogha-Frois "was a safe space for LGBTQ+ musicians from all over Scotland to meet each other and make music together," Pedro explains. And while the gigs were great fun, "just being in the same room as all these wonderful musicians was amazing for me… I think it's beautiful that this rainbow helped me and many other musicians find their place."

After nearly five years of Bogha-Frois, Cameron decided to take a break and scale back his musical adventures for a while. But he's enormously proud of what he and his fellow musicians achieved. "It was a beautiful thing, and I've made lifelong friendships from it," he says. "It's been so inspiring and so amazing. I've done more in the last five years than many musicians could dream of."

"Sometimes I get concerned because I look around at the news cycle and things can seem really bleak," MacGregor tells me. "I know Gaels who have experienced queerphobia in a very real way and I don't want to minimise that at all." As if to underline that, a few days after I spoke to MacGregor, a high-profile female folk artist deleted her social media post about her attraction to another woman after getting "the fear", which a brief look at the mouth-breathing replies to some of her other posts suggests was entirely justified.

But there are many reasons to be optimistic. "You can't really look around Gaeldom and not see Kim Carnie and Pedro Cameron and Marcus McIntyre and all the prominent queer girls who are out there just loving life," MacGregor says.

They tell me about a folk artists' Pride party in Partick they recently attended where "there were twenty or thirty of us there, everyone from uni age to our thirties, and I definitely felt like a geriatric millennial there. As small a community as Gaelic music is, there are heaps of us and we are engaged, and we are visible, and we're all on social media and I really love that." MacGregor smiles. "Things are changing."

I think that change is as much a societal one as a musical one. Folk music reflects the societies it comes from – and Scotland, especially young Scotland, is increasingly open and diverse. As Cameron told me, "Folk music is progressing enormously, and it's a different place for queer people now. I think the world has something to do with that, and the time we live in has something to do with that."

CHAPTER 16:
CHOSEN FAMILY

Not every queer musician has the global impact of a Shirley Manson or a SOPHIE, but they can still change their own part of the world. While Lexi Campbell's name might not be known more widely, "there is a piece of them in every melody, a bit of them in every bassline, a fragment in every phrase coming out of Dundee's music scene."

That's Dundee singer/songwriter Jack Jones, speaking to me about LexFest, a celebration of Lexi's life and love of music. In 2024, it returned for its second year to keep Lexi's name and memory alive and to raise money for good causes, following their passing in 2022. My own band was honoured to be among the artists asked to perform.

A talented, creative and genre-hopping musician, Lexi's love of music started young. "Our Filipino heritage meant that music was always a part of our family gatherings," Lexi's sister Shona told me. What began with karaoke machines and "our botched attempts singing Tagalog into the microphone" became Lexi on guitar and Shona singing, and as the pair grew up their soundtrack encompassed everything from Nirvana to Northern Soul.

Lexi was a musical butterfly and a social one too. In

Dundee, "if you stuck around long enough, it wasn't hard to get to know everyone," Shona says. "Lexi made an effort with everyone they ever met. They loved to host and they knew how to work a room." A naturally generous and gregarious music fan, Lexi was the person "who would encourage you to just try, to play the open mic, start the band, write the song." Lexi played in multiple bands simultaneously including the rocky Kashmir Crows and the joyful Corde Du Roi; they helped turn the ailing open mic night at The George Orwell bar on Perth Road into a packed weekly event for musicians and fans; and they became a linchpin of the Dundee scene.

"The music scene then was mostly cover bands in bars and open mic nights," Jones tells me. "I'd stopped playing music altogether when I came to Dundee, worn down from playing bars and disenchanted with the scene. It was Lex that got me playing again."

"There are many people with that story. Folk that hadn't performed in years, or who had never performed in front of people at all, did it because Lex convinced them that they ought to. Part of it was their genuine desire for others to flourish, and part of it was the environment they created that emboldened people to come forward and give it a go."

"They loved music, red wine and buying books they didn't need," Shona says. Most of all "they loved people, which I think is what made people love Lexi."

"I think Lex would be over the moon to see that many of the people they first encouraged to play are in decent-sized bands playing on the regular now," Jack says. He misses the mixing of genres and musicians that Lexi was at the heart of. As the scene has grown, "genres rarely mix and, at times, regular performers intentionally or unintentionally act as gatekeepers, as opposed to helping new talent as Lexi did. I think Dundee's music scene really misses Lex's unique ability to transcend petty divisions with their unconditional love for people and music."

Lexi's story shows both how far queer people have come in Scotland and how far we still have to go. A mixed-race, gender-queer person whose colours became so much more vivid after they came out, Lexi was clearly adored by the musicians they helped and was something of a local celebrity: whenever I've spoken to people about them, I'm struck by the similarities to the way people talk about the charisma and energy of Billy Mackenzie. Lexi isn't here for me to experience that energy or to make any more music, because Lexi took their own life, aged just twenty-five. The good causes we're raising money for in their name – over £12,000 to date – are suicide prevention charities.

Writer Amie Flett became close to Lexi's family in the wake of Lexi's death and, in a column published by *The Courier*, wrote about the mental health issues Lexi struggled with. "Being queer doesn't cause these problems," Flett wrote. "But issues such as discrimination, homophobia or trans-phobia, social isolation, rejection, and difficult experiences of coming out can all take their toll [...] What I learned from my discussions with those closest to Lexi is that sometimes it isn't enough for your family, friends and even city to accept you as who you are."[176]

"This was someone who was kind, brave and immensely talented," Flett continued. "Someone who was so much more than just their pronouns."

I think that had Lexi lived longer, they would have become the heart of a collective like Hen Hoose, POWA or Popgirlz Scotland, groups whose goal is to make Scots music less of a boys' club and to encourage and support musicians on and off stage. The music made by collective members is as diverse as their memberships.

One such collective is OVER/AT, a trans, non-binary and gender-diverse music-making group that encompasses live performance, workshops and recordings featuring an ever-changing cast of collaborators. OVER/AT's first EP, *Folks' Songs*, was shortlisted for a Scottish Award for New Music.

OVER/AT was founded by composer and musician Rufus Isabel Elliot, formerly of Tower Hamlets and now living in Skye. Rufus has worked with a variety of arts organisations including The Night With festival, Red Note Ensemble, Magnetic North, ATLAS Arts, Drake Music and the Nevis Ensemble. Elliot's work, described as "stunningly intimate" by *The Quietus*,[177] has been performed by a range of organisations including the BBC SSO.

As Elliot told the American Composers Forum, "I was writing a lot of music that was engaged with my experiences – my body, gender, voice, whatever – and was aware that there were a lot of other trans artists who were speaking to similar areas. I wanted to have a gig where we could all speak together and have it be a conversation rather than each speaking alone in our rooms. We can do a lot more if we're speaking together – not necessarily raising our voices in unison, but being part of a conversation."[178] Elliot is at pains to stress that it doesn't want to be having the *only* conversation, but one of many: "The idea of 'first trans role on the Met Opera stage' or 'first trans' anything is just another way of not engaging. It's tokenising."[179]

As we've explored, there's a big difference between representation and tokenism. Cartoonist Alison Bechdel made the difference hilariously clear with her eponymous test, originally coined as "a little lesbian joke" for her webcomic *Dykes to Watch Out For*.[180] The Bechdel Test is a simple way of identifying tokenism regarding women in fiction: to get over its *very* low bar, the story must have at least two women in it, those women must have a conversation with each other, and that conversation must be about something other than a man. It's amazing how many stories fail the test – and if you swap women for people of colour, queer people, trans people or any other marginalised people you'll get similar results. It's a pretty effective tokenism detector. True representation is about reflecting diversity, not checking a diversity tickbox.

Some of the loudest, most joyful queer voices you'll hear in unison are in queer choirs. Choirs have long been part of LGBTQ+ activism and joy: the Pink Singers, the UK's biggest and longest-running gay choir, was founded in 1983 and performs a mix that includes Mozart and Massive Attack. It would be 2005 before the first LGBTQ+ choir was founded in Scotland. Loud and Proud began in Edinburgh in 2005 as part of LGBT Health & Wellbeing's community activities with just three singers, but the choir has since grown to over sixty regulars.

Edinburgh's Gay Men's Chorus was founded two years later. It too came from small beginnings and now has over fifty regulars performing barbershop choruses, traditional Scots music and, of course, pop. Their cover of Girls Aloud's 'Sound of the Underground' is spectacular.

In addition to the joyful performances by queer choirs, you'll also find other Scots musicians celebrating and promoting work by queer artists and composers. For example, in summer 2024, Edinburgh's Calton Consort, one of Scotland's most prominent chamber choirs, celebrated Pride Month by performing work by LGBTQ+ composers from around the world including Derri Joseph Lewis, Judith Weir, Kerry Andrew, Jake Runestad and Mari Esabel Valverde.

I love choirs: one of my very favourite memories is being entranced as a teen on holiday by the Spanish-language choir

I stumbled across one Christmas Eve after a little too much of the Christmas spirit. So I didn't need to be asked twice to go and listen to a Scots queer choir perform to a packed venue. Outside, it's autumn, the wind bitter enough to turn your cheeks scarlet in seconds, but I'm inside, warm and cosy, listening to a gorgeous choral version of Rina Sawayama's 'Chosen Family'. It's a song I'd only previous heard as an Elton John duet, with Elton hamming it up as only Elton can, but here it's much more delicate, introduced by a chorister who says that if it weren't for their chosen family, they wouldn't still be here to sing. Many of the chorus and the crowd clearly feel similar.

The twenty people on stage are all members of Glasgow's LGBTQ+ choir, which was created not just to sing but to provide a safe space for community members to meet and make friends. It's been doing that since 2017 when a Facebook post hoping to bring fifteen people to the compact and bijou Category Is Books in Glasgow's Southside brought sixty to the hastily rearranged venue of Queens Park Govanhill Parish Church, where the choir – now known as Queer Voices Glasgow, or QVG for short – has rehearsed ever since.

Queer Voices Glasgow's performances are fascinating, joyful and genre-hopping, where songs you might expect – Pet Shop Boys' 'Liberation', Lady Gaga's 'Born This Way' – rub shoulders with songs you might not, such as suffragette song 'Bread and Roses', Persian feminist protest anthem 'Woman's Anthem' (aka 'Song of Equality'), and Aerosmith's 'Eat the Rich'.

What unites these disparate songs, other than the choir's obvious delight in singing them, is a mix of pride and inter-sectionality: pride in the varied identities and abilities of the people on stage, and an understanding that while we may not all share the same struggles, we have many of the same enemies.

I was first introduced to QVG by Graham Muir, whose song 'eLiGiBiliTy' – a lyrical riff on the acronym LGBT and the choir's unofficial anthem – he performs today with a twelve-string guitar and the swelling vocals of his fellow choristers. Muir is also the singer in the spiky post-punk trio This Questionable Life, and after the show I ask him what drew him to this rather different kind of music.

"As someone who only came out publicly in my mid-fifties, I'd never really built up any LGBTQ+ networks in my life, so I began to visit queer-friendly bars and attend Pride events," he told me. "At the 2019 Pride march I met people from Bi+ Glasgow and started going to their get-togethers; a couple of their members mentioned that they were also QVG members and it felt natural that [joining] would be the next step for me."

Like most LGBTQ+ choirs, QVG is as much about creating a place for queer people to be themselves as it is about the music – which is one reason Muir does the fifty-mile round trip to each rehearsal. "QVG has become an important part of who I am now," Muir says, crediting it for helping him emotionally, socially and musically and for providing an online lifeline during the COVID lockdowns. "It's so rewarding just to see the smiles on the audience's faces knowing that they fully understand why we're standing in front of them doing what we do."

There's a reason why choirs have been around since at least the second century (singing goes back much further, but sadly the historical records don't): there's something uniquely human and beautiful about singing together, and while we tend to associate choirs with religion, their history is much older and much more fun than my memories of miming interminable Protestant dirges at Sunday school – hymns whose performances were beautifully skewered by Suzy "Eddie" Izzard as sung by "the only people who could sing 'Hallelujah' without making it sound like a hallelujah [...] God must be up there going, 'Jesus Christ! What on Earth is that?'"[181]

In English, choirs used to be queer – literally. In Middle English, the word was spelt in a variety of versions including *queor, queere* and *queyr*, usually denoting the part of a church where the singers would sing; for example, in the 1549 *Booke of Common Prayer* the text describes how, "The priest beeyng in the quier shall begynne with a loude voyce the Lordes prayer."[182] The spelling was changed somewhere in the 1700s to the version we know today, although the pronunciation was retained.

The word is even older, however, with roots in Latin and in Ancient Greek: in that latter language *choros, khoros* or *horos* meant "dance". Some of the earliest choirs mixed singing and dancing to celebrate special occasions or just communicate the sheer joy of being alive.

For many queer people, that joy can be bittersweet and particularly precious. One of the most famous photographs from the AIDS crisis, taken in 1993, is of a queer choir – The San Francisco Gay Men's Chorus, which was founded in 1978 and was the world's first openly gay chorus. The photo is in colour, but the men appear in monochrome: the men dressed in black, facing away from the camera, represent the choristers lost to AIDS; the men dressed in white are the survivors.

There are 122 men in the photo, but only seven of the singers are wearing white.[183]

There's a sadness to queer choirs and to queer music more widely, I think. That doesn't necessarily mean that the music itself is sad. In fact, it's often the very opposite of that: life-affirming, joyous, euphoric, but I think music made by marginalised people carries a weight, an urgency, a hard-won wisdom that informs the music and gives it depth and emotional heft. It's music made by people who know all too well how necessary and how fleeting its joy and escapism can be.

In 2023, the music charity Help Musicians and the Musicians' Union carried out a Musician's Census in which they surveyed 5,867 professional UK musicians to ask about their mental health. In total, nearly one-third of the musicians they surveyed said they were experiencing poor mental wellbeing, and the figures were considerably worse for queer musicians.[184]

The study found that 28 percent of straight male musicians reported low mental wellbeing. For gay male musicians, the figure was 33 percent, and it was higher still for lesbian musicians: 37 percent. The figures rose further – 47 percent of bisexual musicians, 49 percent of disabled musicians and 50 percent of asexual musicians – and the highest proportion reporting negative mental wellbeing were those who identify as a gender other than male or female. Among those musicians, the percentage who reported negative mental wellbeing was a whopping 63 percent, more than twice the percentage for people whose gender identity matched the one they were assigned at birth.

There are multiple factors here, but they all come under the same banner: marginalisation. People from marginalised groups may experience what's known as minority stress: life can be difficult for all of us, of course, but it can be even more so for people who are marginalised because of who they are or who they love. Marginalised people are often paid less, offered more precarious work, denied opportunities, expected to be carers for other family members – and may encounter discrimination or worse at school, at work, at home, in healthcare, and in public. Many people are members of multiple marginalised groups, with the difficulties they face intersecting and amplifying each other.

As Help Musicians points out in its report, some of the key factors affecting musicians' mental wellbeing include low wages and poor financial security; difficulties in finding work; physical health problems; and discrimination, and those are just inside the industry. Queer people face many other obstacles in the rest of their lives.

Again and again in this book I've spoken to musicians who found music as a safe space, as an escape, and clearly, many LGBTQ+ musicians have plenty to escape from – and plenty of reasons to try and make a better world through their art. I think collectives, grassroots groups and choirs are a way of bringing people together in an attempt to create that world, even if it's only in this space, in this moment, in this song.

In the introduction to his influential book *Cruising Utopia: The Then and There of Queer Futurity*, José Esteban Muñoz argued that queerness *itself* is about making a better world. He wrote, "The here and now is a prison house […] we must dream and enact new and better pleasures, other ways of being in the world, and ultimately new worlds […] Queerness is essentially about the rejection of a here and now and an insistence on potentiality for another world."[185]

Or to paraphrase David McAlmont: our instinct for survival is to celebrate.

CHAPTER 17:
CRIMINAL RECORDS

When Edinburgh's Young Fathers spoke to journalist Kate Mossman after the release of their 2015 album *White Men are Black Men Too*, Graham Hastings talked about being a teenage Scots hip-hop fan in the era of Eminem, Big Boi and D12. "We weren't into the other side of hip-hop – everyone being angry and calling each other 'faggots' the whole time," he said. Hastings, who met his bandmates Alloysious Massaquoi and Kayus Bankole at a hip-hop night in the now-bulldozed Bongo Club next to Waverley Station, recalled, "We hated the aggression. Because we knew the guys who were doing it and it was all fake, it was all emulated. Most of them were middle-class boys. Hip-hop was seen as rebellion."[186]

There are plenty of working-class kids in Scottish hip-hop too, of course, but irrespective of whether the kids come from the schemes or the suburbs, that particular F-bomb has been part of mainstream hip-hop's punctuation for a very long time, so it's perhaps unsurprising that in Scots hip-hop there appear to be very few openly gay rappers of any gender. When I reached out to one particularly well-connected artist and producer, they couldn't think of a single gay male rapper.

"There's lots of bi folk cutting about," they offered. "Not that they advertise it." I've asked the same of other hip-hop heads and had similar responses.

Yet hip-hop has queer roots. It grew from the inclusive New York club scenes of the 1970s such as The Gallery, where gay DJ Nicky Siano pioneered beat-matching and EQ-ing and where Black and LGBTQ+ and Black LGBTQ+ people found community;[187] the electro sounds of the 1980s came from a scene defined by gay artists such as Man Parrish, latterly of 'Male Stripper' fame;[188] and rappers who rhyme about their experiences of life in marginalised communities are part of a lineage that you can trace back to Bessie Smith, the Nicki Minaj of the 1920s, a queer woman who attracted plenty of condemnation for her rejection of gender stereotypes and for her assertive sexuality.[189]

Unfortunately, homophobia has been present in hip-hop's culture from the very beginning. The disco-inspired 'Rapper's Delight' included a homophobic slur (levelled against Superman, of all people) and while that other iconic rap classic, Grandmaster Flash and The Furious Five's 1982's 'The Message', was performed in outfits that could have been borrowed from the Village People, it nevertheless included a few homophobic lines. Dr Dre, DMX and Public Enemy's Professor Griff are among many notoriously homophobic hip-hop artists;[190] when a very uncomfortable Busta Rhymes was asked on camera in 2007 if he believed that hip-hop would ever accept a gay rapper, he walked out of the interview.[191]

Even that most right-on of rappers, Beastie Boys' Ad-Rock (Adam Horovitz), would end up apologising to the LGBTQ+ community for the homophobic language in the Beasties' early work – language that clearly didn't really reflect their views, as the band would later pay for their former label boss Donna Lee Parsons' gender confirmation surgery. The Beasties knew

Donna wouldn't accept such a large gift, so they pretended the money was newly discovered royalties from their 1982 debut recording *Polly Wog Stew*, which Parsons financed and contributed backing vocals to.[192]

Homophobia wasn't specific to hip-hop – rock musicians were pretty dreadful too, with Guns N' Roses' gormless slur-filled 'One in a Million' on their *Lies* EP in 1988 a particularly low point, and dancehall DJs like Buju Banton or Beenie Man made some of hip-hop's homophobes sound positively playground, but there was a crucial difference. That music wasn't being played *in* playgrounds. Hip-hop was, with Eminem's cartoonish Slim Shady fulfilling the same role in pre-millennial schools as the equally entertaining Madness had played in mine.

If you were a young Scots rap fan in the late 1990s or early aughts, the biggest rapper in the world was vocally homophobic. My publisher's budget doesn't stretch to getting permission to reprint Eminem's lyrics, and that's probably for the best: it means you don't need to read the deliberately inflammatory lines from his 2000 single 'Criminal' that concludes with positive confirmation of "hating fags".

A persona? An act? Ironic? Maybe. Eminem did perform his hit 'Stan' with Elton John at the 2001 Grammys a few months later, so he can certainly claim that some of his best friends are gay; he's spoken up for equal marriage, and his youngest child Stevie is non-binary (add your own "Emintheythem" joke here). It's also debatable whether school kids spitting slurs from 'Criminal' in 2000 or from 'Rap God', released seventeen years later, even know what they're copying. Last year I discovered that my youngest, then aged ten, could rap two hip-hop tracks word-perfect: the Eminem parody 'Charles II: The King of Bling' from the kids' TV show *Horrible Histories,* and Eminem's 'Rap God'. They knew that the words in 'Rap

God' were naughty, and that was most of the appeal: they repeated Eminem's slurs with the same glee they have when they repeat my occasional in-car expletives.

That said, I doubt teenage rap fans are so innocent, or that they're necessarily aware of or continuing any satirical intent, and I'm not convinced that the LGBTQ+ people who hear the rhymes, or hear others repeating the same words, should be expected to give the people who use those words the benefit of the doubt. As with other slurs, there's a huge difference between members of a community reclaiming a word, as some of the Black rap community has done with the N-word, and people from outside that community using it against others for shock value or laughs. What may seem amusing or edgy to straight kids can feel like a message to others: this music is not for you.

As we headed towards the millennium, hip-hop was the genre that took rock's place as the dominant musical movement, and it really felt that queer people weren't welcome in that movement.

There are lots of reasons for that. The US hip-hop artists whose music crossed the Atlantic were often from poor, God-fearing communities where queerness was considered sinful. Marginalised communities often create hierarchies that marginalise their own, and young men in particular are often cruel and assert themselves by picking on people they consider weaker, and America at the time was far from being a queer utopia, or even queer-friendly. The homophobic Defense of Marriage Act, which defined marriage as solely between a man and a woman, was signed into law in 1996 – not by the reliably villainous Republicans, but by Bill Clinton. Despite the law being ruled unconstitutional twenty years previously, Texas's legislation criminalising gay sex was on the statute books until 2023, and was only repealed after the sponsors of the bill to remove it agreed to make a concession: their bill was amended to say that "homosexuality is not a lifestyle acceptable to the general public".[193]

All of these aspects played their part, but the main reason for the lack of openly queer artists in hip-hop was simpler. If you were gay, no hip-hop label would sign you. Coming out, or being outed, would mean the swift end of any aspiring rapper's career.

Of course, there were queer rappers, but they kept their private lives private. For example, Queen Latifah didn't come out until 2012, by which point she was long established as rap royalty. In the 2009 memoir by former industry insider Terrance Dean, *Hiding in Hip Hop: On the Down Low in the Entertainment Industry*, multiple closeted big names from the hip-hop community on both coasts of the US are strongly hinted at even if they're never quite named, presumably on legal advice. If they were indeed in the closet, they're still there today.

Homophobia hasn't gone away, but queer visibility in hip-hop improved considerably through the 2010s and beyond, with stars such as Jay-Z and Kanye West calling out homophobia in their community. Frank Ocean's coming out was particularly lovely: in a 2012 letter to fans, which is still on his Tumblr, he wrote beautifully about his first love, one that clearly inspired his groundbreaking album *Channel Orange*.[194]

Shortly after the letter was posted and widely reported, the huge US retail chain Target decided not to stock Ocean's highly anticipated album. It firmly denied allegations that the decision was due to Ocean's letter,[195] claiming the reason it had decided not to stock the record was due to multiple non-homophobic factors – particularly the decision by Ocean's management to release the album one week early to

Apple's iTunes Store to try and prevent piracy, which at the time often came from people obtaining CDs in advance of the on-sale date and uploading them to file-sharing services. Kanye West and Jay-Z's *Watch the Throne* album had done the same just a few months before for the same reasons and that record had suffered no such sanction. If you were a closeted queer rapper or their management, you might have taken Target's move as a warning.

Hip-hop is a lot more inclusive now, and some of the biggest acts in the world today are proudly, fabulously and sometimes provocatively queer: Cardi B; Lil Nas X; Tyler, The Creator; Azealia Banks; Janelle Monáe; Megan Thee Stallion. It's taken a long time to get there, and there's still a long way to go.

As a middle-aged, middle-class, suburban rock fan and part-time Swiftie, hip-hop isn't exactly my area of expertise, so I reached out to Arusa Qureshi, writer of the excellent guide to innovative women in hip-hop, *Flip the Script*.

Arusa is a woman of many hats: a former editor of *The List* and current editor of *Fest*, a music journalist for *The Guardian*, *NME*, *Clash* and *Time Out*, co-curator of the AMPLIFI series of shows in Edinburgh, and chair of the Scottish Album of the Year Award judging panel.

"I'm pretty proud of what Scotland is doing, hip-hop wise," Arusa tells me. "There are lots of people who are experimenting and collaborating across genres, which people are really embracing." While Arusa says there's a strong hip-hop scene here, it's not getting the attention it deserves: like most music media, hip-hop media is very much focused on London at the expense of Scotland, Wales and Northern Ireland.

As Arusa explains, Scots hip-hop suffered from an image problem in its early days, the country's rappers being seen as pale imitations of their American influences. "When people first started rapping in the UK, they would put on American accents because they thought that's what you had to do to get noticed by the media and industry," she says.

They were right. When Dundonian rappers Gavin Bain and Billy Boyd tried to get record company interest in the early 2000s as rappers who didn't disguise their accents, they were dismissed as "rapping Proclaimers", so Bain and Boyd came up with a plan. They wouldn't just adopt American accents, they would adopt American identities too. The duo became Silibil N' Brains, who claimed to be Californian rather than Caledonian. Sony Music UK gave them a record deal, they appeared on MTV and they supported D12 on tour, all without anyone apparently suspecting they weren't who they claimed to be. The whole story is detailed in Jeanie Finlay's 2013 documentary, *The Great Hip-Hop Hoax*, which at the time of writing is available on BBC's iPlayer as well as on various streaming services.

In the 1990s and early 2000s, Scots music started to sound different. Artists such as Arab Strap, King Creosote, Frightened Rabbit, and Admiral Fallow didn't take on the transatlantic accents of previous generations, preferring to sing in their own voices, and the same changes were happening in Scots hip-hop. "Gradually, in the 1990s, people started using their own accents," Arusa says. "The scene was starting to have its own identity." That identity, as with the use of more authentic accents in music, was a rejection of the previously-mentioned Scottish Cringe. From our language to our art, the largely London-based media has long treated Scots culture as an afterthought at best, a curiosity unworthy of serious attention or support: in tone, it sometimes recalls the description of a dancing dog in Ken Liu's *The Hidden Girl and Other Stories*: "It's not so much how well the dog dances, she thought, but that a dog is dancing at all."[196]

As the rapper Steg G, a legendary figure in Scottish hip-hop (who we'll meet more fully in the next chapter), told me, "We wouldn't see ourselves as artists, we wouldn't see ourselves as entertainers. We'd see ourselves as comedians, maybe, the butt of a joke, but never an academic, never an intellectual […] we'd never seen ourselves in popular music."

The Proclaimers may have been a joke to the London record industry, but as Steg recalls, their 1987 single 'Letter from America' was revolutionary here. 'Letter from America' is an old song now and it has long since become part of the cosy cultural canon, a mainstay of the kind of nostalgic compilations with thistles, saltires or both on their cover and a promise of the best Scottish songs… ever![197] But, "When they came out, they were culturally shocking," Steg says. "Looking back on it now, you can see how they opened the door for everyone to challenge that cultural cringe, because young people who were getting into music at that time realised they could sing and rap in their own accents, be proud of their own identity, have careers in music and be accepted."

"I do see it getting better," Steg says. "We're getting more confident in our abilities. We see ourselves reflected now in media with our voices, our accents, our identities, whether that's Black Scottish or white Scottish or Polish Scottish or LGBTQ+ Scottish. Because we can all be media, because everyone can have a radio station, everyone can be a broadcaster."

"The tapestry of media is wide now," he continues. "If you're a local kid in Govan you can set up your own YouTube and be who you want to be and express yourself. And that's exciting. I think it really helps to make us more rounded as well, because before we only had a pigeonhole to see what we thought was acceptable, what we thought was the norm, and now we see society isn't like that."

Like Steg, Arusa is optimistic: she talks about the rise of grime and garage, and of the mainstream success of artists such as the Northern Irish rappers Kneecap and describes her hope that regionalism will increasingly be seen as a strength by the media and industry, but there's still a long way to go. "I don't think there is anyone locally who has really made it past the border to get the kind of attention they deserve, unfortunately. Rappers like Bemz, and Chef in Aberdeen, are doing great, but a lot of rappers have moved down to London because they felt they had to in order to break out of this bubble of being Scottish and people not taking them seriously."

Arusa is passionate about diversity in music; we first met as podcasters with Scottish Women In Music, an organisation dedicated to improving representation for women and non-binary people. I tell Arusa that from my outsider's perspective, there don't seem to be many openly LGBTQ+ artists in Scots hip-hop. "I think there are definitely queer scenes in hip-hop now as a result of things like social media and people finding their communities," Arusa says. "But in Scotland I can only think of one rapper who is openly out. That's not to say there aren't more, but there's only one person I know of." Arusa suggests that the more visible and traditional hip-hop scene is still quite masculine, while the club scenes are much queerer: those are the scenes that produced artists such as SOPHIE and TAAHLIAH.

One of the clubs Arusa highlights is Glasgow's Peach. Peach was co-founded by DJ Kacie McAdam, who performs as K4CIE, to create a club night focusing on hip-hop and R&B which put women at the forefront. As she told PRS For Music, "There wasn't anything current and most importantly, it was only ever men in attendance and zero women on the lineups."

Peach set out to create something better and more inclusive. "As a gay woman it was vital to create a space for all of us," she said. "What other rap-focused club night would you see that has gay, trans, straight and all ethnicities in the one room, vibing together? Peach is special and vital for the Scottish scene. It is an outlet for all of us."[198]

Aberdeen's We Are Here Scotland has been another crucial platform for queer musicians. The organisation was created to support and amplify the voices of Black and People of Colour creatives across Scotland, works closely with events such as Edinburgh's AMPLIFI and collaborates with artists such as Glasgow's Eyve, whose music reflects her experiences as a queer Black woman and mixes ballroom culture with her own Zimbabwean heritage.

Eyve credits Glasgow's queer ballroom scene as the place where she found family in Scotland, telling *The Skinny*, "It wasn't until coming to Glasgow – now ten years later since leaving Zimbabwe – that I felt free enough to include my culture in my music."[199] And she's keen to offer the support she found in Scotland to others: her 2024 EP, *Sista! Beyond the Sky Isn't the Limit* was a collaboration with the Cross Borders team at the Scottish Refugee Council, with Eyve setting out to include queer women of colour in the project through House Ball Scotland and the queer, trans and intersex Black, Indigenous and People of Colour (QTIBIPOC) collective I.DIY.

One of the initiatives that aims to shine a spotlight on these grassroots scenes and artists is the Scottish Album of the Year Award, or SAY Award for short. Funded by the Scottish Music Industry Association, the SAY Award and their classical and young musician spin-offs aim to champion "the strength and diversity of Scotland's recorded output [and] inspire the listening, learning and creation of music, especially by young people."

It's easy to be cynical about industry awards, which often seem focused only on sales figures and continually rewarding the most well-kent faces. But the SAY Award, as well as the similarly eclectic Scottish Alternative Music Awards, consistently highlight lesser-known artists including many queer artists.

Arusa has inside knowledge here: she's been a SAY judge previously and is now the annual chair of the award judging panel. As she explains, the representation of queer artists and other marginalised artists isn't tokenistic but organic. "Each album is really talked about and everyone really takes time," she says, "even if it's not a genre or artist they would typically listen to. I think that's a credit to the Scottish Music Industry Association for choosing the judges they do; they're from a wide range of places. I feel like it shows how much great stuff is going on in Scotland."

The goal of the SAY Award is to raise awareness of great Scots music across all genres – its longlists have featured not just rock, pop and hip-hop, but folk, classical, reggae, electronica, and more – but frustratingly, Scottish music awards get virtually no coverage outwith Scotland. That's an issue Arusa says also applies to Scots music more generally. "[Publications] used to come up, but it feels like they don't anymore. It's all about money and people not having budgets, but then you see the national papers sending writers up from London to review Taylor Swift here."

Awards like the SAY and SAMAs, which shortlisted Eyve in their 2024 hip-hop category, do their very best to sing the praises of Scots music in all its diversity, but that's only effective if media's willing to listen to and amplify what they're singing.

CHAPTER 18:
SUNNY DELIGHT

I want to know more about Scottish hip-hop, and I know exactly where to go. If you want to feel its pulse, you need to take a walk not on the wild side, to the east side or to the west side. You need to go to the south side – the Southside of Glasgow, that is.

If you walk west along the south bank of the river from the centre, you'll pass the rotunda from which Beat 106 FM used to broadcast and the shiny steel-and-glass frontages of the STV, BBC and Science Centre buildings that sit where some of the old docks used to be.

Many of the ships that took Scots and our music around the world were made here, as well as many warships and some celebrity cruisers too: the QE2 was launched from these docks in 1967, but the decline, or as some people see it, the destruction, of the shipbuilding industry left the former Prince's Dock, now Pacific Quay, near-derelict for two decades.

What was left of Prince's Dock was cleared to make room for the Glasgow Garden Festival – A Day Out of This World – which took place through 1988 and was designed in part to counter Glasgow's long-held reputation as No Mean City. The festival was part of a wider, years-long renewal project that included Shettleston advertising man John Struthers' "Glasgow's Miles Better" campaign, which he persuaded his friend, *Mr Men* creator Roger Hargreaves, to lend his Mr Happy character to. That predated the festival, Mr Happy first appearing on the skyline in 1983 (and so annoying Edinburgh Council a few years later that they banned Glasgow's Miles Better ads from their buses because of what they perceived to be an ongoing campaign telling Scotland's more genteel capital to go fuck itself). Glasgow's 1980s regeneration also saw the opening of the Burrell Collection, also in 1983; the relocation of the transport museum from Pollokshields in the Southside to the Kelvin Hall in the West End in 1988; and Glasgow taking the mantle of European City of Culture in 1990.

The Garden Festival is itself part of ancient Govan history now: it's long gone, replaced by the "media village"; Glasgow's Science Centre; an IMAX cinema; and the Science Centre Tower, Glasgow's tallest building and the tallest freestanding structure anywhere in Scotland. The Science Centre has been there since 2001; STV moved in in 2006; and BBC Scotland moved from Queen Margaret Drive to Pacific Quay in 2007.

This part of Glasgow, already very different from the industrial Govan of its recent past, is still changing. Glasgow University is building a new campus and "innovation hub" here; brownfield land is rapidly filling with new-build flats; and there's a newly opened bridge linking Govan to Partick, the southernmost part of Glasgow's affluent West End.

If you walk across the Clyde bridge from the BBC to the former Queen's Dock, you'll find Glasgow's three biggest entertainment venues clumped together: the Scottish Event Campus, formerly the SECC, which opened in 1985 with room for up to 10,000 people in its largest hall (and bloody awful acoustics, as many a gig-goer can attest); the 3,000 capacity Armadillo, known to nobody as the Clyde Auditorium, which opened in 1997; and the pie-shaped Hydro, which opened in 2013 with a capacity of 14,300. The Finnieston Crane, the last giant cantilever crane to be built on the Clyde, is a few hundred yards away, across the VIP car park. Completed in 1932, the Crane once loaded steam locomotives onto Clyde-built ships; the docks it served were closed in 1969 and today it's the background to thousands of show-goers' selfies and many BBC news broadcasts.

This is one of the hubs of Scotland's changed economic landscape. As of 2020, the arts, culture and creative sector contributed £4.4 billion in annual gross value to the Scottish economy,[200] and Glasgow plays a large part in that. According to the OECD, Glasgow has, "one of the highest concentrations of creative and cultural sectors (CCS) in Scotland (accounting for around 40% of Scotland's CCS employment in 2019 and over one third of all CCS firms in 2020)".[201] That's partly because of the presence of the BBC and STV on one side of the river and their magnetic effect on related businesses and freelance workers, and it's partly because of the multiple live music venues on the other.

A lot of money moves through the three venues and the hotels around them. As of 2019, the Hydro was the second busiest concert venue in the world,[202] and according to the Glasgow Chamber of Commerce it contributes £150m a year to Glasgow's economy and supports 2,000 jobs.[203] But unlike the Hydro's rapidly gentrifying northern neighbour Finnieston, despite the economic engine just over the water, Govan remains a very poor part of Glasgow – itself a city with higher levels of deprivation than any other in Scotland.

The car parks of the media hubs at Pacific Quay may be packed with the expensive EVs and SUVs of the Range Rover class, their bike racks busy with the Bromptons of commuters who cycle from their Hyndland homes, but walk slightly west and you'll see a very different Glasgow. As Steg G, tells me, "Lifespans here are eighteen years lower than across the motorway in Pollokshields. Women's life expectancy dropped by three weeks this year."[204]

Govan, like many former industrial parts of Scotland, was dependent on heavy industry – in its case, shipbuilding. That industry went into steep decline after the Second World War, and like other former industrial centres, today's Govan has high unemployment – especially among young people, who are 50 percent more likely to be outwith employment, education and training than the Glasgow average.[205] It also has higher-than-average child poverty.

The Scottish Government uses a tool called SIMD (Scottish Index of Multiple Deprivation) to class the most and least deprived areas of the country on a scale of 1 to 5, where 1 is the most deprived and 5 the least. Partick is level 5; Govan, a stone's throw across the water, is a 1.

I'm here to visit Sunny Govan Radio, which Steg G co-founded and runs. It broadcasts on 103.5MHz FM and online from modest, bustling premises at the foot of a tenement block roughly halfway between the centre of Govan and one of the few remaining shipyards.

Sunny G, as it's affectionately known, first broadcast in 1998 and became a full-time broadcaster in 2007. It's more than a radio station: it's a community charity that provides help and training to local people, particularly marginalised people, but it's the radio station I'm here to talk about with Steg G and his friend and colleague, Delaina Sepko. Delaina is a broadcaster and sound engineer who's worked with a variety of acts including Pet Shop Boys, Tinchy Stryder, Trans-Global

Underground and Get Cape. Wear Cape. Fly.

Sunny G isn't a hip-hop station; it's an everything station with an open and eclectic music policy, and it's as rooted in punk rock as it is in hip-hop, but its hip-hop shows such as Steg's *Live In the Mix* and Delaina's *Beats & Breaks* have long been a highlight, providing a platform for music that for many years wasn't given much airtime on either local commercial radio or the national broadcaster.

Steg has been a fan of hip-hop since its early days. "I got into it in '84," he tells me. "I used to be a breakdancer. That's an element of hip-hop that doesn't really get talked about, how thirty years ago young men in schemes were dancing in the streets. For a couple of summers, all the schemes had a breakdance crew. They were all out dancing, using their agility to express themselves. And that was a phenomenal thing." Breakdancing is still an important part of some hip-hop shows: Steg's latest music video, for the joyful and propulsive 'Just Don't Stop', was filmed at an event in Glasgow's Queen's Park and features multiple breakdancers in constant motion.

"One of the things I liked about hip-hop was the community aspect," Steg says, noting that it was particularly wide-ranging and exciting in the early days before American hip-hop became more homogenous and aggressive in the mid-to-late 1990s. "You were listening to records like [Grandmaster Flash & The Furious Five's] 'The Message', Melle Mel's 'White Lines (Don't Do It)'." Steg nods in recognition when I talk about how the cartoonish madness of 'The Show', by Doug E. Fresh & The Get Fresh Crew, was everywhere in my school around that time. "Yes, with the *Inspector Gadget* samples," he says. "It was fun. Hip-hop was very creative and experimental."

"I was always into music, and I played guitar a little bit, but then I discovered hip-hop and I put the guitar down. I thought, 'This is the music I've been waiting for.'"

Glasgow's schemes are half a world away from the streets of New York, but Steg felt an immediate connection with the music: "This is quite a poor community too, so I gravitated towards the stories they were telling."

While hip-hop is a broad church, at heart it – and related genres that draw from it, such as grime, garage and jungle – is the sound of the streets: the projects of the US, the housing estates of London, the schemes of Scotland. In 1988, Chuck D of Public Enemy told *SPIN* magazine that for its Black, working-class musicians and fans "rap serves as the communication that they don't get for themselves to make them feel good about themselves. Rap is Black America's TV station. It gives a whole perspective of what exists and what Black life is about."[206] Steg believes Scottish hip-hop did the same for working-class Scots. "Hip-hop is modern folk music," he says. "People singing about their lives, their ups, their downs." While a lot of mainstream hip-hop, especially in the US, currently likes to present an image of affluence and of financial success, at heart hip-hop "is usually the poorest people in the poorest communities."

"I always knew hip-hop was a good vehicle for people to get out of the schemes, out of the ghettos, out of the places they didn't want to be in," Steg says. "And Sunny Govan built on that."

Delaina's love of hip-hop started young too: "It was my first love," she says. When she was ten, she obtained a cassette of Ice-T's 1991 *O.G. Original Gangster.* It was "fairly hardcore" for a ten-year-old, she says with a grin. "I just latched on and went, 'Yes! I need more of this!'"

Delaina trained as a sound engineer and musical researcher and built a successful career in recording studios, often working with grime artists. As a white gay woman working with Black straight men, Delaina didn't talk about her sexuality. "I was white in a culture and form of music that came up very strongly through the Black community," she tells me, "and it wasn't obvious that I was gay; being white and a woman were big enough hurdles in my day-to-day, so I decided to pick my fights. They were two very obvious things that I couldn't do anything about that were hard enough already, and I think that's probably why I never really took up that third fight." Delaina is a fighter: she's spent many years as a very vocal advocate for women in the music industry and in hip-hop.

"I feel a little bit more bold and secure in where I've gotten and who I am and what I get up to," Delaina says, as she describes how she found a vibrant and welcoming community in the Scots hip-hop scene. While she's long used her platform on Sunny G Radio to highlight hip-hop by women and by LGBTQ+ artists of all genders, such as Sweet Rogue, Eyve and Erin Friel, she hadn't really talked about her own sexuality publicly until the summer of 2024, when she and artist Doctur Normul co-hosted a special Pride Month show on Sunny G to play hip-hop by queer musicians. During the show, both women talked about their place in both the LGBTQ+ community and the musical community. It's available online on Mixcloud; listening to it, I could hear how nervous Delaina was at the top of the show, something that's out of character for the experienced and accomplished broadcaster. "I felt way out on a limb," Delaina says. "It's not something that comes up – not for any particular reason, like wanting to hide anything about myself. But I've never really found a time or place for it […] because I've been so vocal about supporting women in hip-hop it sometimes felt like that was already a big enough fight that I didn't need to take on another one."

Although Delaina makes it clear that she's never encountered any negativity about her sexuality from within the Scots hip-hop community, I think many queer people can relate to the fear of how people might respond if they don't keep quiet about who they are. "I think there was a bit of personal protection in that," Delaina says. "So finally making the decision to go for it and fly that flag was something that went back and forth a lot in my head. I spoke to a few people about it just to make sure that I wasn't making a mountain out of a molehill."

It seems that it wasn't a mountain to listeners either. "Delaina didn't really get any reaction when she put her thoughts and feelings about who she was out there," Steg says. "And I think that's probably a good thing. We're at a tipping point now where we expect people to be honest about themselves, where we're getting more familiar with these textures of humanity. And I think that's why there's no reaction, whereas maybe twenty-five years ago there might have been something. People have changed. Scotland has changed."

As Steg says, hip-hop has changed too. "The biggest artist in American hip-hop is Tyler, The Creator, who's openly gay and we're all playing his songs." The week Steg, Delaina and I meet, Tyler had just announced a huge show at the Hydro across the water. "That's a huge change from thirty years ago, and it's great to see."

Steg and Delaina also cite Kendrick Lamar's 'Auntie Diaries', a song about his transgender aunt. "I like how an artist like Kendrick can do a song about his auntie being [LGBTQ+], how that's affected him growing up and how he has love for her," Steg says. "I think that changed hip-hop. A lot of old-school artists who were dropping the F-bomb were looking at things like that and thinking, 'You know what? My auntie was gay, my uncle was gay, so what? We're all friends and family.'"

For Steg, the changes are "early bells": "Scotland's just finding its voice in music, and it's a little bit behind, but I hope it brings a lot more diversity and that we'll see a bigger range of topics sung and rapped about. That'll be the thing that gets the next generation interested in rap and hip-hop, because they'll see themselves in it. They'll see topics that relate to voices that speak to them and resonate with them. And that's exciting. A lot of young people in this community are really open-minded, and they'll be the first people to call you out on homophobic stuff."

Steg and Delaina tell me about a recent and highly anticipated show by a much-hyped rapper where, "He went on stage and just rapped the most horrendous song." The crowd's verdict was swift. "He got cancelled straight away from the young team, from everybody," Steg says. "The guy's vanished now. Everyone was excited, everyone was a fan, and then he decided to do this anti-LGBTQ+, anti-trans thing and the young team were like, 'No. Unacceptable, unacceptable, unacceptable.' I was super proud of that."

At Sunny G, diversity isn't about ticking boxes. "It's why we're here," Steg says. "We always recognise how diverse our community is and we try our best to promote that, in different languages as well, knowing that sometimes it's a bat signal that people need to see to engage with us."

Steg and Delaina talk about bat signals a lot during our conversation; it's a phrase both of them have been using for a few weeks now, and while all three of us recognise and smile at the cheesiness of the phrase I do love the mental image it conjures up of Steg and Delaina as Govan's Commissioner Gordons, shining a Klieg light from the radio station's rooftops into the Scottish sky.

"We have to send out bat signals over the air," Steg says as Delaina nods in agreement. "Radio isn't just a passive listening thing. It's – 'I'm going to be involved' whether it's an LGBTQ+

issue, a recovery issue, if it's dance music, if it's hip-hop. We try to reflect everybody and we don't have barriers between different styles, attitudes or genres."

Through projects such as Sunny G radio, people are, "getting exposed to lots of things you wouldn't normally get, deep conversations about people's personal issues, music from other cultures, people taking about their cultures, their history, this culture and the culture of New Scots as well."

"We encourage people to talk with their own voice," Steg says. "Whether that's an African voice, a Govan voice, an English voice, an American voice, a Chinese voice. Bring that to us and we all learn together. I hate the term 'melting pot', but when we come together something extra happens. That's the magical bit that keeps us motivated."

"We've always seen Glasgow as a tapestry, a big quilt," Steg says about Sunny G's approach. "You're a patch and it's this colour and this texture. And you're a patch, and it's that colour and that texture. Put it all together and it's amazing. We're happy to reflect that. We *love* reflecting that."

I wonder aloud whether Scots hip-hop is taken as seriously as other art forms, especially by arts organisations, or if it's seen as a poor relation. Steg and Delaina both shake their heads at the latter suggestion. Steg tells me about the Scots newspaper journalist who reviewed his demo tape two decades ago. "He said – and this shows you what time it was – he said, 'You know the film *White Men Can't Jump*? Well. White men can't rap.'" While there may have been that perception in the past, Steg says that lately, Scottish hip-hop is not considered inferior to other genres or art forms.

"Before, funders wouldn't want to fund you. But now there's not the perception that, 'These people are going to be rapping 'Fuck the police' or whatever, dropping F-bombs'. I think we've matured and grown into this culture, this community, and we're in a situation where our voices do get heard." So while Creative Scotland "probably don't have enough hip-hop voices chapping at the door, they do recognise that hip-hop is the biggest music form in the world, and probably one of the biggest forms in Scotland at the moment." However "that's not reflected in their budget spend in terms of where the money goes."

To help address that, Sunny Govan has been working with Creative Scotland on devolved funding. "We get money from Creative Scotland and then we put an application form on our website for hip-hop artists to apply for bursaries. It's a super easy process." It's also massively oversubscribed, with over eighty applications for the twenty bursaries available.

"A lot of the people who work in or try to get involved in hip-hop come from the poorest parts of the community," Steg says. "They don't have access to traditional music skills or anything like that. So it's vital that funding goes to those areas of the community. Because not only is it helping to support hip-hop, it's helping to support confidence, employability, health, and wellbeing. I think Creative Scotland realises that as well. It's good to support the high arts, but we've got to support the people's music too."

That support means doing more than just playing music. Sunny Govan works with multiple organisations including schools and secure units where hip-hop can be used to break down barriers and reach young people in particular. "We're thinking upstream," Steg explains. "Let's help the kids get skills. What do we do? We know music, and a lot of kids like hip-hop music. So let's combine that, let's do workshops aimed at increasing their confidence, their employability, getting them away from the nonsense, the gangs and stuff like that."

As Steg says, "It's not just linked to art. It's linked to poverty.

It's linked to everything. And I think any investment in that community is a good thing." But there's always a need for more. "We only have so many lifeboats."

Prominent and openly LGBTQ+ hip-hop artists are still very rare in Scotland: you'll run out of queer artists long before you run out of fingers to count them on, and when it comes to counting the out gay men in hip-hop you don't need any fingers at all.

"I'd be super excited to see more gay artists in Scottish hip-hop, particularly gay male artists," Steg says. "I think that would be something." Delaina agrees. "It'll happen," she says. "It's a when, not an if."

It's clear that Sunny G's door is open to LGBTQ+ artists but they need queer artists to come knocking; as Steg says, they can only play what they're sent. Both Steg and Delaina point out that marginalised people, including LGBTQ+ people, often have good reason to be wary of media. "I think that for a lot of groups, they need to feel that they can trust a platform before they'll come in and express themselves or talk about their issues," Steg says.

"I know that there is power in example," Delaina says. "Throwing out a bat signal in that way is important, and I almost wish that twenty years ago I'd seen that sort of example. But I never did. There was no one I saw doing that, particularly in hip-hop. As we've all said, it was quite the opposite. So you had to *really* love hip-hop to balance that out."

I ask Delaina about balancing representation with tokenism, of giving women and queer artists a platform without treating gender and sexuality as genres rather than just facets of artists' personalities. "When I programme a show I have a couple of red lines," Delaina says. "One of them is that it has to be gender balanced. And in every show, there's also queer artists that I play. Do I raise that point in the middle of the show? No, no more than I'd call a woman a 'female MC'. But I like to put it all out there on the same table."

"I feel uncomfortable sometimes with adding those qualifiers," she explains. "Why can't we just all be in hip-hop? Why do I need to continue using that nomenclature for those contributors? I want to be satisfied that I've put out something respectful, and the hope is that then reverberates."

It's definitely reverberating with Steg, who says he's much more conscious about the balance in his playlists now. "That's a good change, and if it's happening to me then it's happening to other DJs, other hip-hop DJs, out there as they're cheering these great tunes. The only rule is: is it a banger? Start there. And that's it."

I could talk to Delaina and Steg all day, but they have workshops to run, people to support and beats to drop. A few hours later I'll be watching the 2024 US election results with growing horror, but right now I'm walking into a crisp, cold, sunny Govan day feeling pretty positive about people. I'll be thinking a lot about Sunny G over the next few weeks, reminding myself that even in the darkest times there is light: light from people giving their time, their expertise and their energy to bring people together, to lift others up, to shine bat signals into the sky.

CHAPTER 19:
YOUNG HARD AND HANDSOME

I t's a month to the day since I sat in Glasgow's Royal Infirmary holding my mum's hand for the very last time, and after four-and-a-half weeks of crying I really need to experience something joyful and life-affirming. I'm just down the hill from the hospital, sardine-packed at the back of McChuills bar. I'm here to see a sold-out homecoming show by Walt Disco, Glasgow's twelve-legged "queer glam-goth" pop phenomenon.

Tonight's show is a very early preview of their second album, *The Warping*, which won't be released until the summer of 2024 – almost a year and a European tour with Orchestral Manoeuvres in the Dark (OMD) in the future. Today the band will be interviewed for *Rolling Stone*, which will hail them as one of their "future of music" picks for 2024 and note that "Hollywood superstar and cult queer icon Tilda Swinton called them her new favourite band."[207]

Given the band's fierce styling, I'm surprised by how ordinary the crowd looks. With a few spectacular exceptions, the vibe is more primary school teacher than gender terrorist;

more no-hair than mohair and quite the contrast to the outfits on stage.

There may be significantly fewer feather boas (zero) than I'd expected (lots) and a distinct lack of the leopard prints and faux fur I thought was de rigueur for any queer pop event, but this is without doubt a queer and queer-friendly crowd, and when the opening act – Jacob Alon, a singer-songwriter from Edinburgh whose soaring, multi-octave vocals remind me of both Jeff Buckley and Mary Margaret O'Hara – introduces their song 'Confession' with, "This is a song about being queer and being ashamed of that, and about falling in love with someone who can't love you back", pauses, and then adds, "Relatable", there's a big laugh.

The title of Walt Disco's debut EP, *Young Hard and Handsome*, captures the spirit of the band beautifully: their provocative pop is flirty and funny, self-aware and seductive. Their music is clearly influenced by Bowie and the New Romantics, especially the more theatrical acts of the era. The band cite The Associates as a key influence, along with more modern queer or queer-inspired artists such as Sufjan Stevens, Charli XCX,[208] SOPHIE and TAAHLIAH; TAAHLIAH remixed their single 'Macilent', the song whose lyric gave their debut EP its title.

As singer Jocelyn Si explained to *tmrw* magazine, "We are a band with queer members that champions queer people and attitudes and want to change people's perspectives on that."[209] They do that with tales of gender dysphoria, non-binary lockdown romances, bad sex, and trying to work out where the hell you fit on the gender spectrum. Si looks gorgeous – a proper pop star from another planet – and beams delightedly throughout their show; the band and the crowd crack up when, after a triumphant 'Selfish Lover', someone shouts, "Guan yersel', hen!"

Jocelyn is in a strange place when I meet them for a chat. Not literally – we're in a high street coffee shop – but because right now Walt Disco are supposed to be shouting, "Hello Cleveland!" to North American audiences on the second leg of their tour with OMD. Health issues among the headline band have postponed that to the summer of 2025, so Jocelyn and their fellow Walts are unexpectedly back home under the grey skies of a Scottish autumn.

The band may not be rocking America just yet, but there's still plenty to celebrate. They've just signed a publishing deal that meant they've been able to quit their day jobs and work on their music full-time, and they're about to take their new record, *The Warping*, on a UK and European tour.

It's a great record, ambitious, unafraid and hugely entertaining: for me the highlights are the pristine guitar pop of 'Come Undone' with its echoes of *Young Americans*-era David Bowie, the fragile acoustics of 'Weeping Willow' and the yearning title track, which is particularly devastating if you've ever felt uncomfortable in your own skin.

As good as the music is, what really stands out is Jocelyn's voice. Pop and rock bands from Scotland tend to sing in one of two voices: a mid-Atlantic English/American hybrid one with flattened vowel sounds or the supposedly more authentic working-class Scottish one with harder vowels and rolled Rs. I say "supposedly" because of course there's a long tradition of well-spoken middle-class kids taking the class elevator downwards; for every Arab Strap, Sweet Rogue or Doctur Normul who sings or raps as they speak, I suspect there are just as many artists whose voices become considerably less Scottish when the mics are off – the artistic equivalent of your mum doing her phone voice until she recognises the caller.

Jocelyn doesn't sing like your mum. Their singing is much more interesting and dramatic. I can hear Bowie at his most theatrical and Billy Mackenzie at his most operatic; Jocelyn tells me that they've also been compared to David Sylvian from Japan, among others, so I'm surprised to discover that Jocelyn didn't hear those artists until Walt Disco were already making records. "I think I've just got that type of voice," Jocelyn says. "I have a baritone voice with tenor notes in there, and that was a popular type of voice for those kinds of bands."

"I started singing when I was seventeen," they tell me. "I started writing songs when I was sixteen, but I sounded crap – like Bob Dylan or someone like that. And I wanted to be a *good* singer, not just an, 'Okay, get the job done' singer." Jocelyn's dad was going to singing lessons to work on his breathing and suggested that Jocelyn might enjoy lessons too. Jocelyn did. "My teacher was an opera singer at the Royal Conservatoire, I think. We got on really well; he was gay and I was just buzzing to chat to someone who was openly gay and doing cool stuff." As Jocelyn explains, the lessons mixed pop music, especially by interesting singers such as Bowie, with more classical techniques. "I tried to pick up some of the techniques Bowie used, and then every time I've heard a singer I've been drawn to, I just steal a little bit – or if there's a singer with a note I can't hit, I'll go, 'I want to hit that note now!'" Patience paid off, with songs such as Bowie's 'Life on Mars' – a deceptively hard song to sing – moving from apparently impossible to easily achievable. "And then I heard Billy Mackenzie and wanted to go even higher," Jocelyn grins.

I ask Jocelyn what songs soundtracked their childhood. "Queen. I think that was the safe ground for my mum and dad. I don't know if they had a formal discussion about what music they liked that they'd play us, but my dad was into quite a lot of prog stuff and as a kid, that's not what you really want to hear. Queen was a big one, and so were Scissor Sisters, and that's obviously stuck with me."

For many musicians there's a tension between what they want to do and what their parents want them to do. Jocelyn experienced that too, but in reverse: they wanted to do marine biology, and their dad wanted them to do music. "I went and did marine biology, but then I joined a band and dropped out after two and a half years," Jocelyn says. "So, he was right. It was meant to be. But when you're young it has to feel like it's *your* decision."

As a teen, Jocelyn was drawn to much the same music as everybody else – "The Cure, The Smiths, The Stone Roses" – as well as older music such as Siouxsie and the Banshees, eighties and nineties pop, "new wave, indie, that sort of stuff."

"My mates and I tried to keep an eye on what was new and good, but I think when you're that age you're not as discerning about new acts – we were going to see artists that probably weren't very good, just indie bands all the time; you're easily influenced and you're told to like certain bands." But as Jocelyn's musical awareness grew, they started to seek out more interesting music – and a lot of that was from previous generations.

Jocelyn makes a point that I hadn't really thought about: it's sometimes easier to find really exciting music by older acts than by new acts "because it's had to stand the test of time. You don't hear about the bands who were around at the same time as The Cure, but who weren't as good." It's a good point: the marketing of music is primarily focused on the here and now. It's often easy to mistake what's new for what's good, but as with any art form what's new isn't always good and what's good isn't always new.

That's not to say that Jocelyn and their fellow Walts aren't interested in the here and now, though. The band are huge fans of contemporary pop, and they're particularly drawn to music by queer and/or female artists; that music was a big influence on their previous record, 2022's *Unlearning*, which was written and recorded during the COVID pandemic. "When lockdown hit, we had to make an album on a computer," Jocelyn recalls. "So, we were like, 'What's the best computer music that we listen to?' And the answer was experimental pop, so we made that kind of album."

The newer album, *The Warping*, is still pop, but it's more organic, rooted in more traditional sounds. "The second record [*Unlearning*] was a reaction to the first one, and then we decided that because that was so digital we wanted to make a really acoustic one. And with the songs we're working on now, we know exactly what we want to sound like." The next record will still be Walt Disco. But it'll be a different Walt Disco yet again.

In interviews, Jocelyn has said that Walt Disco isn't a queer band; they're a band with queer people in it. I ask them if that's still an important distinction. "I think so. I think people associate queerness with us a lot because I'm always writing about it, but not all of the band members are queer." We talk about the problem of tokenisation, of "queer" being seen as a genre rather than just a descriptor. "I know it's a clunky way to put it, but I think it's similar to how a female-fronted band gets put in the 'female band' category."

That said, if being labelled a queer band means the music will be heard by more people, so be it. "It's really hard for women, for trans people, for queer people to get in the band scene sometimes because it's a pretty straight and male world," Jocelyn says, nodding at my Garbage T-shirt. "So, if a nice straight male drummer like Butch Vig is able to platform someone like Shirley Manson, then I'm all in favour of it."

One of the things I wanted to ask Jocelyn about was their experience of being so open so publicly: they're a fearless lyricist, and some of the songs on *The Warping* are very frank about Jocelyn's experience of gender dysphoria and of their sexuality. All successful bands do a certain amount of growing up in public, but not all of them are dealing with gender, changing their name and exploring their gender presentation quite so visibly. "There are times I've wanted to just start again with a clean slate, as a band whose frontperson is a butch lesbian with a baritone voice instead of someone who's seen as a flamboyant gay or bisexual man," Jocelyn says after a pause. "So many people are used to that idea, Freddie Mercury and all of that. We've worn those influences on our sleeve and when I started this band, that's who I thought I was."

I suggest that Jocelyn's journey – we both use the word with a raised eyebrow, well aware of its overuse – as a front-person has parallels with many people's coming-out narrative; there can be a rush to do and see and be all the things, to try on lots of different personas until you find the one that fits. "And that can be great," Jocelyn says. "But now, I'd like to slightly change the narrative. Not to second-guess ourselves or un-queer ourselves or anything like that. Just being more genuine." Jocelyn smiles. "Just as queer, but maybe in a less flamboyant way."

CHAPTER 20:
YOU COULD HAVE IT SO MUCH BETTER

O ne of the things I think is crucial about the artists I've discussed is that everybody – and I do mean *everybody* – knew who they were. I watched Bronski Beat on *Top of the Pops* with my parents, read about Horse in the music press and the Scots broadsheets, heard The Soup Dragons do a session on John Peel, but for the up-and-coming artists I'm also writing about, almost all those outlets are gone.

That begs the question: how do the emerging artists of today become the stars of tomorrow? Can today's queer musicians have the same cultural impact as the artists who had such an impact on prior generations? Was SOPHIE the last of the breakthrough queer Scots music superstars?

Over the last two decades, and particularly in the last few years, we've lost huge sections of media that used to cover music. The music press is as good as dead, with the large-circulation weekly and monthly music titles a distant memory; there are far fewer new music shows on radio and far fewer people listening to them; newspapers devote ever fewer column inches to the arts in general and emerging music in particular; and there's precious little music on TV, or viewers for it.

That's partly because music isn't the huge cultural force it used to be. We live in an age where there's more music than ever for us to pay less attention to. There's a near-infinite supply of new music and a near-infinite supply of old music too; our phones and our smart speakers give us access to almost all the music ever made in exchange for a small subscription or a few adverts. That music is now in competition with our many other amusements: online gaming, social media, streaming TV.

Music's appeal has become more selective, but that doesn't fully explain the astonishing speed of music media's decline. Between 2010 and 2020, circulations plummeted so dramatically that many of the biggest names in print media, including Q magazine and NME, ceased publication before being reborn as online brands with little connection to their previous iterations; others, such as Mixmag, paused their print editions during COVID and never brought them back.

There isn't a single smoking gun here; rather, there's a whole arsenal of them including a failure to move with the times, with some mainstream outlets desperately pushing landfill indie and retro rock while R&B and hip-hop became the world's favourite music. Most of the damage was done by the internet, which destroyed the two crucial things underpinning music media: the need for it, and the money that paid for it.

Established artists don't need the media anymore, and neither do their fans: if I want to know what Shirley Manson is up to, or see candid backstage pictures from Lauren Mayberry's latest video shoot, or find out when Walt Disco are next playing near me, I'll go directly to their Instagram feeds instead of buying a music magazine. If I want to hear their new albums I don't need to listen to the radio; I can stream from their socials and pre-save on Spotify.

That's changed the way music is promoted, and where record companies' and tour promoters' money is spent. Why pay for banner or print ads when you can precision target fans on social media instead? Why buy advertising for a tour when you can sell out every venue via the artist's email list?

The same thing has happened more widely with the non-music press. Local and national papers made a lot of their money from people selling houses, advertising old sofas and recruiting new staff, but that was before Rightmove and Zoopla, Facebook Marketplace and Gumtree, Indeed and Totaljobs. What little advertising revenues remain online largely goes to Google and Meta, the parent company of Facebook and Instagram. For much of the media, the good old days are gone.

The advertising crash has been particularly devastating for local media, both print and broadcast, which has become increasingly centralised and homogenised. Today, many playlists and pages are not created locally, but made centrally in far-away business parks for the occasional broadcaster or byline to then sprinkle them with the appearance of local connections. There's a running joke on the r/glasgow subreddit that it's where some local newspaper sites source many of their stories; there's some truth to it. Much music coverage is now based not on what artists say to local journalists, but what they've posted on global social media.

This doesn't really affect established artists who already have an audience, but it's been devastating for up-and-coming ones because it's made it so much more difficult for them to make an impact.

Local newspapers used to be a valuable outlet for very early-stage acts to promote their shows and build up a press kit. Smaller local newspapers never had much space or budget for extensive local music coverage, although there have always been true believers in the likes of the *Ardrossan & Saltcoats Herald* or the *Alloa Advertiser* who'd do their best to try and feature the odd local act or gig. Even that is largely gone now that budgets are even tighter and revenues so much smaller. The same is true in Scotland's larger markets where there's very little coverage of local music of any kind, let alone music by marginalised artists.

When I visited the website of the *Dundee Courier* and *Evening Telegraph* in early 2024 to browse its archive of music stories, of the twenty-five most recent pieces about music only one, the twenty-fourth, was about a local act: The Shambolics. It was preceded by twenty-three stories about Ricky Martin, Shania Twain, Miley Cyrus, Rod Stewart, and U2, and only that last one had a local angle: it was a sharing-friendly nostalgia piece about the band's 1983 show at the Caird Hall. There were another sixteen stories about artists such as Britney Spears before the next Fife musician, King Creosote, in a story that at the time was already six months old.

Aberdeen's *Press & Journal* was better: I visited on the same day and the top posts in its music section were local stories about traditional music, emerging and established local rock acts and HOURS ABDN, a key part of Aberdeen's hip-hop scene. Even then, the news section featured stories about those famously not-Aberdonian artists Beyoncé, Eminem, Ariana Grande, and Shakira.

The *P&J* isn't unique here. Almost all news websites do it because there's virtually no money in online advertising, so to make even a pittance from your pages you need to target the very biggest audiences with the very biggest stories, and with all due respect to The Shambolics, stories about them are not those kind of stories. In fact, The Shambolics are lucky to get any coverage at all. Local newspapers have been cut so far back and now employ so few people that actual journalism

– journalism of the "go out and talk to people" kind – is a dying trade. It's a numbers game now where young journalists in particular are expected to stay at their desk and file multiple articles per day in order to drive online traffic. Inevitably, those targets incentivise the regurgitation of press releases and chasing whatever's trending online rather than time-consuming interviewing and reporting. That's how you end up with the *Dundee Courier* sharing Shakira's views on the *Barbie* movie in its music section (as it did in April 2024), a story whose readers almost certainly won't be local and who equally certainly won't be scrolling on to read about King Creosote.

Some chains are trying to get rid of the journalists altogether. For example, Reach, which owns many Scots local papers and websites, has an AI tool called Gutenbot that "rips" stories from press releases, wire services and other Reach websites, automatically rewriting them so that they can be republished with very little human input at all.[210]

The internet wasn't the only reason our mass culture became so fragmented and so fixated on clicks and ad views, but it was one of the main offenders, and the promises that it would build something better have proven hollow. The internet titles that hoped to replace the inky weeklies and the monthly magazines have largely fallen victim to plummeting advertising revenues, asset-stripping venture capitalists and frankly baffling attempts at brand synergy. I'm writing this as the hugely influential *Pitchfork* site has been rolled into *GQ* after years of declining revenues so it can be defanged and used as another lifestyle brand to sell expensive watches; in the same month *Vice* laid off hundreds of writers and stopped publishing new articles.

The internet changed things in another way too. By enabling editors and publishers and programmers to see down to the individual mouse click how well every single article or stream performs, that inevitably incentivised publishers to chase quantity over quality, to give readers and listeners more of what they already like rather than risk giving them something unfamiliar.

That flattening of culture, that massive reduction in arts media and arts coverage, means the mainstream is less able to give you something really valuable: serendipity.

Serendipity was when you tuned in to Peter Easton's *Beat Patrol* or Mark Percival's *Electronica* on Radio Scotland, Billy Sloan on Radio Clyde or Jim Gellatly on Northsound to hear your current favourites, and you came away having heard a new band.

Serendipity was when the magazine you bought because your favourite singer was in it had a free flexi disc or a cover-mounted cassette containing the greatest song you'd never heard.

Serendipity was picking up the local paper to scour Situations Vacant and finding out there was an intriguing three-band bill happening on Saturday night.

Serendipity was sitting down to see who was on *Top of the Pops* – even though you taped the charts off the radio on Sunday – and discovering something or someone extraordinary.

Let's take one evening at random: Thursday June 7, 1984. If you turned on the BBC for *Top of the Pops* to see Howard Jones, Bananarama or Spandau Ballet, you'd also see Sister Sledge, Wham! and in their very first appearance, Bronski Beat.

I'm cheating a bit, because that was a pretty queer-friendly evening for *TOTP*, but there were many more. For example, alongside Nana Mouskouri on January 23, 1986, there were gender-blurring artists Grace Jones and Eurythmics; on July 16, 1992, Jason Donovan couldn't have seemed more vanilla in a show that also featured Prince and Sophie B Hawkins. It didn't always deliver joy unconfined – if you tuned in to catch

Shirley Manson and Garbage's debut appearance in 1995, you'd pay the price by then having to endure Cast, Simply Red and Menswear – but you get the idea.

There are lots of reasons why we shouldn't miss the monoculture of the seventies, eighties and nineties, but there are some good reasons to miss some of it too. With the possible exception of *Gladiators*, there's no show bringing extraordinarily attractive queer people into our living rooms in prime time, and now mainstream music TV is long gone I'll never get the chance to complain to my kids that I can't hear the words, it isn't proper music and all the other guff my generation grew up rolling our eyes at.

My kids and I don't have that communal experience because it doesn't exist anymore. We share the same sofa, but our musical worlds are siloed on our smartphones, streaming soundtracks that we don't share.

As the channels that helped broaden our musical horizons have shrivelled and died, we've seen a hollowing out of live music as multiple venues have closed. COVID-19 was the final hammer-blow for many, but grassroots venues were already fighting on multiple fronts: against noise complaints from new neighbours, against rapidly rising rents and utility bills, and against the increasing difficulty of persuading people to come out to see live music.

The Barras endures, of course, and bands big enough to fill the Usher Hall, the Hydro or Hampden can happily charge ever-higher prices for strings of sold-out shows, but at the level between the back room of pubs and the bouncing floor of the Barras, we've lost a lot of venues where artists were able to become exceptional. I'd highlight the 2023 closure of Glasgow's 13th Note as a particularly egregious loss to the live music circuit and to queer musicians especially, but it's just one entry on a miserably long list of lost musical opportunities that also includes Inverness's Ironworks, Leith's Central Bar, Dundee's Doghouse and so many more.

According to the Music Venue Trust, in 2023 alone the UK lost 125 grassroots live music venues and there's no sign of that slowing down. The MVT and the Scottish Greens have urged Scotland and the UK to emulate France, where a small levy on big gigs helps to keep local live music off life support. Despite very loud protestations by Spotify and Deezer, France also has a small levy on music streaming services (currently 1.2 percent) that goes to the grassroots too. What little funding exists for music in the UK is under threat: Westminster's ongoing austerity policies have led to underfunded councils scaling back their arts programmes and, in some cases, scrapping their arts support entirely.

The streaming era has not been good for smaller artists. Spotify, which barely pays artists in the first place while showering six-figure sums on podcasts by right-wingers such as Joe Rogan and which has made CEO Daniel Ek richer than any musician in history – as of 2024 his net worth was reported as $4.9 billion, compared to $2.5 billion for Jay-Z, $1.4 billion for Rihanna and $1.3 billion for Taylor Swift and Paul McCartney alike – demonetised more than four-fifths of its music catalogue in 2024. Smaller artists who were streaming their songs on the service for a pittance now won't get paid at all. The demise of radio and closure of venues means that PRS royalties, which are paid for national radio play and live performances in venues beyond a certain size, are shrinking too. Venues are increasingly demanding large cuts of one of artists' few remaining income streams, the merchandise they sell at their shows. As *The Guardian* reported in late 2022, the Academy Music Group, which runs UK venues including the O2 Academy in Glasgow and the former Corn Exchange in Edinburgh, expects a 25 percent cut of merch sales.[211]

There's more to this than an old woman mourning the *NME*s, *Peel Session*s and Thinking Popster columns of her musical youth, although I am absolutely doing that too. In a very short space of time, we've seen music media and coverage of grassroots music almost disappear, and that has had terrible consequences for artists who aren't yet big enough to sell out Bannerman's in Edinburgh's Cowgate, let alone pack the same city's Murrayfield stadium over multiple consecutive nights at £300+ per ticket.

While the likes of dedicated arts magazines such as *The List*, *The Skinny* and *Snack*, fanzines and online outlets such as *Scots Whay Hae* and *Is This Music?* continue to do wonderful things, there's no longer the middle tier of media that would pick up on their discoveries and send record companies scurrying across the border to propel Scots artists into the stratosphere. The days of two dozen A&R men travelling up to sign and invest in new artists are largely gone; even more importantly, so are their chequebooks. Few record companies are in the business of investing and nurturing new artists anymore; today's acts need to come to them fully formed, with a ready-made audience and the streaming statistics and TikTok followers to prove it.

Pop is not dead, but the shift to digital distribution of everything via a handful of global platforms who dominate not just music delivery but music discovery too, has made the musical world significantly smaller and removed many of the regional differences that once provided space for new artists to find their audiences. For emerging artists, that has made everything much harder. They're no longer competing for attention with their peers, but with the whole planet.

How do they break through when the odds are so stacked against them?

I don't know the answers, but I know some people who might.

CHAPTER 21:
DREAMING OF THE QUEENS

Getting marginalised people to take the stage, while important, is only part of the picture. Having stages for them to take, and having people see them play those stages, is crucial too. That's where events such as the AMPLIFI programme of shows at Edinburgh's Queens Hall are crucial.

Halina Rifai is one of the curators of AMPLIFI, has worked extensively in music PR and the arts sector, and is the founder of long-running popular music podcast and blog *Podcart*. She is passionate about elevating marginalised people in music.

I ask her if she thinks Scotland will produce another artist with the impact of SOPHIE. "She was one of a kind," Rifai tells me. "But many of the communities she appealed and appeals to are very much underground still – and these beautiful hidden pockets are far bigger than a lot of us maybe understand."

Rifai cites Sarra Wild of OH141 – "a phenomenal DJ" – as an example; OH141 began as a club night, became a radio show and is a central part of Scotland's vibrant club scene. Wild has also worked with groups such as Grassroots Glasgow to provide support to women, people of colour and LGBTQ+ people, a Venn diagram that has a lot of overlap. As Wild told

The List, "I figured, what better way to get more POC people, queer people and women involved in the scene?" Asked for her advice for the electronic music scene, Wild responded, "Book more diverse lineups and have people present, not just behind the decks but in tech positions. Put minorities in positions where decisions can be made and it will trickle down. My night OH141 or Grassroots is the perfect example of that. Have a POC or a woman of colour or a queer person or someone who isn't a majority at the top and everything changes."[212]

I ask Rifai whether she feels Scots music has become more diverse during her two decades helming *Podcart.* "I've thought about that a lot," she says, "and I don't know if it has become more diverse or if I have become more diverse." Rifai grew up in Dunoon, "pretty much on the west coast and a bit more rural than the city centres", but moved to Glasgow and began joining much more diverse communities both personally and through her work. "I think our audience has changed because of that, because I've changed what I've covered."

Rifai is particularly proud of AMPLIFI, in which she and Arusa Qureshi put on shows centring people of colour and a significant number of LGBTQ+ artists. "We were approached by Edinburgh's Queens Hall about doing this series, and one of the best things about it was that they were taking a risk. We could book what we want, who we want, and let it evolve."

Although Rifai used the word risk, she's not sure that's the best way to describe the booking policy, asking, "Why should these people be deemed a risk when it's just representation of communities?"

The tagline for AMPLIFI is "The sounds of modern Scotland" and, for Rifai, the diversity of its lineups is key. "We're not your token hip-hop night. It's genre diverse, and because we're billed as guest curators, we're not gatekeepers.

We can move on, and we can bring other people in to continue the work."

Representation is a process, not a one-off event, and as Rifai points out there can still be an imbalance when it comes to gender. "One of the things I've noticed and that we've talked about is that even when it's a Black or POC collective booking nights for Black and POC artists, it tends to be very male – especially with hip-hop artists. That's something we really want to challenge." As she explains, it's about "ensuring that the diversity of Scotland's population is represented in terms of that cultural activity."

"So, I don't know if it's risk," Rifai says with a smile. "I prefer to use the term 'faith'."

Halina's co-curator at AMPLIFI, Arusa Qureshi, helped me understand the Scots hip-hop scene. Arusa has also worked as the music booker for Edinburgh's gorgeous Summerhall venue, a space where I've seen some of the best shows I've ever experienced. As she explains, AMPLIFI and shows at Summerhall aren't just about putting artists on the stage, they're also about "getting those artists in front of the people who are booking shows, and the people writing about shows." As Arusa tells me, it's gratifying and a little bit frustrating to see the artists they champion moving on to bigger stages; gratifying because that's the whole point of what they do, and frustrating because it needs to be done.

Arusa identifies the press as a particular problem for musicians from marginalised groups. The English press by and large isn't interested in Scots arts, and the Scots press is mostly focused on the familiar. "There just aren't enough people that are published from diverse backgrounds," she says. "If you have the same journalists for ten-plus years and you don't bring in anyone new, or you do bring in someone new but don't nurture them or give them opportunities, then of course we're just going to have the same people all the time and the readers are going to be given the same recommendations all the time. That's not to criticise any journalists; there are people I know who are doing this, who are brilliant and who really care. But I still think that you need new voices to tap into different scenes. It's the only way those artists will reach the wider public."

Arusa is a music booker as well as a music writer, and she says the scene is getting ever harder. "Grassroots venues can't catch a break," she says. "We really can't." As a board member of the Music Venue Trust, the organisation that's lobbying for a France-style tax to help support smaller venues, she's very much in favour of a levy on the very biggest concerts.

We're speaking just days after Coldplay announced a significant donation to the MVT from their 2025 stadium tour, and while Arusa is clearly delighted by that, she also points out that one rock band's donation, however large, is hardly a structural solution to a serious and ongoing problem. "Imagine if Taylor Swift also did it, and if Beyoncé did it, and every other big stadium show did it and fed money into local, grassroots venues where those musicians started out and found their audiences," she says. "But at the moment we're dependent on the charity of rock stars rather than a straight levy." Arusa says that the Scots government are open to the idea of a levy "but I don't know how long it'll actually take to get it across the line."

What would the effects of such a move be? "It'd mean more of a chance of grassroots venues not closing all the time, being able to keep the lights on, put on artists and pay them reasonable, decent fees. Just simple things to keep things going, because at the moment I really do think we're in a dire place." As if to underline that, two days after we speak HMRC issued a petition to wind up Summerhall's management company over allegedly unpaid corporation tax; the company's bank accounts were frozen, leaving staff unpaid and dozens of Edinburgh Fringe performers, companies and artists owed thousands of pounds.[213] The building, believed to be the largest privately owned arts complex in Europe, has now been sold to a property developer[214] and while its future is unclear, the words "luxury flats" are likely to feature prominently.

When news that Summerhall was up for sale broke, an online petition was immediately launched to "Preserve Summerhall as a cultural hub".[215] It's had over 15,000 signatures to date. "But across that period, I didn't see any jump in ticket sales," Arusa tells me. "Had every one of those people bought a ticket… even when we talk about making a £1 contribution, that really does add up. It really does make a difference."

With arts funding increasingly constrained, media taking fewer risks, costs increasing, and venues struggling to attract audiences, Arusa thinks that "something radical needs to happen. I'd like to see people get more angry, rather than just sharing things on social media," she says. "Actually do something."

One of the people who decided to do something is vocalist, multi-instrumentalist and writer EJ Kempson, who relocated to Scotland after studying at universities in Guildford and Brighton. While in Guildford, Kempson was struck by the difficulties their queer friends were experiencing. "So many people ended up quitting because of how they were treated by their university and by their peers," she says, "and a lot of my trans friends ended up either giving up music altogether or reverting to their birth gender because it was easier to make it in the music industry."

As a metal musician, EJ found that while "the fans in the metal scene were incredible, most of the people that were running the scene and most of the well-known bands in the area were just not inclusive at all." So Kempson created Queenz Sounds to help create a more inclusive and supportive music scene. "I didn't want to see minorities who were incredible musicians struggle so much to just get heard," she says.

Kempson moved to Glasgow to do her PhD and continued with Queenz Sounds, with the collective becoming a registered charity. Today it consists of and represents a wide range of LGBTQ+ and women musicians – the current artist roster includes Megan Black, Anna Secret Poet, Emma Dunlop and many more from Scotland as well as artists from further afield. It also organises shows in Scotland, London and Spain, as well as connecting artists with other venues and bookers. Essentially, it's a found family for musicians, providing help, encouragement and support for marginalised artists – some of whom experience multiple kinds of marginalisation, or different kinds of marginalisation in different contexts.

EJ recalls her conversation with Skunk Anansie singer Skin, a supporter of the charity, who is a queer Black woman. "I asked her, did she experience more racism, homophobia or sexism, and she told me that no one really cared about her race, no one really questioned whether she was queer or not, but she had sexism in almost every room that she walked in." That wasn't the answer EJ expected, but as they say, marginalised people's experiences vary widely. However, "the fact is that the more diverse you are, the more likely you are to be persecuted by someone."

"The main thing we do is getting to know people," EJ explains. "It's getting to know the artists that aren't being represented, finding out why they aren't being represented, and understanding the struggles they're facing. Every single person is facing something completely different and has had a completely different experience of the music industry."

"We try and promote people in all sorts of different ways," they continue. "We do a yearly festival, and we contact venues, booking agents and promoters and really just have a chat with them." That chat is focused on creating new connections, finding a good fit between Queenz Sounds' artists and the more established ones that venues and festivals already know. "I think a big part of it is awareness, just making sure they are listening to these artists and see their talent."

Are the industry figures responsive to that? Do they listen? "It really depends," EJ says. "I've had some horrific conversations with some people when I've contacted them and they'll make a sweeping statement such as, 'Oh yeah, we really support women in the music industry,' and I'll go, 'Well, how?' And they'll say, 'We haven't started yet.' But there are others that contact us and tell us that they'd like our help. Those are always the easiest conversations to have because they're ready to have a discussion. You can tell when something is a PR stunt, and you can tell when promoters are genuinely trying to make change: it's not that they're trying to pinkwash or anything; something has made them go, 'Oh. We need to change our ways.'" Pinkwashing, if you're not familiar with the term, is a phrase used to describe exploitative marketing that uses the LGBTQ+ community for positive PR without supporting or standing with that community.

While many organisations EJ speaks to are progressive, tokenism can be a concern. "As soon as you have someone who's a minority, that'll be marketed as part of the gig: 'Our first all-queer bill,' or 'Our first all-women bill'" – queerness or femaleness as a genre. "I've seen both sides of it, and it is really easy to tell which it is as soon as you start talking to people."

EJ admits that the most open-minded, enthusiastic and inclusive people tend to be lower down the music business hierarchy, and often younger. "The difficult conversations are when you're talking to someone who is so privileged, and they don't have an inner circle that's diverse in genre or gender."

That lack of diversity tends to be reflected in who gets attention and who gets booked, and success can be a disincentive to embrace diversity. "The people that are making all the money in the industry are not trying to promote artists that are just starting out, or who are from minorities, because why should they if they're already making money?" EJ says. But among newer businesses, "I've found that the most successful music businesses are the ones that are extremely diverse. People come in with new ideas, with different backgrounds, and they see things that other people will miss."

I ask them what single change would help marginalised musicians. "Minorities supporting other minorities," EJ says. As EJ explains, artists and industry insiders from marginalised communities who do become successful have power, especially collectively, that they could use to move the needle for other marginalised people. "There are so many of us," EJ says. "It's fine blaming the people in power, looking at the biases in writing and in hiring. But taking a step back and just watching it happen means nothing is ever going to change."

CHAPTER 22:
FRIGHT CLUB

I 'm keen to find out what it's like to be an up-and-coming queer artist in Scotland today, and two very different artists were happy to be my guides: Mrs Frighthouse, an industrial noise metal band from Glasgow, and Livingston's Megan Black, who makes loose-limbed seventies-inspired funk and rock with wit and a strong splash of self-awareness: she describes her songs as "old man music but for the gays".

Mrs Frighthouse began as a marriage. Luna Frighthouse and her wife Carys were together for nine years before starting their musical partnership in late 2023. That musical partnership, while thrilling and attracting attention from taste-makers such as Apple Music's editors, who featured the band in their Breaking Metal playlist, isn't always an easy listen: their music is often violently cathartic and unsettling, living up to titles such as 'DIY EXORCISM'. *Metal Hammer* described their music as "like being sucker-punched by a tidal wave" and sounding "like the end of the world cranked up to 10".[216]

I ask Luna, who is trans, what it's like to be a queer musician in Scotland today. "For the most part it is amazing," she says. "There are lots of other queer musicians around, and other musicians are for the most part very accepting." The worry isn't so much the other musicians as other bands' audiences and, sometimes, venue staff. In 2024, she posted on social media after experiencing deeply unpleasant transphobia from a staff member in one of Scotland's best-known venues. Thankfully that kind of thing is relatively rare. "We've been embraced by a lot of people," Luna says. "Not just on the noise scene, but the wider metal scene and the alternative music scene. We all exist very much in different worlds, but we're all part of the same overall alternative music scene."

Luna was born in the mid-nineties and wasn't particularly aware of mainstream queer musicians; while she listened to bands like The Darkness and Queen, she didn't know that Freddie Mercury was gay and The Darkness singer and catsuit-enjoyer Justin Hawkins, while very much in the Freddie Mercury tradition of flamboyant frontmen, has made it clear that "my sexual persuasion is nobody's business but my own."[217]

"And then sort of around 2006 I discovered My Chemical Romance. While they're not a queer band, they've been very supportive of, and embraced by, queer people." Luna's musical tastes grew heavier, and she cites Korn as another example of a band who weren't necessarily queer – although singer Jonathan Davis "has spoken lots over the years about being bullied as a teenager for being gay, even though he was straight" – but who again made Luna feel part of their tribe. "And then I came across Placebo."

Placebo's singer, Brian Molko, was openly and happily bisexual, beautifully androgynous and sang songs with provocative titles such as 'Nancy Boy', and he arrived in Luna's life at the perfect time: she was struggling at college and was feeling very much like an outsider. "I was at secondary school around the time Section 28 ended, and that was when I discovered queer music."

"A lot of pivotal points in my life are linked to certain bands and certain artists," Luna explains. At the time of Luna's coming out and transitioning, one of those bands was Against Me! – whose singer, Laura Jane Grace, has become one of the most visible and admired trans musicians since she came out to *Rolling Stone* in 2012 and released the confessional album *Transgender Dysphoria Blues* in 2014.

At first, Luna tried not to listen. "I was aware of them when Laura came out, but almost on a subconscious level I didn't let myself listen to them because I was like, 'I don't want to open the floodgates,'" she says. Her thinking at the time was, she recalls, "I'm queer, not trans. Then when I finally started accepting myself, I put them on." The band's music would be part of the soundtrack to Luna's transition.

I ask Luna whether, like me, she's found a fearlessness since coming out. "Absolutely," she says. "Living as myself is the scariest thing I've ever done. So doing anything else may be hard, and it may be scary. But it's easy compared to that."

Musicians who felt seen in queer and queer-supportive music are now making their own contributions. Luna cites LA black metallers Agriculture and the excellently named London mathcore band Pupil Slicer as fellow travellers, with the latter being, "a metal band singing about the trans experience, and it's not just queer people that are into them. When you go and watch them, the majority of the people there are just cishet men who love metal, but they're embracing this band. You see that regularly." While queer bands represent a niche within the wider scene, "the people who love music will embrace the bands whoever they are. It creates a space where women and queer people can do heavy music and be accepted."

For someone who grew up feeling isolated at high school in the dying days of Section 28, and who's experienced abuse and even violence because of their queerness, that acceptance is profound. "You can see all these queer bands and know you're not alone," Luna says. "Things are really shifting."

"I grew up in a small town and it was horrendous being queer," Megan Black tells me, her eyes bright behind lemon-tinted John Lennon glasses. Black is bi. "I'm on the asexual spectrum as well. I dated guys in my teens, mainly because I was so scared of coming out." Like many musicians, Black found a creative outlet in music, and – unintentionally – her debut release also turned out to be her coming-out announcement. "I was nineteen when I wrote that song, just before lockdown," she recalls. "I didn't know if I liked anybody, but I've always felt a connection with women – and when I first had a crush on a woman, I wrote a song about it."

The song was a gorgeous piano ballad called 'Fur Coat Queen' and while she's self-deprecating about it – "I had a crush on a girl who used to wear a fur coat," she laughs. "That's kind of as deep as it goes" – it proved to be important. "It was picked up for a singer-songwriter award with the BBC, they interviewed me, and I told them what it was about. And then my parents were like, '*Okayyyyyy…*'"

With her secret no longer secret, Black decided, "I might as well own this. I'm just going to pick up every stigma I can think of about being bisexual and make it into a song." That song, the glam rock-tinged stomp of recent single 'Sweet Bisexual', is a lot of fun, but the words have sharp edges as Black sings about not being straight enough or gay enough and fearing she'll never fall in love; "I'll never be the queen." There's similar self-reflection in 'Funk for Introverts'. "I'm still learning how to be queer," she tells me. "I don't have a clue, I really don't."

Is it liberating to sing about those tensions, those doubts? Black nods. "'Sweet Bisexual' was written during lockdown, and I had nothing else to do but to try and deal with all this internalised misogyny and homophobia," she says. "It's very freeing when I see people sing it back to me. I remember someone saying to me that the song really helped them, and that part is *very* cool."

That's something Black herself experienced with other artists. She cites Bowie as a particularly big influence – "I don't know if he really *was* queer, but he had the vibe" – along with Lady Gaga. "It wasn't necessarily a case of, 'This person's queer, so that gives me permission'; it was more that for me, physical expression is a big thing so there were people I kind of wanted to look like. I didn't really want to look the same as a lot of my straight friends." For Black, there's a strong visual pull from queerness and androgyny. "A lot of artists just naturally camp things up, but I think that representation – seeing someone else doing something a bit strange and thinking, 'Oh, I like that. That's cool. I want to do that strange thing.' It's *yeahhhh*."

I tell Black that when I listen to her music I hear a lot of seventies LA expensive-studio cocaine rock. "That's a great description," she says with a smile before pointing out that while her music may sound like it's made by hedonists, she's usually in bed by 8pm.

The LA coke-rock scene was pretty promiscuous and dramatic, but it was also very straight and, in some cases, pretty problematic. That's something Black is very aware of, citing The Rolling Stones as an example of another band whose music she adores, but whose sexism she abhors. "A lot of the songs make me cringe a little, or a lot," she says. "I don't want to be like that. So how do we learn from it, how do we move on? How can we still make this cool music without objectifying women?" For Black, the challenge is: "How can I play this music I think is cool without being a dick?"

"My queerness is my personal business. I can put it into

songs, and I can celebrate it, and it definitely helps me narrow my target audience: they're the people I want listening to my music, and anyone else who wants to listen to it has to be accepting of that community. But I don't know everything. I'm just a wee queer guy, living my life and figuring things out."

Speaking to artists like Luna and Megan, and to other Scots artists in other parts of the country, I'm struck by the contrast between the musical worlds they inhabit and the much more toxic world of social media: where the former appear to be overwhelmingly open-minded, supportive and inclusive, social media feels very different for queer artists and queer people more generally. Some queer artists I was keen to interview for this book politely declined, citing their experiences of online abuse and harassment.

Part of the difference, I'm sure, is that for some people social media is rather like driving a big SUV: it can insulate you from the world around you and make you feel that you can be a terrible arsehole without facing any consequences, but I can't help thinking that this is also a demographic thing. Scotland's music scene, like any other group of people, has its racists, its right-wingers and its reactionaries. When it comes to anti-queer voices, the most vocal ones almost all seem to be at least a generation older than the teens and twentysome-things they deride. But the kids? The kids are all right.

CHAPTER 23:
MEN LIKE WIRE

I have a theory: I think the most interesting musicians are often the most interested. As much as I also love throwaway music made by idiots, the music and musicians I've really loved, the artists whose songs took up permanent residence in my head, were the ones whose *NME* and *Melody Maker* interviews sent me scurrying to the library, the ones whose passion for artists and art that were new to me expanded my horizons as well as my record collection, the ones who made me want to experience *more*: Bowie, The Smiths, Manic Street Preachers, Pet Shop Boys.

Not all of those artists were queer, but many of the ones who really struck a chord with me were either queer or queer-adjacent, and that leads me on to another of my pet theories: artists who, for whatever reason, are outsiders often tend to be observers, the kind of people who before they become famous are much more likely to pick up a Penguin paperback of Oscar Wilde than go to a wild party. They are watchers, inspectors, *collectors* with an insatiable appetite for art, for ideas, for experiences, and what they collect are base materials from which they create pure gold.

I'm very relieved that when I explain this theory to Hamish

Hawk, he doesn't laugh, look scared or start inching towards the door. Instead, he has his own suggestions of which artists made the best alchemists.

Hamish and I are sitting in an Edinburgh coffee shop on what is a rare day off for him: he's just launched his new album *A Firmer Hand* amid an intense run of gigs – twenty shows in eighteen days – and a short European jaunt supporting Travis. After years of hard work Hamish's star is heading heavenwards: having effortlessly sold out a run of shows in venues such as Glasgow's Saint Luke's, Hamish has just announced a headline show at Edinburgh's beautiful and cavernous Usher Hall and he and his band will be supporting Simple Minds when they play an enormous show at Glasgow's Bellahouston Park in the summer of 2025.

A Firmer Hand is a wonderful record made by the band that bears Hamish's name. Musically ambitious and lyrically provocative, it ranges from widescreen anthems and euphoric floor-fillers to almost unbearably intimate bedroom confessionals. It's unflinchingly honest, sometimes eye-openingly so. Were Alan Partridge to hear it, he'd undoubtedly proclaim, "Lynn! These are sex people!" I think I can get away with saying that because the album is also – intentionally – very funny in places. Hawk's lyrics have an arch sense of humour that reminds me of The Smiths, particularly songs such as 'Hand in Glove', and his songs are packed with vivid imagery, literary references and musical echoes that draw from a range of influences and genres. It's clear Hawk is a very interested artist indeed.

Like most of the musicians we've met in these pages, Hamish's early musical education came via his family. His dad loved sixties and seventies rock – "The Rolling Stones were his thing" – while his mum preferred The Kinks, The Swinging

Blue Jeans and "folkies" such as Kris Kristofferson, Cat Stevens, James Taylor, and Leonard Cohen.

"I had a bit of a tough time at school with bullies and that sort of thing," Hamish recalls, "so my dad would take me out for drives in the evening and after dinner. We'd go for a drive and I – I wouldn't be in the best shape." They didn't talk much during the drives, but each trip was soundtracked; Hamish remembers Bowie's 'Kooks', from *Hunky Dory,* as a regular and a particular highlight. "There's a line in there – if the homework brings you down then we'll throw it on the fire and take the car downtown. It sounds silly, but that was a real thing for me... a song of support, of succour. Just a kind voice."

Hawk was drawn to this pre-Ziggy Stardust version of Bowie. "This sort of maiden-esque figure on the front... I sort of know now, but I didn't know then why those songs spoke to me. I was fascinated not only by his language, but by the images he was putting together."

Hunky Dory, like many of his parents' favourites, was released long before Hawk was born: twenty years, in this case. Even now, *Hunky Dory* is striking: its cover was originally shot in black and white and then recoloured, with Bowie in a pose strongly reminiscent of iconic actresses Greta Garbo and Lauren Bacall, and if you're going to become obsessed with any Bowie album, *Hunky Dory* is an excellent choice: its many riches include the Lou Reed tribute 'Queen Bitch' as well as 'Changes' and 'Life on Mars?'

Hamish was also exposed to his siblings' musical tastes: his elder brother's hip-hop, metal and skate punk and his sister's Britpop: "Blur, Pulp, Oasis... it was Pulp, mainly. I remember hearing 'Disco 2000', 'Common People' and 'Underwear' playing through the walls of her room." As for the school-age Hamish? He was into Disney musicals, particularly the villains. "I'd play the films over and over again and break the tapes, the

VHSes. Just wear them out. It was the songs. It was always the songs," he says, adding with a smile, "If you take little moments out of all those different things and smash them together you really do get my music."

Hamish's first album was The White Stripes' *Elephant*. "I remember feeling at the time that I'd got into music late," he says. "Feeling at ten, eleven, twelve that I was late to the party." But he soon made up for lost time. "I bought Franz Ferdinand's *Franz Ferdinand* and thought, 'Aha!'" he recalls. Hamish became a voracious listener and obsessive gig-goer, and inevitably that love of music led to trying to make it.

I suggest that for most musicians, the first step is trying to emulate your heroes and failing dismally. Who was Hamish trying to be? "I was a big indie kid from the age of about thirteen to seventeen," he says. "It was that burgeoning indie scene in the UK that was post-Libertines: Franz Ferdinand, The Kooks, The Killers… and I liked landfill indie," he grins.

For Hamish, listening to any band would send him down a rabbit hole: if a band he liked recommended another, he'd go out of his way to hear them. That curiosity took him way beyond landfill indie and into much more interesting territory: Sigur Rós, The Flaming Lips, Belle and Sebastian, Soft Cell, Bronski Beat, Orange Juice and endless other artists across multiple genres and generations. "I was spring-boarded from one to the other: Franz Ferdinand have a song about Ivor Cutler so okay, I want to know about Ivor Cutler; they're working with this band called Sparks, so I want to hear about Sparks. I'm a total collector, and if I hear about some kind of association it feels like a secret alleyway that I can go down."

Franz Ferdinand loomed particularly large in Hamish's imagination – "I went to see them and Alex Kapranos stands at the front of the stage, this charged figure, almost androgyne – I know he's from Glasgow, but I'm looking at them as if they're from space. Alex is up on the monitor with his Telecaster like it's a weapon and I was just so totally starstruck."

That set a template that Hamish would later try to follow. "What I want is a distant alien figure on stage, whether it's The Liquid Room or Bar Bloc+ or Stereo or Mono or wherever, that room is not the same room when they're in it. That's what I'm trying to do when I'm on stage."

Back then Hamish didn't know that he'd end up as Franz Ferdinand's support act in 2022, or that another of his idols would sing the praises of his music: when Hawk released his 2023 album *Angel Numbers*, Pet Shop Boys' Neil Tennant posted one of the songs, 'Bridget St. John', to the Pet Shop Boys' Facebook page with the comment, "I really like this wistful song."[218] Hamish is effusive in his praise for Tennant, who he cites as a key influence – "one of the most visionary lyricists of the twentieth century" – alongside Stephin Merritt of The Magnetic Fields and The White Stripes' Jack White.

As a performer, Hawk has long been obsessed with stage-craft – "I was doing acting at school, I loved drama and I was learning a lot about theatre. I was obsessed with performance, what performers did to stages and what stages did to audiences. To this day I'm absolutely enamoured with the whole thing, the smell of the greasepaint and the dry ice. I love it so much that when venues don't necessarily have that vibe, I need to change it, I need people to come into this room and know that when we come on stage it's not going to be the same room anymore, for the next hour the rules are not the same. I like that, the electricity in the air and the fizz of it all. It's a spell and I'm still totally under it."

I mention Neil Tennant's horror at the stagewear of Oasis-era bands, bands who looked like off-duty plumbers rather than glamorous space aliens. Hamish nods and points out that that lack of a persona is still a persona. "If you're choosing to have your performance look like it's not a performance that's a valid choice, but it's still a choice, still a performance."

That's not Hamish's idea of a good time. "When we booked the Usher Hall, I did say – and maybe this doesn't make me look so great – I said, 'We're going to need to get some new clothes.' I need to make sure that on that stage I look like I'm *supposed* to be on that stage."

"I don't mean to sound all highfalutin, but I think I think about it more than anybody else does," Hamish says. "The idea that I'm going on stage not knowing what I'm doing, it's almost insulting. It's too important. I know what I'm doing. Every moment, every flick of the wrist, every movement of the microphone cord, it's no word of a lie to say that I've been studying these things. In watching bands and going to shows I've been collecting features, aspects, moments, moves, in the hope that I could smash them together and create something greater than the sum of the parts. There are magic tricks that I've learnt, and that I'm throwing back out there."

To an extent, I think Hamish's musical career has run in reverse: where many artists start out making urgent, sexually charged rock before moving into calmer singer-songwriter territory, he's gone in the opposite direction. I ask him what he thinks the teenage Hawk would have made of *A Firmer Hand*'s confidence, urgency and honesty. This would be a great opportunity for a glib soundbite, but Hamish takes the question seriously and thinks for a moment. "I think he'd have been shocked," he suggests.

Hamish doesn't find labels particularly useful, but his new record is the first time he's been completely frank about desire: where Hamish's lyrical influences such as Morrissey preferred not to gender the subjects of their songs in order to keep them as universal as possible, this is a record that's clearly mostly about men. "I consider myself attracted to all genders and sexualities," Hamish says. "I'm very open in that sense but I think my teenage self would be shocked at the volume of desire in this record that is so purely for men and for the masculine."

Listening back to his influences, Hamish says the connections between his musical loves and his own identity are more obvious now. "I had a preoccupation with these musicians and it's only now become clear why," he says. "Morrissey was one of them, Stephin Merritt was another, and Pet Shop Boys were another. There was something in their wordplay, something in their creativity, something in the worlds they created."

That something wasn't just musical. "I really do believe that there were things being whispered to me in this music, the significance of which I didn't fully appreciate at the time," he says. "Nowadays I think, *Of course! That's why I liked it!*"

Hamish and I compare notes on the clarity you get from seeing things in the rearview mirror that you perhaps weren't ready to accept at the time, of the almost subconscious connection with songs such as Pet Shop Boys' 'It's a Sin' and its words of shame and guilt and of wanting forgiveness. "There was something about that world that as a partly closeted person freaked me out. It was like, oh god, they're seeing into me too much."

"There's a knowledge that the Pet Shop Boys' music had of me and there's a knowledge that I had of the Pet Shop Boys' music, a completely unspoken secret knowledge that blew me open and challenged me in every corner of my own identity and shone, like came into every dark corner of my identity and shone a torch in it and said, 'Oh are you hiding in here, are you? Is there anything to see in here?'"

"It may sound odd, but I'm grateful to the music for that," Hamish says. "It forced me to reckon with myself. It wasn't always a pleasant thing to go through, but the music never felt threatening or hostile – not hostile to me. But hostile to whatever destructive force is keeping me not owning up to it, not speaking out about it."

"I don't think I've ever spoken at length about the influence of someone like Neil Tennant," Hawk says. But while the Hemingways of music tend to get a lot of attention – "The big-man writers, the tortured, whiskey-soaked guys, the big, barrel-chested lyricists" – and Hawk loves them too, the artists who really captured his imagination were the Neil Tennants, the Stephin Merritts, the David Bowies. "There are little flashes in their music that were like life rafts for me," Hamish says. "I would love to pay tribute in some way to the queer artists who paved the way."

CHAPTER 24:
ARE YOU AWAKE?

I n 1987, the Tories in England used the Conservative Party Conference in Blackpool to demonise gay and lesbian people. In 2023, they went to Manchester to turn their guns on LGBTQ+ people again, particularly trans, non-binary and gender non-conforming people. The faces may have changed, but the bigotry is all too familiar.

During their speeches, the Health Secretary, the Home Secretary and the Prime Minister each took turns to demonise "woke ideology", equality and diversity. They were particularly angry about the existence and human rights of trans people: health minister Steve Barclay vowed to ban trans women from women's hospital wards, ban trans men from men's wards and ban gender-neutral language from all NHS publications and guidance. Prime Minister Rishi Sunak, who had recently reneged on his party's promise to ban conversion therapy, aka bullying people into being someone they're not, puffed up his chest and told the sparse crowd that "we shouldn't get bullied into believing that people can be any sex they want to be."[219] As in 1987, the blue-rinse brigade rattled their pearls in approval and the papers hailed the speech as heroic.

Sunak would continue to demonise trans people and make

scripted anti-trans jokes in Parliament – including in early 2024 when he mocked trans women at Prime Minister's Questions knowing full well that the mother of Brianna Ghey, the teenage trans girl whose murderers had been sentenced just days before, was in attendance. He and his fellow ministers refused to apologise; most of the press excused or ignored it.

After the speeches, a handful of Tories danced for the cameras to live music by late-1990s dad-rockers Toploader, prompting comedian and national treasure Kathy Burke to post on Twitter that "Toploader must be really skint as well as being really shit."[220]

On the same evening that middle-aged Tories danced sexlessly to washed-up one-hit wonders, a much younger, more diverse and considerably more delightful crowd packed out a sold-out Glasgow's SWG3 to see Lauren Mayberry perform her first solo Scottish show, backed by an all-woman and non-binary band.

Mayberry is a brilliant pop star who has frequently used her platform as the singer of CHVRCHES, a band with an enormous queer fanbase and an obvious love of and influence by queer pop music dating back to the synth experiments of Wendy Carlos through the sonic experiments of SOPHIE, to denounce bigotry and stand up for marginalised people. So, it wasn't a huge surprise that mid-show, Lauren gave the Prime Minister both barrels while wearing a T-shirt demanding "safety, dignity and healthcare for all trans people".

"Fuck Rishi Sunak," she said, to cheers. "We need as much queer and trans energy as we can get."

The crowd roared in agreement.

Lauren Mayberry's musical tastes have always been wide: she grew up in a home soundtracked by her dad playing Yes and Brian Wilson and her mum playing Sade and Whitney

Houston, the latter of whom was an enormous influence. "One of those artists that I love purely and completely, but would never try to emulate," she tells me – alongside George Michael ("One of my favourite songwriters – and what a voice.") Music by queer artists has been part of the soundtrack to her life: "In university, I got very into Tegan and Sara and Rufus Wainwright (*Poses*, *Want One* and *Want Two* especially)," Lauren recalls, and she cites Bartees Strange, Ethel Cain and Phoebe Bridgers as some of her favourite contemporary lyricists. Among their many inspirations, CHVRCHES cite hyperpop as a current fascination, and the influence is audible on tracks such as 'He Said She Said', lead single from the *Screen Violence* album.

One of the key bands for the teenage Lauren was Riot grrrl pioneers Bikini Kill, and while she agrees with me that there's not a lot of Bikini Kill in CHVRCHES' music, she credits the fiercely feminist, bisexual singer Kathleen Hanna as a key influence both musically and more widely thanks to her intersectional, inclusive feminism. "I think Kathleen Hanna's ethos and how she has approached her work was impactful for me at a formative time," Lauren says. "Music was the way I was introduced to a lot of feminist ideas and Kathleen was at the forefront of so much of that, but I think her emphasis on intersectionality – and later critiquing lack of racial and other diversity in Riot grrrl – is what keeps her messaging as important in the present day."

The last time CHVRCHES played Glasgow, Mayberry dedicated their song 'Clearest Blue' – "Probably our gayest song ever," she announced with a grin – to Pride month, raising a huge cheer. "I'm really happy that CHVRCHES' music has resonated so much with the queer community," she told me. "It's been fortifying for me personally to have seen the fanbase expand from our original home on very straight, male music blogs to a much more diverse space."

Lauren agrees that for queer listeners there's "a common language in terms of shared influences – Pet Shop Boys, Depeche Mode, Eurythmics" – but she was still surprised by how much the band's queer fans in particular related to their *Screen Violence* album which, at the time of our conversation, is their most recent release. "From conversations I've had with some of our queer and trans fans, the horror inspiration of *Screen Violence* seems to have resonated in a different way, which was something I didn't consider when writing some of those lyrics."

It's not something I'd considered as a listener beyond really wanting one of the band's FINAL GIRL T-shirts, but of course it makes sense. The horror genre is beloved by queer people for many reasons: its gothic glamour, its eroticism, its tales of forbidden love, of body horror, of transformation, of people misunderstood and called monsters. I think for many queer people, horror movies can provide the cinematic equivalent of a rollercoaster: it's scary, but it's safe in a way the real world may not necessarily be.

Mayberry's *Screen Violence* songs of fear and survival are part of that tradition, delivering the same tension, suspense and catharsis as the celluloid that helped inspire them.

Lauren's kinship with the queer community and marginalised people isn't a recent development. Long before CHVRCHES, she was *The List*'s LGBT editor, and she was also a core part of the inclusive feminist collective TYCI (Tuck Your C**t In – "We didn't think too deeply about the moniker behind TYCI at the time – we just wanted something that felt punk and nineties, but now I don't think I would name it that.")

Mayberry's allyship is clearly heartfelt, and in the current climate it's also brave: as a woman in music Mayberry is no stranger to hate, and being such a vocal ally to trans people means being the target for even more abuse. I ask her whether she feels a responsibility to speak for her marginalised fans, and whether she feels she's helping to move the needle for them.

"In terms of allyship, those are things I think about a lot because of how my queer and trans friends have been treated – something that I do think has worsened in recent years because of the more high-profile media narratives," she tells me. That treatment isn't just torrents of online abuse. "I've been with friends when people have heckled them in the street or challenged them about which bathroom they're going into in a pub," she explains. "In this moment, if there's anything I can do that makes it clear which side of history I'd like to be on, I think that's worthwhile."

She continues, "There have been a lot of straight white feminists who have voiced some troubling opinions in recent years, especially when it comes to trans issues, and I don't want to be one of them. Obviously, there is a balance to be struck with how much we expect from public figures or who we put our faith in, but I know, as a fan, what it's like to feel let down by an artist you admire so I am conscious of wanting our LGBTQIA+ fanbase to know that they can feel safe."

That's a view shared by Shirley Manson, who says, "It's disappointing that we're still here having to fight for the rights of the LGBTQ+ community. But things are slowly improving."

"What's glorious," Manson continues, "and I try to remember this every time I feel dismay, is that back then, when we released 'Androgyny' and 'Cherry Lips' and 'Queer', there was no language in common for us to discuss, to explain, to describe, to glorify gender fluidity and the breaking of the binary. We just didn't have that language, and now we really do. And even though there's snide comments made about pronouns and this, that and the next thing, things are advancing whether the fucking right like it or not."

A few months after I speak to Mayberry and Manson, the entire country echoes Mayberry's "Fuck Rishi Sunak" announcement and gives the Tories the biggest electoral kicking in UK political history, while also turfing out notorious bigots from other parties and humiliating the newly formed anti-trans Party of Women, whose candidates lost their deposits in every constituency in which they stood. Most of them couldn't even attract as much support as Phin "Barmy Brunch" Adams of the Monster Raving Loony Party, a man with a baked beans mask on his head who promised to Make Brunch Great Again.

That does not magically make everything okay for LGBTQ+ people. Sunak's successor, Kier Starmer, who gained the nickname "queer harmer" before even taking office, has continued with the Tories' war on healthcare for trans teens, and appears to be as spineless and craven as many queer people feared; and in November 2024, to the absolute horror of most LGBTQ+ people and other marginalised groups, Donald Trump was re-elected as US President and began his second term in 2025 with an unprecedented assault on queer and trans people's human rights. But LGBTQ+ people are more visible, more connected, and stronger than ever before and one thing is very clear: today may be hard, but the future does not belong to the culture warriors, the pearl-clutchers and Toploader.

The future is much more enlightened, much more diverse, and it has a much better soundtrack.

CHAPTER 25:
THE SOUND OF YOUNG SCOTLAND

I n previous chapters, I asked whether today's queer musicians can ever have the cultural impact of their predecessors. I think the answer to that question is probably no, but that's largely because those predecessors had such a huge impact that they changed music, and the wider world, for the better. We're here, we're queer, and people are used to it.

These are still scary times for queer people, but there are more of us living authentically than ever before. In early 2024, a Gallup poll found that compared to 1.1 percent of the silent generation (born 1945 or earlier), 2.3 percent of baby boomers, 4.5 percent of generation X and 9.8 percent of generation Y, some 22.3 percent of generation Z – the generation born between 1997 and 2012 – identifies as LGBTQ+. That same summer, a US survey found that 44 percent of respondents aged eighteen to twenty-four described themselves as "not fully straight".

And the world's favourite music is queer.

I should probably explain.

When Alan Horne's Postcard Records brought us the disco-infused, anti-macho pop of Orange Juice and called it "the sound of young Scotland" he was having a bit of fun. Today, the sound of young America *is* the sound of young Scotland, and that sound doesn't just tolerate queerness but embraces it and celebrates it. Queer music is the very heartbeat of global pop.

I'm writing this in the summer of 2024. Billie Eilish is in the UK top ten singles chart with 'Lunch', her lustful lesbian banger; demisexual, lady-loving pop sensation Chappell Roan is in the same charts with her exuberant queer anthems not once, not twice, but three times; Charli XCX is in there too with singles from her newly released album *Brat*, which includes a tribute to SOPHIE and bears her influence proudly. When I turn on Apple Music to flick through its top video playlists, among the first videos it serves up in its chart hits playlist are Eilish's 'Lunch', Calvin Harris and Sam Smith's 'Desire' and Troye Sivan's 'One of Your Girls': lesbian lust, non-binary yearning and genderqueerness respectively.

Allyship is everywhere too. Another current chart topper, Hozier, has been a vocal ally from the get-go; and when Taylor Swift came to Edinburgh during Pride month, she spotted a woman proposing to her girlfriend during 'Cardigan'. A visibly delighted Swift congratulated them amid the cheers of nearly 70,000 Scots.

Skinny straight cis boys with guitars, while still capable of thrilling crowds and filling venues, barely feature in this new pop landscape and while not everyone is on board with this new normal – after a long hiatus Eminem has dug up his homophobic and transphobic alter ego, Slim Shady, and sits atop the singles chart as I write this – if you look a little further down the chart you'll see something rather lovely. A very beautiful slice of perfect pop, written by three young gay men, is climbing back into the UK charts forty years after it was first released after once again becoming a hit, this time on TikTok.

It's 'Smalltown Boy' by Bronski Beat.

CELEBRATE: A PLAYLIST

As much as I love writing about music, I'm very aware that reading about great songs can only ever be a poor substitute for listening and dancing to them. I've put together a playlist featuring many of the songs from the book by queer artists and by some of the artists who've influenced or been influenced by them, and you'll find it on Apple Music and on Spotify; if you'd rather not stream, it makes a pretty good shopping list too.

While the playlist does include a lot of music from long ago, many of the artists you'll hear are making and playing music right here and right now. In the Spotify era that doesn't pay so well, or pay at all, so I'd love it if you went to their shows, bought their music on physical media or treated yourself to their merchandise, and I'm sure they'd love it too.

Hound Dog - Big Mama Thornton
Didn't It Rain? - Sister Rosetta Tharpe
Hittin' on Nothing - Esquerita
Private Idaho - The B-52's
Magic - Pilot
Ever Fallen in Love (With Someone You Shouldn't've) - Buzzcocks
Flying Saucer Attack - The Rezillos
Party Fears Two - The Associates

A Matter of Gender – The Associates
Rip It Up – Orange Juice
Please Stay – The Cryin' Shames
Baby Honey – The Pastels
You Make Me Feel (Mighty Real) – Jimmy Somerville
The Rattler – Goodbye Mr Mackenzie
Suffocate Me – Angelfish
Careful – Horse
The Road Less Travelled – Horse McDonald
Male Stripper – Man 2 Man ft Paul Zone & Miki Zone
Bits + Pieces – Artemesia
Move Your Body – Marshall Jefferson
Discipline – Throbbing Gristle
Detestimony – Finitribe
Move Any Mountain – The Shamen
Tainted Love – Coil
Mother Universe – The Soup Dragons
Celebrate – HiFi Sean & David McAlmont
Supervixen – Garbage
Queer – Garbage
In Remote Part / Scottish Fiction – Idlewild
These Important Years – Hüsker Dü
If I Can't Change Your Mind – Sugar
Electrolite – R.E.M.
Sunday Morning – Michael Stipe
Hand in Glove – The Smiths
Michael – Franz Ferdinand
Johnny Delusional – FFS
Sweeter Than Honey – Jill Jackson
Other Side of the World – KT Tunstall
Brighter Days – Emili Sandé
Lemonade – SOPHIE
Whole New World / Pretend World – SOPHIE

So I - Charli XCX
Venom - LVRA ft. Spent and TAALIAH
Reason Why - SOPHIE
Folks Songs EP - Over/At *(not available on streaming services; find it on over-at.bandcamp.com)*
Rebel Girl - Bikini Kill
Not Ur Girl - Brat Coven
Tea Jenny - Venus In The Lake
Rise Up! - Steeljoy
Mountains - Man of the Minch
I'm Not Alone - Laura Jane Wilkie
She Moves Me - Kim Carnie
Fever - Kashmir Crows *(not available on streaming services; find it on kashmircrows.bandcamp.com)*
Sound of the Underground - Edinburgh Gay Men's Chorus
Liberation - Pet Shop Boys
Chosen Family - Rina Sawayama
Can't Touch This - Eyve
True Love - Erin Friel
Panda - Sweet Rogue
Just Don't Stop - Steg G & The Freestyle Master
The Warping - Walt Disco
Macilent (TAAHLIAH remix) - Walt Disco
Everyday - Sacred Paws
Real Woman - Comfort
DIY EXORCISM - Mrs Frighthouse
Fur Coat Queen - Megan Black
Sweet Bisexual - Megan Black
Kooks - David Bowie
Juliet as Epithet - Hamish Hawk
Men Like Wire - Hamish Hawk
The Book of Love - The Magnetic Fields
It's a Sin - Pet Shop Boys

Change Shapes – Lauren Mayberry
Final Girl – CHVRCHES
Clearest Blue – CHVRCHES
Smalltown Boy – Bronski Beat

To save you a bit of typing (the web links are long),
I've linked them directly from

CARRIEM.CO.UK/SMALL-TOWN-JOY

ENDNOTES

1 "Tchaikovsky and the secret gay loves censors tried to hide", Dalya Alberge, *The Observer*, 3 June 2018. theguardian.com/ music/2018/jun/02/tchaikovsky-letters-saved-from-censors-reveal-secret-loves-homosexuality.

2 "Was Chopin gay? The awkward question in one of the EU's worst countries for LGBTQ rights", Rob Picheta, *CNN*, 29 November 2020. edition.cnn.com/2020/11/29/europe/ chopin-sexuality-poland-lgbtq-debate-scli-intl/index.html.

3 "Interview with Leon Botstein", Marietta Steinhart, *Austria.info*. austria.info/en/culture/franz-schubert-poet-and-liederfuerst/interview-with-leon-botstein.

4 "George Frideric Handel", *LGBT Archive*, 21 June 2016. lgbthistoryuk.org/wiki/George_Frideric_Handel.

5 "Britten & Pears", Dr Lucy Walker, *Britten Pears Arts*. brittenpearsarts.org/news/britten-pears.

6 "There are places I'll remember… The Beatles' Liverpool… And beyond", *Beatles Liverpool Locations*, 8 April 2021. beatlesliverpoollocations.blogspot.com/2021/04/ john-lennon-childhood-in-photographs.html.

7 "Lou Reed creates a list of the 10 best records of all time", Josh Jones, *Open Culture*, 22 May 2017. openculture.com/2017/ 05/lou-reed-creates-a-list-of-the-10-best-albums-of-all-time.html.

8 "Little Richard Dies Aged 87", *davidbowie.com*, 5 September 2020. davidbowie.com/blog/2020/5/9/little-richard-dies-aged-87.

9 "The Who's Pete Townshend says he used to be pansexual", Charlotte Krol, *NME*, 1 June 2021. nme.com/news/music/the-whos-pete-townshend-says-he-used-to-be-pansexual-2953238.

10 "Yoko Ono Reveals John Lennon Was Bisexual – Which Makes Sense Because We're All On A Sexual Spectrum, Even Beatles", E. Alex Jung, *Vulture*, 14 October 2015. vulture.com/2015/10/yoko-ono-lennon-had-sexual-desire-for-men.html.

11 "The Beatles shaped American culture, explaining their enduring appeal", Randall J. Stephens, *The Washington Post*, 10 December 2021. washingtonpost.com/outlook/2021/12/10/beatles-reshaped-american-culture-explaining-their-enduring-appeal/.

12 Ibid.

13 "Rainbow Europe Map and Index 2015", *ILGA Europe*, 10 May 2015. ilga-europe.org/report/rainbow-europe-2015/.

14 "Religious Affiliation by Birth Decade, 1900-9 to 1980-9", *British Religion In Numbers*. www.brin.ac.uk/figures/affiliation-and-attendance-from-1983/religious-affiliation-by-birth-decade-1900-9-to-1980-9/.

15 "Commons Amendment", *Hansard 1803-2005*. api.parliament.uk/historic-hansard/lords/1921/aug/15/commons-amendment-2.

16 "SNP leadership: Kate Forbes defends gay marriage stance", *BBC News*, 21 February 2023. bbc.co.uk/news/uk-scotland-64715944.

17 "Scottish Tory leadership candidate Murdo Fraser says he still doesn't support gay marriage", Faye Brown, *Sky News*, 23 August 2024. news.sky.com/story/scottish-tory-leadership-candidate-murdo-fraser-says-he-still-doesnt-support-gay-marriage-13201550.

18 "Gay marriages to go ahead after historic vote by MSPs", *The Herald*, 4 February 2014, heraldscotland.com/news/13144026.gay-marriages-go-ahead-historic-vote-msps/.

19 "Four stories of life in Scotland when being gay
meant a jail sentence", Georgia McShane, *The Herald*,
9 July 2017, heraldscotland.com/news/15399288/
four-stories-life-scotland-gay-meant-jail-sentence/.

20 "I'm still haunted by sex abuse hell at the hands of my manager,
admits Pat McGlynn in Secrets of the Bay City Rollers doc",
Jess Lester, *The Sun*, 27 June 2023. thesun.co.uk/tv/22820335/
bay-city-rollers-pat-mcglynn-sex-abuse-tam-paton/.

21 "Bay City Roller Les McKeown died
'with a heavy heart'", Victoria Pease, *STV News*,
September 8, 2021, news.stv.tv/entertainment/
bay-city-roller-les-mckeown-died-with-a-heavy-heart.

22 "John Carpenter: a conversation with the horror master,"
Alex Denney, *Dazed*, 24 October 2017. dazeddigital.com/music/
article/37844/1/john-carpenter-interview.

23 "After a Sex Change and Several Eclipses, Wendy Carlos Treads
a New Digital Moonscape", Susan Reed, *People*, 1 July 1985. web.
archive.org/web/20090604133951/http://www.people.com/
people/archive/article/0,,20091206,00.html.

24 Darryl W Bullock, *Pride, Pop & Politics.* Omnibus Press, 2022,
p. 151.

25 Jon Savage, *The Secret Public*. Faber & Faber, 2024, p. 593.

26 Vic Galloway, *Rip it Up*. MNSE, 2018.

27 "Outpunk Magazine", Queer Music Heritage,
queermusicheritage.com/jul2009qg11.html.

28 Ibid.

29 Ibid.

30 "On this day in 1976 – Sex Pistols play their first
Scottish gig," Alison Campsie, *The Scotsman*, 12 October
2020. scotsman.com/heritage-and-retro/heritage/
on-this-day-1976-sex-pistols-play-their-first-scottish-gig-3000466.

31 "The Clash, the Pistols and the Stranglers: punk revolution in the air", Russell Leadbetter, *The Herald*, 29 May 29 2023. heraldscotland.com/business_hq/23554243. clash-pistols-stranglers-punk-revolution-air/.

32 "Strength in Numbers: A Social History of Glasgow's Popular Music Scene (1979-2009)", Robert Anderson, theses.gla.ac.uk, theses.gla.ac.uk/6459/1/2015andersonphd.pdf.

33 Simon Goddard, *Simply Thrilled: The Preposterous Story of Postcard Records*. Ebury Press, 2018 edition, p. 27.

34 Jon Savage, *The Secret Public*. Faber & Faber, 2024, p. 597.

35 "You've got to say yes to another excess: Alan Rankine on his friend and fellow Associate Billy Mackenzie", Teddy Jamieson, *The Herald*, 7 May 2016, heraldscotland.com/life_style/arts_ents/14476983.got-say-yes-another-excess-alan-rankine-friend-fellow-associate-billy-mackenzie/.

36 Ibid.

37 "The Associates: The Affectionate Punch", Paul Morley, *billymackenzie.com*. http://www.billymackenzie.com/articles/nmeaprev80.htm.

38 Ibid.

39 "Chocolate Guitars and Billy Mackenzie: Alan Rankine Talks About Life in The Associates", Paul Gallagher, *Dangerous Minds*, 6 August 2016. dangerousminds.net/comments/chocolate_guitars_and_billy_mackenzie_alan_rankine_talks_about_life_in_the_.

40 "Goodbye mr mackenzie", Paul Lester, *billymackenzie.com*. billymackenzie.com/articles/uncut0697.htm.

41 Ibid.

42 Ibid.

43 "You've got to say yes to another excess: Alan Rankine on his friend and fellow Associate Billy MacKenzie", Teddy Jamieson, *The Herald*, 7 May 2016. heraldscotland.com/life_style/

arts_ents/14476983/got-say-yes-another-excess-alan-rank-ine-friend-fellow-associate-billy-mackenzie/.

44 "Goodbye mr mackenzie", Paul Lester, *billymackenzie.com*. billymackenzie.com/articles/uncut0697.htm.

45 "You've got to say yes to another excess: Alan Rankine on his friend and fellow Associate Billy MacKenzie", Teddy Jamieson, *The Herald*, 7 May 2016. heraldscotland.com/life_style/arts_ents/14476983.got-say-yes-another-excess-alan-rankine-friend-fellow-associate-billy-mackenzie/.

46 "Alan Rankine of The Associates Passes Away At 64", Alice Teeple, *Post-Punk.com*, 3 January 2023. post-punk.com/alan-rankine-of-the-associates-passes-away-at-64/.

47 Ibid.

48 "Getting Nostalgic With Annie Lennox," Jase Peeples, *Advocate*, 29 October 2014. advocate.com/music/2014/10/29/getting-nostalgic-annie-lennox.

49 Simon Goddard, *Simply Thrilled: The Preposterous Story of Postcard Records*. Ebury Press, 2014.

50 Ibid.

51 "Orange Juice," Andrew Shields, *toppermost.co.uk*. toppermost.co.uk/orange-juice/.

52 "Orange Juice: 'If anything became too smooth, Edwyn Collins liked to fuck it up'", Alastair McKay, *Uncut*, 20 June 2014. uncut.co.uk/features/orange-juice-if-anything-became-too-smooth-edwyn-collins-liked-to-fuck-it-up-7627/.

53 Ibid.

54 "Rip It Up," *anyonecanplyaguitar.co.uk*. anyonecanplayguitar.co.uk/rip-it-up/.

55 "Rip It Up: Most Influential Scottish Artists," Tallah Brash, *The Skinny*, 20 June 2018. theskinny.co.uk/music/rip-it-up/rip-it-up-most-influential-scottish-artists.

56 "Love Songs #12 / Blue Boy", *Ban Ban Ton Ton*, 25 April 2018. banbantonton.com/2018/04/25/love-songs-11-blue-boy/.

57 "Homage Not Fromage: Jimmy Somerville Interview", John Freeman, *The Quietus*, 25 March 2015. thequietus.com/interviews/jimmy-somerville-interview/.

58 Ibid.

59 "The Night They Drove Old Disco Down", Jack R. Johnson, *North of the James*, June, 2023. northofthejames.com/the-night-disco-died.

60 "The night when straight white males tried to kill disco", Hadley Meares, *Aeon*, 28 February 2017. aeon.co/ideas/the-night-when-straight-white-males-tried-to-kill-disco.

61 "The Flip Sides of 1979," Dave Marsh, *Rolling Stone*, 27 December 1979. rollingstone.com/music/music-news/the-flip-sides-of-1979-113608/.

62 "How Bronski Beat's Jimmy Somerville Survived the '80s", Max Dax, *Electronic Beats*, 11 March 2015. electronicbeats.net/jimmy-somerville-interview/.

63 "Homage Not Fromage: Jimmy Somerville Interview", John Freeman, *The Quietus*, 25 March 2015. thequietus.com/interviews/jimmy-somerville-interview/.

64 "Exclusive Interview with Jimmy Somerville: 'A Huge Part of Soho's Culture and History Has Gone – It's Been Wiped Off the Map'", Ray Kinsella, *Madame Soho*, 17 November 2015. madamesoho.com/2015/11/17/exclusive-interview-with-jimmy-somerville-a-huge-part-of-sohos-culture-and-history-has-gone-its-been-wiped-off-the-map/.

65 Ibid.

66 "It struck a chord because it could be anyone's story", Jimmy Somerville, *The Guardian*, 12 November 2006. theguardian.com/music/2006/nov/12/popandrock27.

67 "Exclusive Interview with Jimmy Somerville: 'A Huge Part of Soho's Culture and History Has Gone – It's Been Wiped Off the Map'", Ray Kinsella, *Madame Soho*, 17 November 2015. madamesoho.com/2015/11/17/exclusive-interview-with-jimmy-somerville-a-huge-part-of-sohos-culture-and-history-has-gone-its-been-wiped-off-the-map/.

68 "Fakin' It/Makin' It: Falsetto's Bid for Transcendence in 1970s Disco Highs." Anne-Lise François, *Perspectives of New Music*, vol. 33, no. 1/2, 1995, pp. 442–57. JSTOR. jstor.org/stable/833714. Accessed October 8, 2024.

69 Peter Shapiro, *Turn the Beat Around: The Secret History of Disco*. New York: Faber and Faber, 2005.

70 "You Make Me Feel (Mighty Real) – Sylvester", Jami Smith, songsthatsavedyou.com, 8 June 2023. songsthatsavedyourlife. substack.com/p/no7-you-make-me-feel-mighty-real.

71 "Sylvester (singer)," Wikimedia Foundation. en.wikipedia.org/wiki/Sylvester_(singer).

72 "You Make Me Feel (Mighty Real) – Sylvester", Jami Smith, songsthatsavedyou.com, 8 June 2023. songsthatsavedyourlife. substack.com/p/no7-you-make-me-feel-mighty-real.

73 "Today marks 40 Years (!) since 'Smalltown Boy' was released!", Somerville, Jimmy, *Facebook*. facebook.com/reel/827148235934087.

74 "Musician Horse McDonald: 10 things that changed my life", Lorraine Wilson, *The National*, 3 April 2022, thenational.scot/news/20040560. musician-horse-mcdonald-10-things-changed-life/.

75 "Role Models: Being Yourself – LGBT Lives in Scotland", Horse McDonald, *Stonewall Scotland*, 2021. lgbteducation.scot/ wp-content/uploads/2021/10/role_models_-_web.pdf.

76 "Tegan and Sara on how sexism and homophobia hasn't changed in the music industry", Sam Damshenas, *Gay Times*, 18 September 2019. gaytimes.com/culture/

tegan-and-sara-dont-think-the-music-industry-has-changed-since-their-debut/.

77 ""Male Stripper" by Man 2 Man Meet Man Parrish has always had a v. special place in my heart & I'm always proud to tell people it is (possibly) the best selling", Keith McIvor, @JDTwitch, *X*, 11 September 2018, 11:49pm. x.com/JDTwitch/status/1039647243580653568.

78 "You do know that @DasGiftBerlin thought the words were "I was a male stripper in a local bar", yes?", Stuart Braithwaite, @plasmatron, *X*, 12 September 2018, 12:00am. x.com/plasmatron/status/1039649916304478209.

79 "It never gets old. A great hook. I even like the shoddy remix cover that's doing rounds just now. Always reminds me of the waltzers at the shows", Paul Croan, @alextronic, *X*, 12 September 2018. 09:43am. x.com/alextronic/status/1039796706345451520.

80 "From the archive: romance at Glasgow's dance halls", *The Guardian*, 12 February 2014. heraldscotland.com/news/13091975.from-the-archive-romance-at-glasgows-dance-halls/.

81 "Interview: Yogi Haughton," *In the Beginning*, 26 April 2020, inthebeginningpress.wordpress.com/2020/04/26/interview-yogi-haughton/.

82 "Eterna: Scotland's Undying Techno Love," Ian McQuaid, *Boiler Room*, 16 May 2015. boilerroom.tv/eterna-scotlands-undying-techno-love/.

83 "Marshall Jefferson: Master of the house," Bruce Tantum, *DJ Mag*, 20 January 2020. djmag.com/longreads/marshall-jefferson-master-house.

84 Grant McPhee, *Postcards From Scotland: Scottish Independent Music 1983-1995*. Omnibus Press, 2024, p. 290.

85 Ibid, 292.

86 "Art & Gender: The Interview," Megan Walters, *chrisconnelly.com*, 6 October 2017. chrisconnelly.com/news/music/2017/10/

art-gender-the-interview/.

87 "Rise of the machines: how industrial music took over the world", Jonathan Selzer, *Metal Hammer*, 16 April 2020. louder-sound.com/features/1988-the-year-industrial-broke.

88 "Cult heroes: Optimo (Espacio) – the club night that defied expectation and defined a generation", David Pollock, *The Guardian*, 11 October 2016. theguardian.com/music/2016/oct/11/cult-heroes-optimo-espacio-club-night-keith-mcivor-jonnie-wilkes-djs.

89 "HIV and AIDS in Edinburgh and the Lothians, 1983-2010," HIV/AIDS online resources for teachers. hiv-aids-resources.is.ed.ac.uk/historical-context/#fn1.

90 "How Edinburgh became the AIDS capital of Europe," Steven Brocklehurst, *BBC News*, 1 December 2019, bbc.co.uk/news/uk-scotland-50473604.

91 *Smash Hits magazine* (Issue 215 – 25th February – 10th March 1987), page. 7.

92 "All You Need Is Love (JAMS song)," *Wikimedia Foundation*. en.wikipedia.org/wiki/All_You_Need_Is_Love_(JAMs_song).

93 "Aids campaign: Thatcher 'fought against risky sex warnings'", Justin Parkinson, *BBC News*, 8 February 2021. bbc.co.uk/news/uk-politics-55973726.

94 "Speech to Conservative Party conference", *Margaret Thatcher Foundation*. margaretthatcher.org/document/106941.

95 Kestral Gaian, *Twenty-Eight*, Reconnecting Rainbows Press, 2022.

96 "Dave Grohl discusses how The B-52's 'opened up a whole new world'", Jack Whatley, *Far Out Magazine*, 12 September 2022. faroutmagazine.co.uk/dave-grohl-discusses-how-the-b-52s-opened-up-a-whole-new-world/.

97 "Scottish Pride: An interview with Simon Neil of Biffy Clyro",

Randy Shulman, *Metro Weekly*, 13 April 2017. metroweekly.
com/2017/04/scottish-pride-interview-simon-neil-biffy-clyro/.

98 Old Bad Habits Label, "OBHLP015 – Silent Industry".
oldbadhabitslabel.bandcamp.com/album/obhlp015-silent-industry.

99 "London was everything. Great crowd. My husband Silver
saw us on stage for the first time ever and he loved it. Newcastle
tonight. Pic by Diana Pisani", Sean Dickson (@TheSoupDragons),
X, 1 November 2023, 8:04am. x.com/TheSoupDragons/
status/1719626462242771180.

100 "HiFi Sean & David McAlmont – Happy Ending – album
review," Iain Key, *Louder Than War*, 4 February 2023. louderthanwar.
com/hifi-sean-david-mcalmont-happy-ending-album-review/.

101 "HiFi Sean & David McAlmont," Martin Aston, *Mojo*. archive.
org/details/mojo-march-2023/page/87/mode/1up?view=theater.

102 "McAlmont & Butler's Debut Album 'The Sound of
McAlmont & Butler' Turns 25 – Anniversary Retrospective,"
Patrick Corcoran, *Albumism*, 26 November 2020. albumism.com/
features/mcalmont-butler-debut-album-the-sound-of-mcalmont-
butler-turns-25-anniversary-retrospective.

103 "Liam Gallagher's homophobia has gone unchallenged for
years. I saw him heckle Kylie with "Lesbian!" and Robbie with
"Queer!" at the Q Awards and everyone just", Simon Price
(@simon_price01), *X*, 8 January 2018, 11:10am, x.com/
simon_price01/status/950323750205083649.

104 "ABC FIGURES: NME out of rhythm", campaignlive.
co.uk, 18 February 1999. campaignlive.co.uk/article/
abc-figures-nme-rhythm/59266.

105 "Loaded editor gets straight to the point", *Press Gazette*,
16 July 2007, pressgazette.co.uk/comment-analysis/
loaded-editor-gets-straight-to-the-point/.

106 "The Queerest of the Queer: Listening to Garbage in the
Nineties", Niko Stratis, *Catapult*, 24 January 2022. magazine.catapult.

co/column/stories/niko-stratis-everyone-is-gay-queerest-of-the-queer-listening-garbage-band-nineties-shirley-manson-music.

107 "Recording Garbage", Sam Inglis, *Sound On Sound*, June, 2002. soundonsound.com/people/recording-garbage.

108 "I wouldn't be in a band if it weren't for Shirley Manson. I discovered @garbage at a pivotal time. Shirley's voice, heart+fearlessness inspire me to this day", Lauren Mayberry (@laurenevemay), *X*, 13 February 2018, 5:53am. x.com/laurenevemay/status/963290052196552706.

109 "#waw the amazing Shirley Manson, singer of Garbage. One of the only women in the 90s that really cornered a sound all her own.", Lzzy Hale (@officiallzzyhale), *Instagram*, 19 February 2014. instagram.com/p/knDEGNo39X/.

110 "Q&A: How Evanescence's Amy Lee Got Her Groove Back On 'The Bitter Truth'", Steve Baltin, *Forbes*, 25 March 2021, forbes.com/sites/stevebaltin/2021/03/25/qa-how-evanescences-amy-lee-got-her-groove-back-on-the-bitter-truth/.

111 "Happy Birthday Florence Welch: Revisiting her 2010 interview with Hot Press", Stuart Clark, *Hot Press*, 28 August 2019, hotpress.com/music/happy-birthday-florence-welch-revisiting-2010-interview-hot-press-22786232.

112 "Blonde On Blonde: Lady Gaga Interviews Debbie Harry", Lady Gaga, *Harper's Bazaar*, 5 August 2011. harpersbazaar.com/celebrity/latest/news/a771/lady-gaga-interviews-debbie-harry-blondie-0911/.

113 "Siouxsie Sioux", *Wikimedia Foundation*, en.wikipedia.org/wiki/Siouxsie_Sioux.

114 "25 years of Idlewild: Our Influences Playlist" on Spotify.

115 "Hüsker Dü", *Wikimedia Foundation*, en.wikipedia.org/wiki/H%C3%BCsker_D%C3%BC.

116 "Grant Hart", David Jarnstrom, *Modern Drummer*, 22 November 2011. moderndrummer.com/2011/11/

grant-hart/?srsltid=AfmBOorgukDA2J-
ImKLvEFvdJzIR8jHBO9tI3hHrL5H0d8wAh6eM29aJ.

117 "10 things that changed my life: Idlewild's Roddy Woomble",
Nan Spowart, *The National*, 23 May 2021, thenational.scot/
news/19322269.10-things-changed-life-idlewilds-roddy-
woomble/.

118 "Bob Mould, alt-rock's gay icon, takes on American evil: 'My
head's on fire!'", Stevie Chick, *The Guardian*, 30 September 2020.
theguardian.com/music/2020/sep/30/bob-mould-alt-rocks-gay-
icon-takes-on-american-evil-my-heads-on-fire.

119 "Queer rocker Bob Mould on coming out later in life:
'Why didn't I do this a little sooner?'", Lyndsey Parker, *Yahoo!
Entertainment*, 21 June 2019. yahoo.com/entertainment/queer-
rocker-bob-mould-on-coming-out-late-in-life-why-didnt-i-do-
this-a-little-sooner-184759277.html?guccounter=1.

120 Ibid.

121 Ibid.

122 Ibid.

123 Ibid.

124 "Nine Songs: Roddy Woomble", Ed Nash, *The Line of
Best Fit*, 18 August 2017. thelineofbestfit.com/features/lists/
roddy-woomble-chooses-nine-favourite-songs.

125 "The Smiths: Out to Save Rock & Roll", James Henke,
Rolling Stone, 7 June 1984. rollingstone.com/music/music-features/
the-smiths-out-to-save-rock-roll-62389/.

126 Ibid.

127 "Bigmouth strikes again and again: why Morrissey fans feel
so betrayed", Tim Jonze, *The Guardian*, 30 May 2019. theguardian.
com/music/2019/may/30/bigmouth-strikes-again-morrissey-
songs-loneliness-shyness-misfits-far-right-party-tonight-show-jim-
my-fallon.

128 "For Britain Movement", *Wikimedia Foundation*. en.wikipedia.org/wiki/For_Britain_Movement.

129 "Morrissey expresses sympathy for jailed ELD founder Tommy Robinson", Ben Beaumont-Thomas, *The Guardian*, 7 June 2018. theguardian.com/music/2018/jun/07/morrissey-express-es-sympathy-for-jailed-edl-founder-tommy-robinson.

130 "Morrissey: Unfortunately, I am Not Homosexual", Miriam Coleman, *Rolling Stone*, 20 October 2013. rollingstone.com/music/music-news/morrissey-unfortunately-i-am-not-homosexual-97985/.

131 "Former Smiths guitarist Johnny Marr: Glasgow is one of my favourite places to play, even though there were only 11 people at first gig", John Dingwall, *The Daily Record*, 23 June 2013. dailyrecord.co.uk/entertainment/celebrity-interviews/former-smiths-guitarist-johnny-marr-1978545.

132 BrasoBiadonsky, comment on "Franz Ferdinand – Michael (Official Video)," *Domino Recording Co*, 12 February 2011, *YouTube*. youtube.com/watch?v=ktwlN_ocL-o.

133 "Madonna, Christina Aguilera, Britney Spears and Missy Elliott – Like a Virgin/Hollywoodt (Rehearsal).", *Xtina Daily*, 23 June 2023, *YouTube*. youtube.com/watch?v=e3gaF0lo4JU.

134 "Friends Too Much Penis For A Dress Like That!." Tarpey, Anthony. 15 August 2013, *YouTube*. youtube.com/watch?v=6Jla-_To3HA.

135 "Transphobia on Film: A Look at Ace Venture: Pet Detective." Malmrose Projects, 2 March 2018, *YouTube*. youtube.com/watch?v=yJmxI3dbozc.

136 "Naked Gun 3 1/3: The Final Insult: Cherry cake." Nizzinny. 22 August 2013, *YouTube*. youtube.com/watch?v=KzC6j1QpK5g.

137 "i'm not a fag, i'm a werewolf." Secret C. 15 August 2012, *YouTube*. youtube.com/watch?v=57SSuRbQDxE.

138 "The Blue Oyster Bar 1." Teschner, Christian, 9 April 2013, *YouTube*. youtube.com/watch?v=niumQLDL_k0.

139 "Crocodile Dundee "lady" in bar." Slippin Jimmy. 10 February 2015, *YouTube*. youtube.com/watch?v=n6fgPX3NjyA.

140 "All 235 Dead Lesbian and Bisexual Characters on TV, and How They Died", Reise, *Autostraddle*, 27 February 2023. autostraddle.com/all-65-dead-lesbian-and-bisexual-characters-on-tv-and-how-they-died-312315/.

141 Ibid.

142 "Great LezBritain: Interview with Jill Jackson," *AfterEllen*, 7 February 2011. afterellen.com/great-lezbritain-interview-with-jill-jackson/.

143 "So I thought I would share with you an interested tweet on my account this morning", Jill Jackson, *Facebook*, 3 May 2020. facebook.com/jilljacksonofficial/posts/so-i-thought-i-would-share-with-you-an-interesting-tweet-on-my-account-this-morn/1104900766556680/.

144 "The Queen Tut's Stage @ TRNSMT … Let's Talk About It," abbiemeehan, *industryme.co.uk*. industryme.co.uk/the-queen-tuts-stage-trnsmt-lets-talk-about-it/.

145 Douglas Adams, *The Hitchhiker's Guide to the Galaxy*. Pan Books, 1979, p. 36.

146 "So I thought I would share with you an interested tweet on my account this morning", Jill Jackson, *Facebook*, 3 May 2020. facebook.com/jilljacksonofficial/posts/so-i-thought-i-would-share-with-you-an-interesting-tweet-on-my-account-this-morn/1104900766556680/.

147 "Legendary: The Badass with The Bass, Suzi Quatro", VK Lynne, *Guitar Girl*, 18 September 2017. guitargirlmag.com/interviews/legendary-bassist-suzi-quatro/.

148 "KT Tunstall on Why Kissing Girls Wasn't Just a Phase and Channeling Her Masculinity ('I Feel Like I Have a C★ck," Chris

Azzopardi, *pridesource.com*, 6 September 2016. pridesource.com/article/78022-2.

149 "KT Tunstall doesn't consider herself a 'locked-down straight person'", Sam Damshenas, *Gay Times*, 23 November 2018. gaytimes.com/culture/kt-tunstall-doesnt-consider-herself-a-locked-down-straight-person/.

150 "KT Tunstall on Why Kissing Girls Wasn't Just a Phase and Channeling Her Masculinity ('I Feel Like I Have a C★ck," Chris Azzopardi, *pridesource.com*, 6 September 2016. pridesource.com/article/78022-2.

151 "Emeli Sandé shares first loved-up snaps with new girlfriend after coming out in heartfelt post", Shannon Power, *The Sun*, 2 April 2022. thesun.co.uk/tvandshowbiz/18147618/emeli-sande-first-snaps-new-girlfriend-coming-out-heartfelt/.

152 "Sophie, Who Pushed the Boundaries of Pop Music, Dies at 34", Jon Pareles, *The New York Times*, 31 January 2021. nytimes.com/2021/01/30/arts/music/sophie-dead.html.

153 "Sophie", *A.G. Cook*, February 2021. agcook.com/msmsmsm/.

154 "Pop Producer SOPHIE on Anonymity, Honesty, and Artifice", Michelle LHOOQ, *Teen Vogue*, 7 December 2017. teenvogue.com/story/sophie-producer.

155 "Grimes implies 'numerous' producers have demanded sex from her", *The Guardian*, 15 April 2016. theguardian.com/music/2016/apr/15/grimes-producers-have-demanded-sex.

156 "i said this 3 years b4 sophie came out. apologized to her profusely since, was sheer stupidity on my part.", Grimes (@Grimzsz), *X*, 6 July 2018, 8:30pm. x.com/Grimezsz/status/1015317186267701253.

157 "Pop Producer SOPHIE on Anonymity, Honesty, and Artifice", Michelle LHOOQ, *Teen Vogue*, 7 December 2017. teenvogue.com/story/sophie-producer.

158 "Sophie", *A.G. Cook*, February 2021. agcook.com/msmsmsm/.

159 "Pop Producer SOPHIE on Anonymity, Honesty, and Artifice", Michelle LHOOQ, *Teen Vogue*, 7 December 2017. teenvogue.com/story/sophie-producer.

160 "Pop Is Not A Dirty Word: SOPHIE's live shows are a masterclass in crowdfuckery. I think I sort of love them", Douglas Greenwood, *NME*, 25 October 2018. nme.com/blogs/nme-blogs/pop-not-dirty-word-sophies-live-shows-masterclass-crowdfuckery-sort-think-love-2393356.

161 "Sophie was a stellar producer, a visionary, a reference. She rebelled against the narrow, normative society by being an absolute triumph", Redcar (@QueensChristine), *X*, 30 January 2021, 11:05am. x.com/QueensChristine/status/1355472218462048261.

162 "Charli XCX knows you're obsessed with her", Shaad D'Souza, *The Face*, 19 February 2024. theface.com/music/charli-xcx-interview-new-album-xcx6-vol-4-issue-18.

163 "Matthew Lutz-Kinoy and SOPHIE by Legacy Russell", Legacy Russell, *Bomb*, 11 January 2012. bombmagazine.org/articles/2012/01/11/expanded-benefits-matthew-lutz-kinoy-and-sophie/.

164 "TAAHLIAH, Stormzy, Nia Archives and more win big at the AIM Awards", Gemma Ross, *Mixmag*, 29 September 2022. mixmag.net/read/aim-awards-crown-winners-taaliah-stormzy-nia-archives-more-news.

165 "#2 Deeper into Out of Space | TAAHLIAH", Jim Ottewill, *Substack*, 1 February 2023. jimottewill.substack.com/p/2-taahliah.

166 "Never Constrained by Anything: TAAHLIAH's fearless creativity fuses emotion, pop and experimental electronics", Tope Olufemi, *Mixmag*, 27 May 2021. mixmag.net/feature/taahliah-impact-mix-interview.

167 Ibid.

168 "from kilmarnock to berlin, taahliah is making her mark in clubs around the world", Josiah Moktar, *oestrogeneration*, 28 March 2023. oestrogeneration.org/from-kilmarnock-to-berlin-taahliah-is-making-her-mark-in-clubs-around-the-world/.

169 "Sophie, Who Pushed the Boundaries of Pop Music, Dies at 34", Jon Pareles, *The New York Times*, 31 January 2021. nytimes.com/2021/01/30/arts/music/sophie-dead.html.

170 "Hannah Diamond Is Ready To Be Seen", Harry Tafoya, *Paper*, 7 November 2023. papermag.com/hannah-diamond-picture-perfect.

171 Ibid.

172 "Nevermind the Beatles, Here's Exile 61 and Nico", Ralf Von Appen & André Doehring, *JSTOR*. jstor.org/stable/3877541?mag=creating-the-musical-canon. Accessed 26 October 2024.

173 Ibid.

174 Ibid.

175 "Scotland gets its own School of Rock Chicks", Hannah Rodger, *The Herald*, 28 June 2015. heraldscotland.com/news/13414751.Scotland_gets_it_own_School_of_Rock_Chicks/.

176 "Let Lexi Campbell's legacy be a symbol of hope for queer individuals everywhere", Amie Flett, *The Courier*, 22 April 2022. thecourier.co.uk/fp/opinion/3212120/amie-flett-lexi-campbell-legacy/.

177 "Heart-to-Heart: Rufus Isabel Elliot's Three Sexual Pieces for Violin", Vanessa Ague, *The Quietus*, 17 February 2022. thequietus.com/quietus-reviews/album-of-the-week/three-sexual-pieces-for-violin-rufus-isabel-elliot-harry-gorski-brown-review/.

178 "Speaking Together: Rufus Isabel Elliot on the Trans, Non-Binary, and Gender-Diverse World of OVER/AT", Chrysanthe Tan, *I Care If You Listen*, 28 October 2021. icareifyoulisten.com/2021/10/

speaking-together-rufus-isabel-elliot-trans-non-binary-gender-di-verse-world-over-at/.

179 Ibid.

180 "Comic-Con vs. the Bechdel Test", Kinsee Morlan, *San Diego CityBeat*, 23 July 2014. web.archive.org/web/20150316161800/http://www.sdcitybeat.com/sandiego/article-13243-comic-con-vs-the-bechdel-test.html.

181 "Eddie Izzard – Christian Singing", Carmen, 14 November 2010, *YouTube.* youtube.com/watch?v=kuEuY4BUMfM.

182 "Choir, noun," *The Oxford English Dictionary,* oed.com/dictionary/choir_n.

183 "San Francisco Gay Men's Chorus: Pioneers of a Queer Choral Movement", Krista Thomas, *CalPerformances*, 8 June 2023. calperformances.org/2023/06/08/san-francisco-gay-mens-chorus-pioneers-of-a-queer-choral-movement/.

184 "Musicians' Census: Mental Wellbeing Report," *Help Musicians & Musicians' Union*, November 2023, static1.squarespace.com/static/6398a2cf26f9de4e45e94d-d7/t/655e09ac9064433549b2237b/1700661683250/MC23+Mental+Health+Report+1023+FA.pdf.

185 *Cruising Utopia: The Then and There of Queer Futurity*, José Esteban Muñoz. New York: New York University Press, 2009, p. 1.

186 "Young Fathers interview: Pop needs to represent culture as it really is", Kate Mossman, *The New Statesman*, 27 March 2015. newstatesman.com/culture/2015/03/young-fathers-interview-pop-needs-represent-culture-it-really.

187 "Nicky Siano Talks 'Lifeless' Modern Dance Music and the Return of Libby at MOMA PS1", Elias Leight, *Billboard*, 7 March 2015. billboard.com/music/music-news/nicky-siano-interview-6619943/.

188 "Man Parrish," *Hip Hop Be Bop.* hiphopbebop.com/man-parrish-discography/.

m

189 "How Bessie Smith Influenced a Century of Pop Music", Maureen Mahon, *NPR*, 5 August 2019. npr.org/2019/08/05/747738120/how-bessie-smith-influenced-a-century-of-popular-music.

190 "Hiphopophobia", Zoe Williams, *The Guardian*, 29 April 2003. theguardian.com/music/2003/apr/29/artsfeatures.popandrock.

191 "A Hip-Hop Fan Hunts the Reason Behind the Rhyme", Chris Richards, *Washington Post*, 20 February 2007. washingtonpost.com/wp-dyn/content/article/2007/02/19/AR2007021901224.html.

192 "True Trans Soul Rebel", Norman Brannon, *Anti-Matter*, 2 April 2024. antimatter.substack.com/p/true-trans-soul-rebel.

193 "Effort to repeal Texas sodomy law advances with bipartisan support", Nina Lakhani, *The Guardian*, 6 April 2023. theguardian.com/us-news/2023/apr/06/texas-sodomy-law-repeal-bipartisan-support.

194 Frank Ocean, *Tumblr*. frankocean.tumblr.com/image/26473798723.

195 "Frank Ocean's manager speaks out over US store Target's refusal to stock 'Channel Orange'", Tom Goodwin, *NME*, 13 July 2012. nme.com/news/music/frank-ocean-115-1266982.

196 Ken Liu, *The Hidden Girl and Other Stories*. Gallery/Saga Press, 2020.

197 "Various – The Best Scottish Album in the World… Ever!", Discogs. discogs.com/release/11954894-Various-The-Best-Scottish-Album-In-The-World--Ever?srsltid=AfmBOoq1B9OcWix-SqycwYOI5Khh_VI3nfLa-zMSIJauRIw-RNlKYbipU.

198 "The Sound of Scotland: Grassroots groups and unexpected genres", Arusa Qureshi, *PRS for Music*, 21 March 2023. prsformusic.com/m-magazine/features/the-sound-of-scotland-grassroots-groups-and-unexpected-genres.

199 "Spotlight On… Eyve", Tallah Brash, *The Skinny*, 2 November 2023. theskinny.co.uk/music/interviews/spotlight-on-eyve.

200 "Building a New Scotland: Culture in an independent Scotland", Scottish Government, 2 February 2024. gov.scot/publications/building-new-scotland-culture-independent-scotland/pages/9/.

201 "Culture and the creative economy in Glasgow city region, Scotland, United Kingdom", OECD Local Economic and Employment Development (LEED) Papers, No. 2022/10, *OECD Publishing*, Paris. doi.org/10.1787/54374bc9-en.

202 "The Hydro in Glasgow named world's second busiest concert venue behind MSG in New York", Stuart Hodge, *The Daily Record*, 21 December 2019. dailyrecord.co.uk/news/scottish-news/hydro-glasgow-named-worlds-second-21142635.

203 "Let's hear it for the Hydro", Richard Muir, Glasgow Chamber of Commerce, 1 November 2023. glasgowchamberofcommerce.com/news/ce-and-management-team-blogs/2023/november/01/lets-hear-it-for-the-hydro/.

204 "Glasgow life expectancy gap widens between richest and poorest", *BBC*, 6 August 2021. bbc.co.uk/news/uk-scotland-glasgow-west-58118599.

205 "Children and Younge People's Profiles," *Understanding Glasgow*. understandingglasgow.com/profiles/children-young-people-s-profiles/south-sector/greater-govan.

206 "Public Enemy: Our 1988 Interview With Chuck D", John Leland, *SPIN*, 18 August 2019. spin.com/2019/08/public-enemy-chuck-d-it-takes-a-nation-of-millions-to-hold-us-back-september-1988-interview-armageddon-in-effect/.

207 "Walt Disco: inside a warped reality", Sam Law, *Rolling Stone*. rollingstone.co.uk/music/walt-disco-the-warping-interview-37897/.

208 "Charli XCX Says LGBTQ+ Fans Helped Her Find Herself In New Documentary", Taylor Henderson, *Pride.com*, 2 February 2022. pride.com/movies/2022/2/02/charli-xcx-says-lgbtq-fans-helped-her-find-herself-new-documentary.

209 "The Tale of Walt Disco", Alex Brzezicka, *tmrw*. tmrwmagazine.com/index.php/news/the-tale-of-walt-disco.

210 "Reach using AI to speed up 'ripping' and use same article on multiples sites", Bron Maher, *Press Gazette*, 22 February 2024. pressgazette.co.uk/publishers/nationals/reach-ai-guten/.

211 "'Holding the artist to ransom': musicians struggle to break even as venues and Universal cream off merch sales", Eamonn Forde, *The Guardian*, 15 April 2022. theguardian.com/music/2022/apr/15/holding-the-artist-to-ransom-musicians-struggle-to-break-even-as-venues-and-universal-cream-off-merch-sales.

212 "Sarra Wild (0H141): Representation and feeling represented in a club is huge for me", Arusa Qureshi, *The List*. list.co.uk/news/6776/sarra-wild-oh141-representation-and-feeling-represented-in-a-club-is-huge-for-me.

213 "The Summerhall Crisis", Mike Small, *Bella Caledonia*, 23 October 2024. bellacaledonia.org.uk/2024/10/23/the-summerhall-crisis/.

214 "Exclusive: Summerhall to be sold to housing developer", Euan McGrory, *Edinburgh Inquirer*, 11 October 2024. edinburghinquirer.co.uk/p/exclusive-summerhall-to-be-sold-to.

215 "Preserve Summerhall as a Cultural Hub in Edinburgh", Daniel Connel, *change.org*, 14 May 2024. change.org/p/preserve-summerhall-as-a-cultural-hub-in-edinburgh.

216 "The 13 best new metal songs you need to hear this week", Rich Hobson, *Metal Hammer*, 28 June 2024. loudersound.com/features/best-new-metal-tribulation-beast-in-black-dream-evil.

217 "The Darkness's Justin Hawkins: 'Contrary to expectations, you'd never catch me dogging'", Paul Lester, *The Guardian*,

23 August 2010. theguardian.com/culture/2012/aug/23/
darkness-justin-hawkins-30-minutes.

218 "I really like this wistful song by Hamish Hawk, 'Bridget St
John' from his new albums 'Angel Numbers'", Pet Shop Boys,
Facebook, 8 February 2023. facebook.com/photo.php?fbid=744202
333733214&id=100044303610159&set=a.263716241781828&
locale=pt_PT.

219 "Rishi Sunak tacks to right with comments on sex education
and transgender rights", Christopher McKeon, *The Independent*,
5 October 2023. independent.co.uk/news/uk/politics/rishi-su-
nak-gender-speech-transphobic-b2424369.html.

220 "Toploader must be really skint as well as being really shit.",
Kathy Burke (@KathyBurke), *X*, 4 October 2023, 8:51am. [Post
since deleted.]

ACKNOWLEDGEMENTS

Writing *Small Town Joy* has been an absolute blast, in large part because of the artists who took time out to share their experiences, their insights and their enthusiasm with me. I'd like to thank them for their generosity and their thoughtfulness, and thank the managers, publicists and pals who put us together. I'm also very grateful to the promoters, journalists, organisers, fanzine writers, podcasters, and fans who helped me understand their scenes and histories.

I'd like to thank my amazing editor, Kirstyn Smith, and my equally amazing publishers Laura Jones-Rivera and Heather McDaid. It's been wonderful to get the band back together for this, our second tour. And of course I'd like to thank Kara McHale for the gorgeous cover.

I'd like to thank the booksellers, librarians, book festival curators and helpers, book bloggers, bookstagrammers, and booktokers who do so much for writers and readers alike, and I'd like to thank the many wonderful writers I've met through them.

I'd like to thank David and Ruth Marshall for everything, and Louise Blain and Ely Percy for their wisdom, their patience and their encouragement. I'd like to thank Dave Fraser and Karie Westermann for stifling their yawns during my endless mid-book info dumps.

I would also like to thank Creative Scotland, whose Open Fund for Individuals helped give me the space and time to do this story justice, and to all at the Moniack Mhor writing retreat.

Most of all, I'd like to thank the beautiful humans who give their time and their energy to helping LGBTQ+ Scots and other marginalised people survive and thrive, to ensuring that their voices are heard, that they are listened to rather than talked about or shouted down. That should not be controversial, difficult or dangerous, but in the current moral panic it often is.

And I'd like to thank you. Thank you for reading or listening to this story. I hope it brings you some of the joy that all of this music has brought me.

C x

ABOUT THE AUTHOR

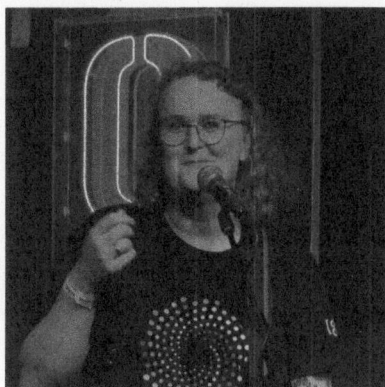

Photo credit: Chris Phin

Carrie Marshall has been a professional writer for three decades and an unprofessional musician for four.

As a writer Carrie has written, co-written or ghost-written over twenty non-fiction books under various names, and her memoir about coming out as trans, *Carrie Kills A Man* (404 Ink, 2022), was shortlisted in the Discover category of the British Book Awards.

As a musician Carrie has been heckled, bottled, threatened with knives, harassed by the police, molested, mocked in national newspapers, electrocuted, ripped off, chased by screaming girls, and even set on fire, although not all at the same time. She is the singer in the band Unquiet Mind.